Critical Muslim 12

Dangerous Freethinkers

T0333237

Editors: Ziauddin Sardar and Robin Yassin-Kassab

Deputy Editor: Samia Rahman

Senior Editors: Aamer Hussein, Hassan Mahamdallie, Ehsan Masood, Ebrahim Moosa

Publisher: Michael Dwyer

Managing Editor (Hurst Publishers): Daisy Leitch

Cover Design: Fatima Jamadar

Associate Editors: Alev Adil, Nazry Bahrawi, Merryl Wyn Davies, Abdulwahhab El-Affendi, Marilyn Hacker, Nader Hashemi, Vinay Lal, Iftikhar Malik, Shanon Shah, Boyd Tonkin

International Advisory Board: Waqar Ahmad, Karen Armstrong, William Dalrymple, Farid Esack, Anwar Ibrahim, Robert Irwin, Bruce Lawrence, Ashis Nandy, Ruth Padel, Bhikhu Parekh, Barnaby Rogerson, Malise Ruthven

Critical Muslim is published quarterly by C. Hurst & Co. (Publishers) Ltd. on behalf of and in conjunction with Critical Muslim Ltd. and the Muslim Institute, London.

All correspondence to Muslim Institute, CAN Mezzanine, 49-51 East Road, London N1 6AH, United Kingdom

e-mail for editorial: editorial@criticalmuslim.com

The editors do not necessarily agree with the opinions expressed by the contributors. We reserve the right to make such editorial changes as may be necessary to make submissions to Critical Muslim suitable for publication.

C. Hurst & Co. (Publishers) Ltd.,41 Great Russell Street, London WC1B 3PL

ISBN: 978-1-84904-452-3 ISSN: 2048-8475

To subscribe or place an order by credit/debit card or cheque (pound sterling only) please contact Kathleen May at the Hurst address above or e-mail kathleen@hurstpub.co.uk

Tel: 020 7255 2201

A one year subscription, inclusive of postage (four issues), costs £50 (UK), £65 (Europe) and £75 (rest of the world).

The right of Ziauddin Sardar, Robin Yassin-Kassab and the Contributors to be identified as the authors of this publication is asserted by them in accordance with the Copyright, Designs and Patents Act, 1988.

A Cataloguing-in-Publication data record for this book is available from the British Library.

The British
Museum

Discover
the Islamic
World

From early scientific
instruments to
contemporary art,
explore how Islam
has shaped our
world through objects
for centuries

Great Russell Street,
London WC1B 3DG
⊖ Tottenham Court Road,
Holborn, Russell Square
britishmuseum.org

Mosque lamp. Enamelled glass.
Syria, c. AD 1330–1345.

HALAL FOOD FOUNDATION

Halal Is Much More Than Food

The Halal Food Foundation (HFF) is a registered charity that aims to make the concept of halal more accessible and mainstream. We want people to know that halal does not just pertain to food – halal is a lifestyle.

The Foundation pursues its goals through downloadable resources, events, social networking, school visits, pursuing and funding scientific research on issues of food and health, and its monthly newsletter. We work for the community and aim at the gradual formation of a consumer association. We aim to educate and inform; and are fast becoming the first port of call on queries about halal issues. We do not talk at people, we listen to them.

If you have any queries, comments, ideas, or would just like to voice your opinion - please get in contact with us.

Halal Food Foundation

109 Fulham Palace Road,
Hammersmith, London, W6 8JA
Charity number: 1139457
Website: www.halalfoodfoundation.co.uk
E-mail: info@halalfoodfoundation.co.uk

 @HFF_UK

 Halal Food Foundation

The Barbary Figs

by

Rashid Boudjedra

Translated by
André Naffis-Sahely

Buy a copy of Rashid Boudjedra's *The Barbary Figs* at
www.hauspublishing.com or by calling +44(0)20 7838 9055
and a recieve a copy of Khaled al-Berry's memoir
Life is More Beautiful than Paradise free.

RASHID AND OMAR are cousins who find themselves side by side on a flight from Algiers to Constantine. During the hour-long journey, the pair will exhume their past, their boyhood in French Algeria during the 1940s and their teenage years fighting in the bush during the revolution. Rashid, the narrator, has always resented Omar, who despite all his worldly successes, has been on the run from the ghosts of his past, ghosts that Rashid has set himself the task of exorcising. Rashid peppers his account with chilling episodes from Algerian history, from the savageries of the French invasion in the 1830s, to the repressive regime that is in place today.

RASHID BOUDJEDRA has routinely been called one of North Africa's leading writers since his debut, *La Répudiation*, was published in 1969, earning the author the first of many fatwas. While he wrote his first six novels in French, Boudjedra switched to Arabic in 1982 and wrote another six novels in the language before returning to French in 1994. *The Barbary Figs* was awarded the Prix du Roman Arabe 2010.

CM12

October–December 2014

CONTENTS

DANGEROUS FREETHINKERS

ARTS AND LETTERS

REVIEWS

ET CETERA

Subscribe to Critical Muslim

Now in its second year, *Critical Muslim* is the only publication of its kind, giving voice to the diversity and plurality of Muslim reporting, creative writing, poetry and scholarship.

Subscribe now to receive each issue of Critical Muslim direct to your door and save money on the cover price of each issue.

Subscriptions are available at the following prices, inclusive of postage. Subscribe for two years and save 10%!

	ONE YEAR (4 Issues)	TWO YEARS (8 Issues)
UK	£50	£90
Europe	£65	£117
Rest of World	£75	£135

TO SUBSCRIBE:

CRITICALMUSLIM.HURSTPUBLISHERS.COM

41 GREAT RUSSELL ST, LONDON WC1B 3P
WWW.HURSTPUBLISHERS.COM
WWW.FBOOK.COM/HURSTPUBLISHERS
020 7255 2201

DANGEROUS FREETHINKERS

THE CIRCUMFERENCE OF FREETHOUGHT

Ziauddin Sardar

'This cannot happen again.' Sprout just did not want to lay any more eggs. Inside her overcrowded coop she couldn't move, flap her wings, or even sit on her own eggs, which were collected by the farmer's wife who complained constantly that they were getting smaller and smaller. Even when allowed on the farm, she couldn't stroll around and see the world flourishing outside the barnyard. She yearned for freedom. In her discontent, she became frail, unable to produce eggs. Disgusted, the farmer's wife removed Sprout from the flock and threw her into the 'Hole of Death', to die or be devoured by the weasel. But Sprout survived; gathering enough energy to escape with the help of Straggler, a friendly mallard. When she returned to the barns, other animals shunned her for being different and having ideas above her station. Even to stay on the outskirts of the farm, she needed to follow the rules. 'What if I don't like the rules?', she asked. 'Don't be ridiculous', she was told, 'everyone follows the rules'.

Sprout decided to follow Straggler and another duck outside the farm; and she learned to find food, survive in the wild, and outwit the eager-eyed, lean and hungry weasel. When the other duck was killed by the weasel, Sprout found an abandoned egg. She decided to brood the egg, with Straggler standing watch for the deadly weasel and bringing food to keep her going. She continued to concentrate on keeping the egg warm, even after Straggler became another victim of the weasel. When the egg hatched and the 'Baby' turned out to be a duckling, Sprout realised that her adopted son was the offspring of Straggler and his mate, the beautiful white duck that had fallen victim to the weasel. She raised her Baby with selfless devotion. Both mother and Baby were torn between their desires and natural inclination. Sprout tried to teach her Baby to fly but she knew she couldn't fly. 'Why can't we fly anymore?', she asked.

Sun-Mi Hwang's *The Hen Who Dreamed She Could Fly* is a simple, moving, beautifully-written allegory, in the style of *Charlotte's Web* and *Jonathan Livingstone Seagull*. It is a story of family and love, devotion and sacrifice, courage and loss, and above all, the value of freethought in the face of conformity. The feisty Sprout wants to break out of her physical and mental confinement. Even the name she has chosen for herself symbolises freedom and hope: 'Sprout is the best name in the world. A sprout grew into a leaf and embraced the wind and the sun before falling and rotting and turning into mulch for bringing fragrant flowers to bloom.' She knows there are other worlds – dangerous though they may be – beyond her own; she knows she can nurse and nourish other beings and other ideas besides those she has learned on the farm; and she knows that life and death are intrinsically linked. Death, as Sprout witnesses on the farm and in the wild, can be violent and cruel. But as she realises in her own case, it can also be meaningful and liberating when it serves to foster new life.

Freethinkers are a bit like Sprout. Restless and rebellious, eager to break out of convention, longing to be free from tradition that crushes individual and social creativity and spirit. Like Sprout they ask: there must be more to this world than the confinement of our given space? Sprout exhibits unconditional maternal love that transcends species; freethinkers have, or should have, uncompromising love for thought that surpasses the boundaries of race, ethnicity, ideology and religion. Freethought is about dissecting received and perceived truths, breaking out of dominant paradigms and discovering new ways of knowing, being and doing.

Why should freethought, and freethinkers, be deemed dangerous? After all, thought or our ability to reason, as Davies notes in her 'Last Word', is integral to what makes us human. But as Davies also points out, 'thought operates always in a context, the context of the world, the culture, the time and circumstances in which we live. Pure thought is a true utopia, a nowhere no place that is as delusional as it is illusory'. Much of what goes under the rubric of 'freethought' in the West is deeply embedded in the context of the conflict between Christianity (seen as 'religion') and science (seen as 'reason'). Google 'freethought' or 'freethinking' and see what I mean: you will find countless sites devoted to attacking religion and defending science, secularism, and 'no belief'. This is not freethought but another form of dogmatism: cynical antagonism towards all other forms of knowing, including religion. It is an irrationality that justifies itself in the name of reason. So amongst the dangers of freethought is that what often masquerades as freethought is nothing more than an illogical, dangerous fantasy. That freethought itself becomes a kind of religion is its prime danger. Indeed, for dogmatic humanists, secularist fundamentalists and romantic atheists it is already a religion.

Genuine freethought is something much more profound. Freethinkers don't just value knowledge, they embody it. That means they are aware of recent advances in most fields and disciplines, have thought about the ethical, social and cultural consequences of advances in knowledge, and have their own highly developed, rounded critiques of what constitutes the new. They understand what history has achieved, what the present is achieving, and have some insight into what the future may yet bring. But it also means that they are aware of their own ignorance. The knowledgeable know that humility is a prerequisite for true understanding. Genuine freethinkers know how to say: 'I don't know, I don't know yet, I may never know'. This is the conclusion Alev Adil reaches when she sets out to discover whether Aisha, the young wife of the Prophet, was a freethinker; a conclusion she wraps in her (partly) fictional story, 'the Aisha Project'.

Freethinkers are seen as dangerous simply because freethought challenges, or attempts to undermine, the conventional, the orthodox, and the dominant perspectives. If you are going to ruffle feathers you should not be surprised to discover that you are, like Sprout, shunned and exiled. As Davies puts it playfully, freethought 'means pondering the way of things as they are, asking questions without restraint, traversing the known knowns with a quizzical intent, interrogating the known unknowns and venturing forth into the realms of the unknown unknowns, daring to contemplate that there are things we do not know. Whoever thought I would end up quoting Donald Rumsfeld, US Secretary of Defence and architect of the Iraq War? This strange circumstance, surely, is the essence of free thinking: finding the hooks that lead to productive thought in unexpected places and with meaning and purpose quite other than its source may have intended or suspected. It only goes to show that not every useful utterance needs to come from a free thinker or indeed a revolutionary, some can be gleaned from reactionary warmongers as well'.

Indeed, freethinkers have no natural monopoly on 'useful utterances'. Often their utterances end up fortifying the very thing they are attempting to critique. Like most of us, freethinkers too are in danger of succumbing to the lure of power, the enticement of an all-embracing idea, the attraction of 'anything goes'. Three celebrated freethinkers illustrate this well: Mahmoud Muhammad Taha (1909–1985), Abdolkarim Soroush and the illustrious mystic Mansur al-Hallaj (c. 858–922).

The Sudanese reformer Muhammad Taha was so fascinated with power that he jettisoned his carefully argued and developed principles and liberal credentials to side with those in power, dictators included. Despite his rather unusual deconstruction of Islam and liberal ideals, his free-wheeling thought led him to a cul de sac. He argued, writes Abdelwahab El-Affendi, that 'the believer, by immersing himself in the Qur'an and engaging in spiritual exercises of fasting and seclusion could receive "revelation"' – and who better to receive revelation than Taha himself who concluded that he was the ultimate authority on Islam – a Prophet in fact. Anyway, how are we to determine 'when a revelation is authentic as opposed to a mere hallucination?' This not a whimsical question, nor just a theoretical problem, El-Affendi points out: Sudanese history is full of individuals claiming to be the Mahdi. 'Some, like the Sudanese Mahdi, have demonstrated deep convictions and admirable selflessness. But does that guarantee authenticity?' Taha has many followers – most notably the Sudanese scholar Abdullahi An-Na'im, who is universally feted as a human rights champion. But apart from the obvious ideals that most sensible, intelligent people subscribe to, Taha's thought turns out to be, to use Davies' words, 'as delusional as it is illusory'.

The Iranian freethinker, Abdolkarim Soroush, has explored numerous taboo subjects, most importantly, as Mohammad Moussa notes, 'subjective elements of revelation, particularly the Qur'an'. Few would argue with his assertion that Islam is 'no longer guarded by the certainties of the past' and 'urgently requires a rethinking in the here-and-now' or that 'the absence of the elements of knowledge and modernity lead to the deleterious effects of treating Islam as an identity which takes it towards fundamentalism' or that 'official politics and intellectual thought in post-revolutionary Iran had converged to mistakenly privilege the discourse on cultural authenticity'. His attempts to promote 'transcultural encounters' can only be lauded. But should we bury all Islamic traditions to liberate Islam from this impasse, as Soroush seems to suggest? 'No genuine engagement with the intricacies of the Islamic tradition', writes Moussa, 'is made by Soroush which could lead to a creative rethinking of its elements'. His own alternative does not inspire much confidence either. 'What is of serious concern in his thought is a rather uncritical embrace of modernity in its entirety; Islam must follow the trajectory of the Western civilisation, the apex of human achievement', notes Moussa. But Soroush's freethought not only leaves modernity untouched, it is equally uncritical towards secularism. He reduces Islam to a 'minimalist religion' with no social or progressive concerns about justice and equity. His reverence for the authority of his Western teachers such as Popper, and the defining power of a dominant civilisation, is total.

Al-Hallaj allowed his free thought to consume his self, a kind of self-indulgence not too dissimilar to that of Taha. A giant of Sufism, he is regarded as a great mystical poet. But the figure 'who had dared to declare his unity with God by declaring "*Ana al-Haqq*" (I am the Truth)', is more a product of mythology than historical fact. Much of this mythology, as Robert Irwin shows, was created by Louis Massignon, the Catholic scholar of Islam. Massignon's *The Passion of Al-Hallaj* provides a theatrical and poetic account of al-Hallaj's death; but as Irwin notes, 'it is also to a significant degree fictional'. Al-Hallaj invoked God constantly, and saw Truth – His Truth? – everywhere. But he was not simply a 'primitive rebel'; his theological and literary works were highly sophisticated. What makes it unusual is that he favoured taking his mysticism to the masses – to the irritation of most Sufis. 'He preached to the poor in the suburbs of Baghdad, as well as to nomads, robbers and bandits. After preaching to criminals, he was even alleged to have trimmed their hair and beards'. But in the end, al-Hallaj's perpetual immersion in the love of God, his disdain for authority, and rejection of all norms and values of society, were counterproductive. Irwin cites Ali Shariati (1933–1977), the distinguished Iranian social and religious thinker, who observed: 'Hallaj was constantly immersed in the burning invocation of God, and this was a true source of exaltation for him. But imagine if Iranian society were to consist of twenty-five million Hallajs. It would be nothing but a vast lunatic asylum.'

What al-Hallaj, Soroush and Taha demonstrate is that freethought can take us out of one straitjacket and place us into another. Perhaps it is worth noting at this juncture that the most ardent advocate of freethought in the West, Karl Pearson, the author of *The Ethics of Freethought*, was a champion of eugenics and a Nazi sympathiser. So freethought can be dangerous in that it has equal potential to take us into the darker alleys as well as to bright futures. Thus freethought per se is not a panacea. We should not be swayed either by the fact that freethinkers are often persecuted. Al-Hallaj was eventually executed probably as much for his thought as for his disdain for the norms of society. Taha too died on the gallows. Soroush has suffered harassment for his thought and was forced into exile. But persecution, which should always be denounced and resisted, is not an indication of the quality or relevance of freethought.

Fortunately, Islamic history is full of freethinkers who take us in a different direction. It is, as Aziz Al-Azmeh shows in his lecture on Abbasid freethinkers, a rich and diverse history that goes back to the eighth century. It includes all types of characters, believers like historiographer and scholar of world religions al-Shahrastani (1086–1153) and al-Razi, who 'though a rationalist, was no sceptic' but 'sought to think beyond the aporias of theological reason', and hardened atheists such as the celebrated poet Abu Nawas. Al-Azmeh identifies 'two registers' of Abbasid freethinking: 'one is unstructured, playful, often frivolous, jocular impiety and blasphemy, often associated with libertine individuals and milieus of the courtly and literary elite'; the other is 'high-minded, serious, systematic, and theologically and philosophically engaged'. In most cases, this freethought was a missile aimed at orthodoxy; not surprisingly, the guardians of belief and custom took suitable action to avoid the hazardous projectiles.

The theologians, philosophers and poets Al-Azmeh surveys demonstrate that freethought is certainly against dogmatism, but it can, and has to be, much more than that. Al-Azmeh looks at three representative but very different freethinkers who move in different milieus: Ibn al-Rawandi (827–911), critic and 'substantial theologian'; Abu Bakr al-Razi (d. 925, perhaps a decade later), polymath, natural scientist and physician; and Abul-'Ala' al-Ma'arri (d. 1058), a 'poet among philosophers and the philosopher among poets'. From their different perspectives, they arrived at a common ground that Al-Azmeh presents as four theses: organised religion is not necessary, prophecy is irrelevant, religions are self-contradictory and contradict one another, and religions are full of dogma and rituals that are absurd and insulting to reason. Quite clearly, these are dangerous assertions for a society knee-deep in conservative theology. Yet, this was not a total rejection of God. It is just that these freethinkers preferred a belief in a supreme being based on reason rather than revelation. Or as al-Azmeh put it, 'underlying all this chaos and disturbance is a diffuse divinity of deistic description, which might, under conditions never specified, be conducive to human improvement'. Al-Razi was not a sceptic. Al-Maarri sought to correct 'what established religion took for God's criteria'. And Islamic theology has no answers for some rather simple questions raised by ibn al-Rawandi, such as 'can the Muslim paradise be pleasing to anyone but a rustic' and 'why did the Heavenly Host of avenging angels help Muhammad's army at the Battle of Badr, while at the Battle of Uhud they stood by as onlookers'?

The danger here is not so much to religion but to the religious state. The Abbasid freethought rebellion, as illustrated by ibn al-Muqaffa' (d. 756), 'a prose stylist of prodigious talent and intelligence', was against religion that has become 'a political artefact in the hands of the sovereign manipulating the rough and credulous demos', a 'rank unreason belonging wholly to the reason of state'. One need not look further than Saudi Arabia and Iran to find contemporary examples. Islam has been covered with layer upon layer of manufactured dogma that is as absurd as it is dangerously obsolete. The purpose of freethought is to cut through this dogmatism and take us closer to God. Freethinkers have, or rather ought to have, a better understanding of the Divine than those who parade their dogmatic religious knowledge.

Two noted freethinkers demonstrate this well: Adonis and Nasr Hamid Abu Zayd (1943–2010). Adonis is undoubtedly the most prominent modern poet to emerge from the Arab world. He is seen as a heretic but what exactly is his heresy? As Stefan Weidner shows, no one has tackled the Divine more forthrightly than Adonis. The importance of God to Adonis is evident from the opening lines of his famous 1961 collection *The Songs of Mihyar the Damascene*, which is littered with references to Allah: 'He is not only said to encompass opposites (*he is the reality and its contrary, he is the life and its other*), thereby escaping any definition, but has neither a bodily outward appearance (*He has the shape of the wind*) nor an ancestry (*he has no ancestor and his roots are in his footsteps*). Furthermore, he has abilities which are marked by power over life and death: *He fills life and no one sees him. He whips it into foam and drowns in it*, and, *he scares and vivifies (...) he peels man like an onion*'. One of his most controversial poems is 'The New Noah'. Noah, of course, is an important Prophet of Islam. But Adonis wants to replace the Noah we know with a new Noah, who speaks in the poem. 'Towards the end of the poem', writes Weidner, this new Noah says that he does not 'listen to the words of God, but *long[s] for another, for a new Lord*. Although once again the heretic impact of the poem is quite obvious, it is remarkable that the notion of God is not completely dismissed; rather, there is a longing to replace the traditional God with a new one, and the new Noah's most important role is to be one of his prophets. While the meaning of God and Noah as well as the worldview they convey may have changed, what we may call the divine structure remains: there is still a god and there are still prophets – they are, however, to symbolise new values'. If Adonis is a heretic, then his heresy, and his freethought, is rooted in his attempts to understand the Divine.

We can say the same about the Egyptian thinker Abu Zayd who saw 'Islam as a message of equality and justice' and questioned how far the meaning of the Qur'an had been manipulated. Abu Zayd described the Shari'a as 'man made', and argued, in the words of Nazry Bahrawi, that 'Qur'anic exegesis was fossilised as dogma because the commentators and interpreters did not fully account for the historical elements of the Qur'an, leading them to interpret the holy book in a literal manner'. He developed the notion of 'humanistic hermeneutics' that aimed to provide a more humane appreciation of the Divine. Exposing the manipulators, as many as stars in the sky, is obviously dangerous. Abu Zayd was declared an apostate and asked to divorce his Muslim wife. He was eventually driven into exile when Ayman al-Zawahiri of Al-Qaeda called for his assassination for his alleged apostasy.

Both Abu Zayd and Adonis illustrate that freethought can be profoundly reflexive. Like Sprout, freethinkers want to nurse different eggs, think outside the boundaries of convention, tradition and orthodoxy. They begin with the conviction that there must be more to God and His universe than the hodgepodge of dogma, the obscurantism of theologians, and the absurd utterings of the Mullah. Freethinkers create new and different spaces, circumscribed by what Richard Scholar calls 'freedom and constraints'. Freethinkers think freely but they know that freedom depends on constraints without which it cannot function. Freethought is not free of everything, it is not absolute relativism, it is not about 'anything goes'. If all is true and 'anything goes', then everything stays, defeating the very purpose of freethought – to break out of the status quo. Freethinking is the art of navigating a passage out of the ossified and banal beliefs and conventions without turning freedom into a licence.

It is this notion of freethought that we find in three classical scholars: Jahiz (776–868), ibn Rushd (1126–1198) and al-Biruni (973–1048). For Jahiz, as Montgomery writes in his erudite contribution, 'society needed freethinking to ensure it was a fit response to God's revelation of the Qur'an.' He did not regard himself as an authority to be followed unquestionably. 'Rather his writings were designed to promote freethinking and thus function as society's guide (in the same way that Plato's Socrates was both gadfly and midwife of Athens)'. But 'his unwillingness to accept the views of others unquestioningly, his style of writing as an invitation to challenge and examine his own views through a mode of reading that required of the reader profound and extensive scrutiny, were dangerous and thought to be subversive.' Jahiz was mocked, 'branded as capricious, as volatile, as a sophist. His books were read for amusement, or out of antiquarianism, or as an example of style.' Yet, as Jahiz would himself have said, there is nothing dangerous about his ideas: 'the application of reason would lead inexorably to the same conclusions as its application had led him'.

Ibn Rushd's dangerous idea was in fact profoundly simple: the disputes between theologians, interpreters of the Qur'an, grammarians and lawyers, that were then plaguing Islam and have plagued Islam for centuries, should be decided on the basis of reason and evidence. Or, as Oliver Leaman put it 'in the battle of ideas, ibn Rushd came down decisively on the side of philosophy.' But his philosophy was seen as so dangerous that it was totally ignored by Muslim society; and ibn Rushd himself banished.

Al-Biruni, my favourite freethinker, managed to escape this fate. He was, as Bruce Lawrence observes, a freethinker 'not only in his own epoch, but also across the ages, in all the annals of Islamic history extending to culture and religion as well as mathematics and astronomy.' Al-Biruni sought to free us from artificial disciplinary boundaries, from the servitude to a single Method, from instrumental reason, and from the orthodoxy of philosophy itself. If freethinkers are dangerous, then al-Biruni was a nuclear device. We could move from discipline to discipline, he showed, provided we respect the method of each discipline. But no scientific answer obtained through reason and experience, experimentation and dissertation, was considered by al-Biruni to be absolute. He was the most exact of scientists without being fooled into believing that the method of experimental sciences could lead him to eternal truths, or be applied to religion or the humanities. This is why for al-Biruni there is no single method for studying science but methods for acquiring all types of knowledge in conformity with the innate nature of sciences in questions. The answers you get depend on the nature of the questions, the way the questions are formed, the area under study and the methods used. He moved freely from discipline to discipline, making invaluable contributions, changing his questions and methods according to the dictates of inquiry. He studied Hinduism and Yoga according to their own concepts and categories, becoming, in the words of Lawrence, 'not just the first but the unrivalled Muslim observer, commentator, and analyst of Hindu belief, thought and practice'.

While philosophers may regard themselves as being above mortal beings (and most classical Muslim philosophers certainly did), they do not always ask the right questions. Thus, al-Biruni had no hesitation in challenging the preeminent philosopher of his time: ibn Sina (980–1037). Lawrence writes: 'because ibn Sina had commented on the material nature of the universe, Biruni initiated a correspondence with him. He puts forth a number of questions that critique the presuppositions of Aristotelian physics. Bluntly, but also politely, he asks ibn Sina to respond to these questions, in effect, to justify his own predilection for, and reliance on, Aristotle'. The questions were radical in nature and presented a serious challenge both to ibn Sina and Aristotle: 'once it is possible to prove that some part of Aristotelian natural philosophy does not fit all the evidence, the entire system becomes suspect, its formulations unhinged. The stars and planets, that is, the heavenly bodies, are the subject on which Biruni begins his set of queries to ibn Sina. Some may sound obscure or overly technical to a non-scientist. For example: how do you explore and explain weight in space? How do you determine whether or not heavenly spheres are heavy or light? But one issue is germane to all physical and metaphysical reflection: are there other worlds than the cosmos, as we know it from mathematical astronomy? For Aristotle, as for ibn Sina, the answer was no. For Biruni, the answer was maybe. Though we cannot prove the existence of other worlds, neither can we disprove their existence', he argues.

Al-Biruni illustrates so well that freethought is something profound – a progressive ideal that seeks to liberate humanity from all variety of misery and authoritarianism. Including, one must add, the authority of freethought based on instrumental reason itself. This is why we cannot do without freethought. We need freethought both to fight repression and to expand the horizons of human thought and knowledge. Freethought is necessary to counter 'any form of oppression, political falsity, group-think or received ideas', as Czeslaw Milosz discovered. It was, as Eva Hoffman notes, 'a crucial part of Milosz's moral and intellectual development'; and it should be an integral part of the thought and work of any self-respecting intellectual and thinker.

Freedom, Sprout discovers, requires commitment, caution, and hard work, as well as courage and sacrifice. Sprout shows tremendous courage against all odds to rear her Baby, just as freethinkers have to overcome resistance and hostility from orthodoxy both to communicate their ideas and to survive. She makes two supreme sacrifices. When her Baby is ready to fly off with a flock of mallards, Sprout struggles between the desire to be with her progeny and her realisation that his natural place is with the ducks. In an ultimate act of love, she releases her claim and allows him to be among his own kind. A time comes when freethinkers too have to let go of their ideas – allow them to develop and progress in different pastures. Sprout's final act of love and compassion is towards her arch enemy – the weasel. She too is a mother, and starving. 'Go on, eat me', she urges. 'Fill your babies' bellies'. After these two supreme acts of love, sacrifice and compassion, Sprout feels 'transparent and buoyant'; and finally learns to fly.

Freethought, as Richard Scholar demonstrates in his study of Montaigne, is a finely balanced relationship between three essentials: the freedom to reject the authorities of the past including one's own teacher; the careful use of doubt as a means of searching for truth, including doubt about one's own position; and employing 'constraints' when necessary. But even after that freethought has the potential to become an authoritarian enclave. That's why Scholar only gives it 'two cheers'. To be able to fly, as Sprout shows, freethought has to be anchored on love and compassion for all.

JAHIZ: DANGEROUS FREETHINKER?

James E. Montgomery

Freethinking is characterised by a reliance on reason anc autonomy rather than authority or institution. It is an inquisitive and questioning state of mind, one that readily slips into scepticism and possibly even relativism. As Richard Scholar has recently argued, freethinking 'flourishes wherever a thinker encounters an obstacle in the search for truth'. I do not consider secularism or irreligiosity (or even atheism) to be essential to the notion of freethinking. In my view freethinking is characterised instead by a reliance on independent, reasoned thinking driven by a quizzical stance with regard to received knowledge.

Jahiz (d. 868–9), the ninth-century thinker, certainly relied on reason and the questioning of received or inherited beliefs. He was not a sceptic, though he saw doubt as an indispensable moment on our path to truth. He was not a relativist: right and wrong were identifiable and unchanging moral qualities accessible to the human reason. And he was most definitely not anti-authoritarian. For him authority came from God and was vested in the caliph and in the apparatus of the caliph's government, however semi- or loosely institutionalised that apparatus was.

Jahiz was a thinker who put his freethinking at the service of the caliph and his regime. For Jahiz and his society to attempt anything else would have merited God's wrath: society needed freethinking to ensure it was a fit response to God's revelation of the Qur'an. Jahiz would have been dismayed to learn that there was anything dangerous about the promotion of his brand of freethinking. And yet, by the end of his long life, he was castigated as an intellectual lightweight, written off as a doddering wit, and subsequently read largely as a stylist of antiquarian interest.

Let us begin *in media res*, with a typical example of Jahiz's style of writing and thinking. The following passage is from volume 7 of a work called *The*

Book of Living, by far the most ambitious work of Jahiz to have survived.
Jahiz raises the question of whether birds have a language:

Every species of animal knows how to survive and get what it needs, how to evade
its predators and catch its prey. It works out how to trap the animals that are
inferior to it and how to protect itself against those superior to it. It chooses places
to hide and defend itself and moves when it thinks they are unsuitable.

Birds use a language whereby they understand what others need. They have no
reason to have or use a better language than the one they have. After all, their needs
determine and shape the ideas they want to express. A wise philosopher was once
asked, 'At what age did you begin to think?' 'The moment I was born,' he replied.
When he saw that no-one believed him he said, 'Okay then. I cried when I was
afraid. I demanded food when I was hungry. I demanded to be suckled when I
needed to be. I was quiet when I was given what I wanted. Such was the extent of
my needs. If you know the extent of your needs when you are granted or denied
them, you do not at that exact time need to think any further. This is why the
Bedouin poet composed the following couplet:

> May God bless the land where the gecko knows that it is safe, where the plants
> are succulent
>
> And where, on the top of a rock, it built its home. Every man thinks about how
> to survive.'

Should someone retort, 'This does not qualify as a language,' here is the response:
'The Qur'an says that it is a language, poems refer to it as such as do the Bedouin.
Maybe you refuse to classify it as clear communication and claim that it is not a
language just because you do not understand it? But you do not understand the
languages spoken by the other peoples of the world, and if you call their languages
an incoherent babble and not clear speech, then you have made yourself liable to
the accusation that you are disqualifying their languages and the words they use too.
These peoples do not understand the language and the words that you use, so
logically they are quite entitled to refuse to classify your language as a form of clear
communication and speech.

Surely these languages are a form of clear communication and speech because their
speakers understand each other's needs, and because the languages constitute
structured expressions produced by tongues and mouths? So then are not the
sounds made by the various species of birds, and wild and domestic animals, also a

form of clear communication and speech, given that you acknowledge that they are structured and organised, and articulated and given shape, that they understand each other's needs thereby and are produced by tongues and mouths? Even if you only comprehend a tiny part, all these different kinds of animals only comprehend a tiny part of what you say. The structured sounds they make are determined by the limits of what they need and what they have to communicate. The structured sounds that you make are determined by the limits of what you need and have to communicate. You can teach a bird to make certain sounds and it will learn them. A man can be taught a language and he will speak it. This is the case with children and foreigners. The difference between men and birds is that, in the case of the birds, the notion that they talk is called a form of speech and a language through a comparison with human beings and on the basis of a valid connection. The notion that humans talk applies to them, no matter what.

So when the poet described the birds as capable of thought, the words he used were predicated upon this comparison. The poet could not apply these attributes to the birds absolutely and without qualification, and so you in turn are not able to refuse them these attributes in any way or in any circumstance.

You must understand this. May God help you to understand this! Almighty God has commanded you to ponder, acknowledge and heed His lessons. In the Qur'an God says that Sulayman declared: 'We have been taught the language of the birds.' (27:16). The Almighty referred to it as a language and singled Sulayman out as someone to whom He had given comprehension of the thoughts and ideas expressed in that language, someone whom He had put in the position of the birds. And what's more, if He had had Sulayman say, 'We have been taught the language of domestic animals and predators,' then that too would constitute an indicative miracle, a sign from God. God taught Isma'il the language of the Arabs when he was fourteen years old. This took place without any instruction or teaching, and without any need for pedagogical supervision or drills. Isma'il did not even grow up there. That is why this qualifies as a convincing proof, a miracle, and a sign from God.

I hope that once the reader, who may never have heard of Jahiz before, let alone read any of his words, has a chance to get her bearings, she will appreciate the sprightly nimbleness of thought, the pace of argument, the inexorable dilemma the addressee finds himself at the end of the passage. I hope also that a host of questions spring to mind. What is the point of the argument? Is it mere sophistry, an empty battle of words? Did anyone really care whether birds are said to have a language tropically and figuratively, by way of a comparison with humans, or in a literal sense?

I will attempt to answer some of these questions. But let me make one point at the outset. In ninth-century Arabic intellectual culture, the meaning and interpretation of words were of vital importance. Muslim intellectuals thought long and hard about how to develop the correct responses to the Qur'an, how to read it and understand it, and how to fashion a linguistic and interpretative tradition out of it. It was important to get this right, because almost all ninth-century Muslim intellectuals believed that the fate of their souls depended on their getting it right. To make an erroneous interpretation, to get it wrong, meant quite literally to be consigned to eternal damnation. So whether birds can be said to have a language or not goes right to the very heart of how we interpret the Qur'an.

Writer and Legend

Jahiz composed many works during his long life: we know of some 245 titles. Not all have survived, of course, and there is considerable overlap between some of these titles. A conservative estimate would fix his corpus at around 200 compositions. His writings are greatly cherished. He is admired and loved as the 'father of Arabic prose.' Few would nowadays refer to him outright as a buffoon, but most discern in his joyous (childlike) sense of wonder a childish fascination with the mundane and the everyday. Many read this presumed childishness in his mercurial and tumultuous corpus of writings and in his style of composition—full of digressions, asides, meanderings, a helter-skelter inability to stick to the point, an exuberant relish for arguing both sides of a case, because they think he loved argumentation so much but also because they think he could not decide which side to root for. He is notorious for his witty and often apparently irreverent caricatures, for his indefatigable curiosity, and his sophistry.

Jahiz's works are alive with a vital presence; they must have been uttered by a strong personality. What kind of a man wrote such remarkable pieces of prose? When we try to reconstruct Jahiz's biography, we discover that Jahiz the Writer has created Jahiz the Legend and concealed Jahiz the Man.

This is certainly true of the classical biographies of Jahiz which have survived and it also applies to their modern avatars.

The legend of Jahiz is constructed out of key moments in, and unusual features of, his books. Take the name 'Jahiz.' This is a rare word from a root which means 'to suffer from bulging eyes.' The only occasion I can recall encountering it in a ninth- or tenth-century text is in a treatise on physiognomy. 'Jahiz' is a cognomen, a nickname that means 'Pop-eyes' or 'Goggle-eyes.' We do not know how he acquired it. We normally assume that it indicated a physical deformity, but perhaps, as was sometimes the case, he was given it because he had used it in a memorable phrase and so came to be known as Jahiz, 'the man who used the word *jahaza*.' At all events, Jahiz became legendary for the ugliness of his ocular deformity.

Jahiz was not only legendarily ugly, Mahbub his grandfather is said to have been black. Jahiz's full name was Abu 'Uthman (his teknonym, meaning 'Father of 'Uthman'), 'Amr (his given name), ibn Bahr ('son of Bahr', his father's name), ibn Mahbub ('son of Mahbub', his grandfather's name). He also had two titles which indicate tribal affiliation: al-Fuqaymi and al-Kinani. The Banu Kinana were a tribe related to the Quraysh, the tribe of Prophet Muhammad. Mahbub ('Beloved') is an unusual name and may indicate slave status. The tribal affiliations would then indicate the clan and the tribe who owned Mahbub and with which he was connected when he was manumitted. In technical terms this would indicate that Jahiz's was a family of *mawali*, non-Arabs who enjoyed the protection of a network of contacts, presumably the family of the owner of Mahbub, within the tribal conglomeration known as Banu Kinana. A curio within the Jahizian corpus is a work entitled *Treatise on the Vaunting of Blacks over Whites*, in which the author argues in favour of the superiority of the black races to the white races. There are a couple of problems with moving back from this work to the man however. The text as it survives is not complete: it exists in an excerpted form within an anthology. We have really no way of knowing which position, if any, Jahiz supports in the work because he regularly uses a variety of talking heads when he writes: he ventriloquises all sorts of positions, but adopts none.

Jahiz grew up in Basra, a city which he often describes in his writings and where he returned at the end of his life. As a child Jahiz is said to have attended the *kuttab*, the elementary Qur'an school. Of course Jahiz must have received some form of education. However another unusual work within his corpus is *The Treatise on Teachers* and it is natural to connect this work with Jahiz's own life.

A life of idleness ensued. Jahiz may have sold fish for a short time, and he whiled away his life among the lower classes—artisans, tradespeople, sailors, hucksters and criminals—but he was drawn to the congregational mosque where lectures, classes, discussions and debates were held on the most important topics of the day. He also frequented the Mirbad, the camel depot on the outskirts of Basra where the Bedouin tribesmen came to trade, and where the sciences of Arabic philology, grammar and lexicography are said to have been born, as the great scholars of Iraq questioned the Bedouin about Arabic language. (The Bedouin were thought to have kept alive a purer form of Arabic, one closer to the Arabic that Prophet Muhammad spoke and that pre-Islamic poetry was composed in, than the degenerate forms of Arabic spoken in the garrisons and townships.) However if we turn to Jahiz's body of writings, several works seem relevant: *An Epistle on the Crafts of the Leading Exponents* in which Jahiz analyses the speech patterns of all manner of tradesmen, from street-cleaners to horse-surgeons; his most famous work *The Book of Misers* contains a celebrated description of the habitués of Basra's congregational mosque; his abiding, scientific, interest in Arabic as a language and in the correct use of that language is celebrated in his four volume masterpiece *The Book of Clarity and Clarification*.

It was through exposure to these cultural currents, to osmosis, that Jahiz is thought to have acquired the expertise that distinguishes all of his works. It was also in Basra and in the mosque that Jahiz met a man who was to exert an enormous influence on his intellectual development: Abu Ishaq al-Nazzam (d. 836 or 845), a charismatic scientist, theoretician, poet, and nephew of the famous speculative thinker Abu al-Hudhayl (d. 841-2).

Abu al-Hudhayl and Nazzam were avid critics of the newly emergent translations into Arabic of the philosophical and scientific legacy of Greek Antiquity. Nazzam was a serial controversialist who engaged Christians and Manicheans in debate. He developed a radical cosmology which replaced 'spirit' for the neo-platonic and Aristotelian 'soul' and devised a theory of causality based on the properties inherent in a series of primary natures. Jahiz fell under the spell of Nazzam and became a card-carrying member of the Mu'tazila school of thought. In the process he gained access to the latest works of Greek philosophy and science in translation.

In Jahiz's masterpiece, *The Book of Living*, the presence of Nazzam and Aristotle is most evident. Jahiz relies extensively on current translations of Aristotle's works on animals (*Historia Animalium*), and often does not acknowledge that he is doing so, but equally he is vociferous about his disagreements with Aristotle. In fact one of the aims of *The Book of Living* is to excavate ancient Arab Bedouin knowledge of animals and nature and place it alongside the insights and ideas of the Stagirite. It is also clear from a close reading of the work that Jahiz has adapted and modified many of the principal theories of Nazzam—that he was the best kind of disciple, an engaged and constructive critic.

The legendary Jahiz slips out of focus until his death in December 868 or January 869. According to a very late and unreliable source, Jahiz died in frail old age when a pile of books collapsed and crushed him to death.

The Ideologue

Jahiz saw his role as that of a spokesperson for his society. He thought that his pronouncements and compositions could save society. This is an unlikely role for the legendary Jahiz, but it is apt for an intellectual who positioned himself as both apologist and ideologue. He emerges from the mists of legend into something like the cold light of history, because of a comment he makes in *The Book of Clarity and Clarification* written in the early 850s. The Imamate was the burning political and theological issue of the day—who had the spiritual and thus temporal right to lead the Islamic community: the descendants of 'Ali ibn Ab' Talib (the Shi'a), the best man in the community (the Zaydiyya), or the descendants of al-'Abbas (the 'Abbasids)? It appears that sometime around 815-16 Jahiz was invited to write on the subject:

Ma'mun read my books on the Imamate and found them to be as he had commanded. So I was given an audience. He had ordered the grammarian Yazidi to examine them and furnish him with an account. Ma'mun said, 'We have been informed by an individual of commendable intelligence, a man whose word we trust, that these books are extremely well crafted and very useful. We said to him, 'Descriptions often exaggerate: they do not agree with what we see with our own eyes'. But when I read the books, what I saw for myself was far superior to what Yazidi had described. Then, when I picked over them, I realised they were in fact far superior to when I read them for the first time.

A number of Jahiz's works on the subject of the Imamate have survived in partial and excerpted form: *An Epistle on the Affirmation of the Imamate of 'Ali ibn Abi Talib*; *That 'Ali Acted Correctly in Appointing the Two Arbiters*; *On Meriting the Imamate*; *The Responses and Meriting the Imamate*. *The Tenets of the Zaydiyyah and the Rafidah*, a work on the two principal branches of Shi'ism prevalent in Jahiz day, touches on the issue of the Imamate.

Caliphal approval of these writings led to a move to Baghdad. Jahiz found employment in the imperial chancellery as secretary to Ibrahim ibn 'Abbas al-Suli (d. 857), an influential politician and scion of an old Turkic family. This appointment may have been short-lived though: Jahiz's tenure in some sources is said to have been a mere three days. The sources make scant mention of further official employments. A brief spell as tutor to the caliphal children was reputedly terminated because the princes were too scared by his grotesque appearance.

So from around 820 until his death in 868–9 it seems that Jahiz was unemployed. Yet suddenly in the 840s he bursts onto the scene as a member of the entourages of some extremely powerful figures. The shadow cast by his reference to the success of his works on the Imamate led Charles Pellat, the twentieth century's foremost expert on Jahiz, to argue that Jahiz 'acted as an adviser to and apologist for the government, and seems to have exercised this role quite openly.' It is of course difficult to accept this broad generalisation without some qualification. There was no 'government' in the sense that Pellat may have intended, but if we substitute 'elite' for 'government' we can begin to get a good sense of Jahiz's role as ideologue and apologist.

Jahiz's patrons included many of the then controllers of the Islamic world, such as the philosophically inclined Caliph Ma'mun (r. 813–833); the Vizier Muhammad ibn 'Abd al-Malik al-Zayyat (d. 847), head of the imperial administration; the Hanaf' Chief Cadi Ahmad ibn Abi Du'ad (d. 854), a formidable intellect, the chief of the imperial judiciary; his son and deputy Abu al-Walid Muhammad (d. 853); and the caliph Mutawakkil (r. 847–861), stabiliser of the imperium, the Caliph who prepared the ground for what is today known as Sunni Islam. Jahiz's opponents included the pious scholar Ahmad ibn 'anbal (d. 855); and the philosopher Kind' (d. c. 866), the first intellectual to attempt in Arabic a synthesis of the Islamic monotheism and Greek-Arabic philosophy.

So what did Jahiz do for a living during these thirty years or so spent in the company of the leaders of the empire? Jahiz was admitted into the entourages of the caliphs Ma'mun, Mu'tasim and Mutawakkil and into those of his other powerful patrons as a scholar and a special adviser—as both a counsellor and an expert in religious, legal, political, scientific and historical matters. He wrote as proselytiser, apologist and ideologue. He advised, counselled and admonished the imperial elite. He offered them and their gubernatorial agents a vision of how to regulate their society through a correct theologico-political system and in the process offered his readers a way to save their souls. His was a vision of their society informed by his beloved Mu'tazilism.

The portraits I have drawn of Jahiz the Writer, Jahiz the Legend and Jahiz the Ideologue present us not with an anti-authoritarian freethinker but a member of the establishment, a spokesperson of the elite, a communitarian and consensualist thinker driven by a desire to save his society. So why did posterity neglect his ideas? What was it that was so dangerous? In order to answer this question we need to think about the role of theological and political belief in the ninth century; to look at the details of how Jahiz viewed man and God's creation; and to consider reading as freethinking.

Kalam and the Mu'tazila

Abu al-Hudhayl and Nazzam were among the figures claimed as founding fathers and spiritual progenitors by the theological movement known as the Mu'tazila. The origins of his group are fairly obscure. The name, which means 'those who withdraw' may have originally been a derogatory term, as was the case for most of the theological groups who emerged during the eighth and ninth centuries – though it is not clear what precisely the Mu'tazila withdrew from. Jahiz prefers the term 'the people who profess divine justness and unity, '*ahl al-'adl wa-al-tawhid*. Jahiz seems to have been instrumental in writing the history of the movement and defining its principal contours.

The Mu'tazila, and other theologico-political movements, identified themselves as practitioners of the craft of *Kalam*, a style of thinking and debating. They were *Kalam* masters or experts, *mutakallimun*. Jahiz was renowned as a *Kalam* master. By the 840s the *Kalam* was well established as a set of identifiable, epistemological and social practices. It could boast of a cadre of exponents, the *Kalam* Masters. It had established an etiquette and code of conduct for its regularly heated and always fully committed debates – the fate of one's soul was at stake.

There were two complementary sides to the *Kalam*. N*azar* (speculation) was the rational and logical exploration of problems. *Jadal* (eristics) was the process of subjecting them to debate. As its name suggests, the *Kalam*, literally, 'talk', 'speech' or 'discourse', was a pronouncedly and profoundly oral activity, practised in groups, usually in the mosque but also in refined salons and in the doorways to people's houses and even on walks in the outskirts of the city. This is one of the reasons why we do not have any books of *Kalam* from the ninth century.

The defence of the religion was widely recognised as a core component of *Kalam* activity. There was a close intimacy between *Kalam* as a profession and the conduct of forensic inquiries. The *Kalam* and so many other intellectual activities of the period were predicated upon the question and answer style. And it has often been remarked that many early solutions to theological questions were legal solutions: most theologians were jurists.

Yet it would be wrong to think of the Mu'tazila as in any sense an organised group. What beliefs did Mu'tazilite thinkers share? Until about fifty years ago, it was fashionable to think of the Mu'tazila as the 'freethinkers' of early Islam. Their prioritisation of reason and their openness to the logic and argumentation of the ancient Greeks as represented in the *Organon* of Aristotle made them seem the most 'western' of the Islamic creeds. The Mu'tazila were thus feted as 'rationalists,' as continuators of the Greek tradition of logical analysis, and as the promoters of free will. They seemed to many scholars to prefigure the modern virtues of rationalism and philosophical mindedness. Of course this is not only an untenable retrospective history, a distortion based on a limited number of sources previously available, it is also a complete misreading of ninth-century society and Mu'tazilism as a complex system. The Mu'tazili notion of 'reason' has very little in common with rationalism.

An account of Mu'tazila beliefs should begin with 'divine unity.' For the Mu'tazila God was absolutely one, and they recognised no qualifications to His oneness. They were vehement in their opposition to any form of anthropomorphism (the idea the God shared any attributes or characteristics with man) and contemptuous of corporealism (the idea that God was or had a physical body), notions common to some early Shi'i groups and the emergent Prophetic Hadith movement. This meant that the Mu'tazila paid extremely close attention to how God can be described in human language, for they were wary lest any statement implied that an attribute such as 'knowing' was somehow co-eternal or even co-extensive with God. This led them to develop an uncompromising stance on the question of the Qur'an. The Qur'an is God's speech. Did God always have the power of speech? If He did not, how, why and when did He acquire it? If He did, was speech then co-eternal with God, for if it were, then a qualification to His absolute unity would have to be admitted.

The Mu'tazila were also marked out by their highly developed theory that the Qur'an was created in time, and not eternal. They tasked themselves with ensuring that an uncontaminated form of monotheism prevailed. This not only established caliphal legitimacy and authority, but also guaranteed that if the End Time were to come (and the Caliphs and their entourages were convinced it could come at any moment), the Caliph would not be judged by God to have been deficient in his promotion of the one, true faith. The Caliph, after all, was responsible for the salvation of his subjects and without the means for the enforcement of belief, a rightly ordered society could not be produced.

The desire of the Mu'tazila to preserve God's absolute unity at all costs also led them to locate moral responsibility for good and evil firmly within the human domain. This is part of what is meant by the notion of 'divine justness.' God may have the power to create good and bad (though some thinkers denied the latter), but He would never exercise the latter. Instead man was charged with the responsibility for his own actions.

The Mu'tazila argued that man had the ability to choose between right and wrong in his actions, though we should remember that a belief in moral responsibility and an ability to choose between right and wrong are not quite the same as holding a doctrine of free-will (many Mu'tazila seem to have held a sort of compatibilism: man could choose but God in His omniscience knew what man would choose). How could man make such a choice? The Mu'tazila argued that God had equipped man with a special faculty, that of the *'aql* (reason). It is here that the Mu'tazila encountered a conundrum: if God wanted man to choose between good and evil, and had given him reason to make his choice, how does man know what good and evil are? If the answer is through God's revelation, then He is not giving man that much moral responsibility in the end, is He? The Mu'tazila did not like this answer. It was too great a compromise for the notion of 'divine justness' and of man's moral responsibility for his actions. Many seem to have ended up arguing that 'good' and 'evil' were universal verities. They were aware that this seemed to compromise the notion of 'divine unity,' but seemed prepared to live with it. Their opponents were not, however.

The ideas of divine justness and man's moral responsibility led some Mu'tazila, Jahiz among them, to worship a providential God and to devise a theodicy according to which God's creation was optimally designed for man to discharge his moral responsibility. This in turn led Jahiz and others to develop notions about the optimal form of political system in which man could achieve this. Like many ancient thinkers, Jahiz was optimistic about man's ability to discharge his moral responsibility, but profoundly pessimistic about man's base and animal nature. Therefore man required restrictive political structures in which to operate: he had to be protected from himself.

The best social structure for Muslims was one which was stable and operated on the basis of a strict segregation according to birth and social function. The Caliph was at the head of this structure, as the Imam, God's chosen representative of the Prophet Muhammad, a spiritual and temporal leader. Then came the *khassa*, the 'special ones': the aristocracy (the caliphal family, descendants of the Prophet, ancient Arab nobility), the elites (such as the old Turkic families who had come from Khurasan when the 'Abbasids toppled the Umayyads and in 817 when Caliph Ma'mun returned from Merv to Baghdad), the senior civil servants within the imperial administration and the scholars (in Jahiz's system the scholars were those who professed Mu'tazilism, though it was in fact a highly contested category). Then came the *'amma*, the ordinary people and tradesfolk who thronged the streets of the cities such as Baghdad. The 'people of the Book', the religiously sanctioned belief systems incorporated within the community: Christians, Jews and Zoroastrians, were accommodated within this model and could belong to the civil administration, the community of scholars (as doctors or philosophers, for example), or the common people. These broad categories were to a certain extent porous at the level of the individual or the family unit: thus an individual skilled in the use of Arabic or a gifted poet could rise from fairly humble beginnings to a position of some privilege among the *khassa*. And this is precisely what Jahiz did, according to his legend.

What was it that held them together, that ensured this structure remained in place and functioned as well as it possibly could for man to achieve his God-given mandate to exercise moral responsibility? Jahiz's answer was Mu'tazilism. Jahiz promoted Mu'tazilism as a middle-way between the extremes of Shi'i charismatic authority and the denial of reason required by allegiance to the Hadith-based method for constructing the Sunna, the paradigmatic life and practice of Prophet Muhammad. Without such a middle way, society would be thrown out of kilter.

It is time to let Jahiz speak. The following passage occurs in *The Proofs of Prophethood,* his exploration of why Muhammad should be accepted and recognised by all creeds as God's Prophet:

You must understand that the only reason Almighty God made men's natural tendencies differ was in order that He might reconcile them, but He did not want to reconcile them in a manner contrary to their wellbeing. For if people were not subject to differing motivations and under compulsion in matters which suited and did not suit them, then, each and every one of them could conceivably choose to be merchants and craftsmen, or each and every one of them could conceivably seek kingship and rule.

This would make it impossible for men to live and would be disastrous for their wellbeing – it would spell perdition and ruin. If they were not subject to motivations and bound by incentives, they would avoid bloodletting, animal surgery, butchery and tanning altogether. All classes of people have a reason for thinking highly of what they do for a living. It is this which makes it easy for them to bear. Thus if the weaver sees some shoddy work or poor technique or clumsiness on the part of his colleague he will say to him, 'You oafish blood-letter!' and if the blood-letter sees some shoddy work on the part of his colleague, he will say to him, 'You clumsy weaver!' This is why they will only permit their sons to follow their own professions: weaving, blood-letting, animal surgery and butchery.

Had Almighty God not intended to make difference a cause of agreement and sociability, He would not have made one person short and another tall, one handsome and another ugly, one rich and another poor, one a man of reason and another a lunatic, or one clever and another a dolt. He made them all different to put them to the test, for it is through being put to the test that they obey and through obedience that they are given true happiness. Therefore He made them distinct that He might bring them together and He wanted to bring them together in obedience in order to bring them together in the reward to come.

Praise and glory be to the Exalted One! How good and fitting is His test, how magnificent His fashioning, how perfect His governance! For if everyone were to avoid the stigma of weaving, we would walk around naked, and if, to a man, people were to avoid the labour of construction, we would live in the open fields, and if they were to avoid agriculture, foodstuffs would disappear and life would basically be unsustainable. Therefore He subjected them without distressing them and He filled them with desire without rousing them.

If it were not for the difference in people's natures and incentives, they would only choose the most attractive things, the most temperate regions and the most central cities. If they were to make this choice, they would come to blows in their quest for central locations, and would contend for the high lands; no region could contain them all and no peace treaty would be observed. Therefore they have been led to the utmost contentment by God's subjugation. How can it be otherwise? If you were to move the forest dwellers to the deserts, the plain dwellers to the mountains, the mountain dwellers to the oceans, and the tent dwellers to brick houses, their hearts would be eaten up by anxiety and they would be consumed with excess competitiveness.

For Jahiz human society is the way it is because God has created it thus. And He created it thus as a test, in order that difference become a cause of agreement. We could be forgiven for finding in this passage an intimation of Isaiah Berlin's concept of 'positive freedom' whereby reason becomes an instrument of control, interference and oppression.

Jahiz the Thinker

So how did Jahiz view man? What did he think man's role was, as part of God's creation? Let us begin with epistemology, and the surviving traces of Jahiz's *Questions and Responses concerning how we Know*. This work, which survives in scattered and disjointed excerpts, was originally a doxography, that is it presented accounts of competing epistemologies as articulated by other Mu'tazilite thinkers. In this section Jahiz presents his own views. He seeks to clarify those conditions under which we assume the moral responsibility imposed upon us by God for it is only then that we will be held to account for our response to the decisive proof which He has sent in the form of His messenger and the Qur'an. We will see that Jahiz sets some very stringent conditions for men to qualify as responsible under God's moral obligation:

Now I will describe my doctrine on knowing and respond to my opponent on the meaning of 'capacity,' on the modes of capacity in which moral obligation is appropriate and good and the decisive proof is established, and those modes in which moral obligation is inappropriate and bad and the decisive proof is not established.

My first point is this: God does not impose on anyone the performance or avoidance of any action, except of course for those beyond excuse and impervious to the decisive proof. Moral obligation is only imposed on a person who has a healthy body, a well-balanced temperament, and ample means to act; when he has cleared his mind of distractions and knows how to perform the action; when the opportunity for wishing it done are present; when his thoughts are in equipoise and he is cognisant of what he may do and what he ought to do.

He will only be capable in a real sense when these features and the well-known conditions enumerated obtain. They are the basis on which actions occur. They result in choice. Man's moral obligation is seemly and good, his religious duties are incumbent, the Punishment is possible and the Reward is meet because of them. If a man were capable simply because his body is sound and healthy, then we would be capable of climbing up a height without a ladder. A man will only choose to act and be capable in a real and not a tropical sense when his incentives are exactly equal to his disincentives. Thus when you compare what he hopes to receive with what he is afraid of, when you compare his preference for pleasure with his fear of the afterlife, when you compare his experience of what is unpleasant here and now with his hopes of the world to come, you will find them equal in terms of how they attract and dispel hardship and ease.

Furthermore, it is only when he is known to persist in this last condition that a man can be deemed to be under moral obligation. This is because the reasoning intellect is there to act as guardian whereas nature, in which our soul is vested, is to be guarded against. If the guardian is stronger than its natural inclinations, the soul will yield naturally because it is the way of the soul to yield to the stronger of its two guardians and the more robust of its two causes. When the two faculties are equivalent in force, action occurs through choice and is no longer to be defined as coerced. However coercion varies in severity and leniency, and may be less evident in some cases and more evident in others. Take for example when a man, who has no motives for enduring a scorching wind through staying put, runs away, whereas he flees more quickly, leaps further and moves more swiftly from the flames of a fire!

When nature prevails over the reasoning intellect it debilitates and alters it. When it is debilitated and altered, the ideas in his brain are altered and projected to him as images which are not their true ones. When like this, a person is too weary to perceive what he is due to receive in the world to come – his desires make indulgence in the present world attractive. But when the strength of his intellect is superior to the strength of the elements of his nature, these elements are debilitated. In this situation, his preference is for resolute behaviour and he opts for the pleasure of the afterlife over pleasure in the here and now. It becomes his nature. He cannot fight against it – it is compulsory and he is incapable of anything else. Only when his humours are well balanced, the motives are equal, and the causes equiponderant, does the soul choose in a real sense and avoid the actions of nature.

Thus when God gives balance to man's constitution, shapes his reasons and teaches him his rights and obligations, man is in a real sense capable of action, and moral obligation becomes incumbent upon him as a result of the conclusive proof provided by God.

The 'reasoning intellect' is my translation for *'aql*, a word often rendered simply as 'reason' and sometimes in philosophical texts as 'rationality' or 'intellect'. This reasoning intellect and nature are 'two faculties'. The soul is in the sway of human nature, though it is not identical with nature. It is rather a third entity between the two faculties. One's fate in the afterlife will be determined by the outcome of the conflict between the two faculties and the soul seems to be both battleground and prize.

Jahiz implies that it is not a good thing at the outset for the reasoning intellect to overpower nature too easily, but does not say why. I presume that the reason it should not be too hasty to dominate nature and the soul is because this might make it liable to an unquestioning acceptance of opinion and belief (which Jahiz thought was a very bad thing to do). It seems that equiponderance between reason and nature is required for there to be choice and that regular choice leads to habituation and presumably moral improvement.

Choice and moral accountability can only occur when a man is in a state of emotional and mental equipoise, when his fears balance his desires, when his reasons for doing something match his reasons for not doing something. Thus man is only really free when he is not under duress. And when he is not under duress he will perceive with clarity that it is in his best interests to act in this life in ways that will secure for him a life in Paradise.

Much of this will seem strange to readers unfamiliar with ninth century anthropology and ethics. I agree – the thought-world is unusual and its expression dense. What is this reasoning intellect that must overcome nature and control the motives, inclination, disinclinations, anxieties, fears and desires that seem to rage in the soul?

The Reasoning Intellect

There is a telling passage about the reasoning intellect in an ethical treatise Jahiz composed exhorting a young charge to be careful of loose and inappropriate talk. It is known as *On keeping a secret and holding one's tongue*:

I have two criticisms to make: you say the wrong things at the wrong time; you cannot keep a secret. The task I am setting you, the burden I am asking you to assume, is neither easy nor light. I know this only too well for in the course of my life, I can think of not one single person out of all the people I have met, whose control of his tongue I approve of and whose ability to keep a secret I applaud. And I am thinking here of those who seek leadership and authority through membership of the elite and inclusion in the upper ranks of society, who pride themselves on their learning, their imperturbable gravity and seriousness, their self-control and composure. This is because there is nothing harder to achieve than circumventing one's passions, and overcoming one's desires.

Desire has long held sway over judgement, and it is desire which is the motive for spilling a secret and letting one's tongue loose with too much talk. The reasoning intellect is called the intellect because of the way in which it restrains and forbids – Almighty God said, 'Surely the man guided by his restraining intellect sees that this is by God's decree?' (89:5) The intellect puts a halter and bridle on the tongue. It deters it by binding its legs. It manacles excess speech and restrains it, preventing it from charging headlong down the path of crass incivility, making mistakes and causing damage. This is exactly how a camel is restrained. It is how the orphan is prevented from disposing of property at whim. The tongue is the heart's translator. The heart is a strongbox where thoughts and secrets are deposited, and where good and bad things are stored by the senses. It is where the effects generated by our appetites and desires, and the products of wisdom and learning are kept.

The breast is not a receptacle for physical matter. It stores what it does thanks to a power given it by God, a power which we humans do not comprehend. It is constructed in such a way that it is too narrow and constricted to hold its contents. It finds its burden onerous and seeks relief in disburdening itself. It derives pleasure from unloading its contents onto the tongue. It is scarcely able to find consolation by talking in private to itself about its contents and so these contents are communicated to others who do not preserve or keep them safe. This is what happens when desire dominates the tongue and goes in for excessive thinking. This in turn leads to excessive speech.

So the task of the reason, the intellect, is to keep the passions and appetites in check. It is man's principal, God-given, mechanism for moral and spiritual improvement. This is a different conception of reason from that of the rational intellect we are familiar with from the philosophical tradition.

Doubt was one of the strategies which the Mu'tazila thought were at the disposal of the reasoning intellect. For Jahiz, doubt could either be destructive and lead to the spiritual emptiness of scepticism, or it could take the form of the aporia and become constructive. According to Jahiz's vision of the *Kalam*, the aporetic query was a vital step in the progress towards certainty. Without the aporia, without questioning not only the first principles of an argument but all our inherited and cherished beliefs, we could not truly be said to have hobbled and curbed all our desires and appetites, incentives and disincentives.

The term which Jahiz and his contemporaries used to describe this all too human trait of unquestioning and uncritical acceptance was *taqlid*. The man of reason should not accept any belief or opinion, any item of information or meme from anyone, no matter who that someone was, no matter what their authority, no matter how attractive the memeplex was, without first subjecting it to the most robust and engaged form of scrutiny. Even the authority of Prophet Muhammad was subjected to such an inquiry and of course vindicated fully and without qualification, as Jahiz's treatise on *The Proofs of Prophethood* demonstrated. Jahiz would not, however, have expected his readers to take his word for this – for this would itself be *taqlid*, uncritical and unquestioning acceptance of Jahiz's authority. He would have expected his readers to subject his arguments to the severest aporetic doubt. That is why Jahiz's writings exist in a perpetual state of epistemic postponement. They aim to convince but require scrutiny and questioning before any reader can give them his assent.

This is what I mean by Jahiz the freethinker: the thinker who applies doubt to any obstacle in his path to certain knowledge, in order to free himself of any notion he may unwittingly give assent to. And this style of writing in a state of perpetually deferred and postponed assent is also a style of freethinking: it is writing which expects its reader to reciprocate and engage in the application of aporia and doubt before assent is conceded – before we agree with its author. In fact, I would go further and claim that in many works, Jahiz writes in such a way as to make it impossible for his readers to assent. These works are exercises in freethinking as a cognitive enterprise.

Jahiz was also obsessed with language and correct speech. Speech is what makes humans human. Jahiz wrote a wrote in which he argued for *The Superiority of Speech to Silence*:

I have not found silence to be in any way superior to speech. Analogical reasoning supports this, because you describe silence with speech but do not describe speech with silence. If silence were superior, if quietness were more appropriate, there would be no way of knowing that human beings were superior to other creatures, and there would be no way of separating them from any other living creature or any other kind of creation, in terms of their primary substance and different natures, separate states and classes of body, in their essential identity and variety.

Indeed, it would not be possible to tell the difference between men and erected idols and graven images. Every act of being seated and standing, of moving and being at rest or being erected and fixed in the ground would be completely alike, in one ontological condition and in a similar category, since both would effectively be lifeless, because of the effect that silence produces. However humans and statues are distinct by means of reasoned discourse, because of the effect that speech produces.

Jahiz does not mean that idols and statues move, though they can be depicted as reclining or standing. The point is that without speech there is no essential difference between a statue fashioned in a sitting position and a man sitting down. People are distinguished from the rest of creation, animate and inanimate, through the faculty of speech. When silence is the accident which applies to them, they are as mute as statues or corpses, but when they assume the accident of speech, they can distinguish themselves both from the inarticulate and from each other, because not all of the sons of Adam are equal in their reasoned discourse. This has an obvious bearing on how well people can articulate their religions and on how they can express the testimonies of their faith (it being taken for granted that Islam is the consummate religion because of the Arabic of the Qur'an). Speech is how God has asked man to respond to Him:

Speech (*kalam*) is so esteemed and reasoned discourse so valued that God made speech the means to glorify and praise Him – it is speech which points to the waymarks of His religion and the revealed paths of His faith, and is the sign of how to meet with His satisfaction, for when any of His creation embraces the faith, only explicit declaration will satisfy God. He has made the tongue the means of doing this, and clarity (*bayan*) its method. He made the tongue that which voices what the believer keeps hidden in his breast, that which clarifies the information he provides, and that which enunciates what he does not otherwise have the capacity to state clearly. It is the heart's interpreter, and the heart is a capacious receptacle.

For Jahiz, verbal enunciation was only one of the five means of achieving clear communication (*bayan*): the other four are pointing, dactylonomy (counting with the fingers or knuckles), writing and the physical-ontological location of a thing. Speech however is privileged. And speech incorporates writing.

Jahiz took this idea of clear communication further. He saw it not only as man's distinguishing feature but also as the task God has set man as the grateful response to His beneficent and providential creation. Out of all of creation, man alone has been given the gift of the ability to read God's signs – and Jahiz thought that all creation was a giant and extensive semiotic system that pointed to God's providential care for His creatures.

There was another reason for this interest in language. Jahiz and his contemporaries were interested in not only the production of language but in its use and in how to interpret it. Or to put it differently: they were interested in both speaking and listening. Writing and the written word were viewed as essentially another form of speaking – the Qur'an is the word of God. Therefore this interest in listening to an utterance and interpreting the intention of its speaker included reading. And let us recall that for Jahiz reading was an exercise in seeking to rid oneself of *taqlid*, uncritical acceptance of beliefs. This meant that reading the Qur'an involved interpreting it afresh, for oneself, to the exclusion of the inherited exegeses and interpretations developed by others, unless and until in the course of his reading the man of reasoning intellect reached an interpretation reached by others.

The primary task Jahiz and his contemporaries set themselves was to understand how to listen to and read the Qur'an properly. To this end, Jahiz and the Mu'tazila generally explored a distinction in language usage which they saw as fundamental to all speech: the distinction between literal and figurative language.

The Qur'an contains numerous verses which refer to God in human terms: God sitting on a throne, or the hand of God for example. There were some in the ninth century who argued that Muslims should accept these descriptions of God, without asking or seeking to explain what they mean (the *bi-la kayf* doctrine). The Mu'tazila, on the other hand, could not bring themselves to accept these descriptions at face value. For them this constituted anthropomorphism at best. At worst it was outright corporealism – the belief that God was a material body. It involved a complete violation of the principle of divine oneness (*tawhid*) and the related principles of divine simplicity and ineffable superiority to His creation (*tanzih*). But how could they revere God's word in the Qur'an and remain true to their vision of Him? The answer lay in tropical or figurative speech.

In his *Attack on the Anthropomorphists*, Jahiz rehearses and refutes a number of positions, such as the idea that God is a physical body:

The proponents of anthropomorphism disagree as to how they understand it. Some say, 'We say that He is a body and every body is long.' Others say, 'We say that He is a body but we do not say that He is long, because we make Him a body simply to take Him out of the category of non-existence, for when we make a statement about a thing we render it intelligible and conceivable, and body is the only intelligible and conceivable thing. We have no need to make Him long and His being a body does not necessarily entail that He be long, because a body can be long and not be long, such as when it is circular, triangular, square and so on. But a thing must be intelligible and that which is intelligible must be a body. This is why we have made Him a body but have not given Him length.'

God have pity on you! The proponent of this position has no option but to make God wide if he does not make Him long; or if he does not make Him wide, then he must make him circular; or if he does not make Him circular, he must make Him triangular; or if he does not make Him triangular, he must make Him square. If he identifies any shape whatsoever, then he has ended up where he really did not intend to go. Yet every circle, triangle, square, pentangle, cruciform, polygon – every shape I am familiar with is too ugly to utter in this context and to vile to conceive.

In other words, no matter how perfect the circle or any other shape, be it in word or in thought, it still pales into comparison with the perfection of God and is inappropriate as a way to refer to Him.

His argument leads to his final, decisive rebuttal of the incoherence of the anthropomorphist position:

God only uses expressions which can be understood in one way or another, whether that be the primary use, upon which the meaning of the expression is predicated, or the secondary and derivative use which the Arabs call 'tropical'. So let us consider God's speech when He says: 'Deaf, dumb, blind – it is they who do not understand!' (2:171). In our view God is just and does not do wrong, so we know that if those to whom He refers actually were disabled and incompetent, they would have been obligated to fulfil something they were unable to. Now, a deity who obliges his worshippers to fulfil something they are not able to is a wrongdoer and is unjust. That description does not befit Him. Therefore we know that they must have been fully competent, and not incapable or disabled. Given this, it becomes obligatory to rule in favour of the secondary, tropical, use, and to abandon the primary use, that upon which the tropical use is predicated.

So the notion of divine justness takes interpretative priority and becomes the basis for the proper reading of the verse of the Qur'an.

Thus an understanding of tropical, figurative language was central to how Jahiz thought the Qur'an should be read. And the Qur'an had to be read with the reasoning intellect, the *'aql*, the hobble of interpretation, in a state of mind in which the right-thinking human being could exercise choice and seek to evade the pernicious effects of *taqlid*, uncritical reading. Choice was only possible in a state of equilibrium, when motives, incentives, disincentives, and distractions had been neutralised by the reasoning intellect. This was not just a hermeneutic or epistemological position. It was personal (mistaken readings could consign one's soul to eternal damnation) and political (an anthropomorphic regime was an outrage against God).

Reading as Dangerous Freethinking

As the spokesperson of his society Jahiz did not seek to position himself as supreme authority. Rather his writings were designed to promote freethinking and thus function as society's guide (in the same way that Plato's Socrates was both gadfly and midwife of Athens). It might be thought that such freethinking and reading could constitute a danger to society. Would it not lead to anarchy, or relativism, or to the predominance of interpretive error, whim and caprice? Jahiz would have countered that it would lead to no such thing, that there was no such threat: the application of reason would lead inexorably to the same conclusions as its application had led him.

Others disagreed, in particular Ibn Qutayba (d. 889), a younger contemporary who may have studied with Jahiz. Jahiz's rejection of an unquestioning acceptance of authority was too much for how Ibn Qutayba wanted to shape the next generation of writers and intellectuals who sought authoritative hegemony, who saw their moral task as speaking with society's voice, as speaking on behalf of their society. Thanks to Ibn Qutayba's withering critique, Jahiz was branded as capricious, as volatile, as a sophist. His books were read for amusement, or out of antiquarianism, or as an example of style.

Jahiz's positioning of reading as freethinking constituted a threat to an authoritarian style of writing, a style of writing in which authorship was synonymous with authority. The threat of reading as freethinking had to be removed. His unwillingness to accept the views of others unquestioningly, his style of writing as an invitation to challenge and examine his own views through a mode of reading that required of the reader profound and extensive scrutiny, were dangerous and thought to be subversive. The task for the next generation was how best to promote a tempered form of *taqlid* through control of the reading and interpretation of the Qur'an. They had no desire to subject it to Jahiz's reasoning intellect. They had little time for reading as freethinking.

And here's a paradox to end on: Jahiz, the communitarian voice of the elite who argued so passionately in favour of freethinking as central to the articulation of his society and inveighed so consistently against *taqlid*, the unquestioning acceptance of authority, was read as a threat to the proper articulation of society.

IBN RUSHD'S DANGEROUS IDEA

Oliver Leaman

The discussion of how radical ibn Rushd is as a thinker involves not only an understanding of his views, but also a view of what one takes to be radical. He is often taken to be something of an Enlightenment thinker a long time before the Enlightenment. He is often taken to be linked with the Arabic renaissance, the *Nahdah*. His arguments and ideas are certainly very different from the *Nahdah*, so we are being very creative if we link him with it, or even with what came to be known in Christian Europe as radical Averroism. On the other hand, we should not be too literal here. Interesting thinkers tend to have ideas that continue to develop and grow after their time, and it is difficult to deny that those ideas are connected with where they in fact originated.

Abū l-Walīd Muḥammad bin 'Aḥmad bin Rušd (1126–1198), commonly known as ibn Rushd and as Averroes in the West, is a defining figure in *mashsha'i* philosophy, the peripatetic trend that dominated Islamic philosophy for a brief but very rich period between the ninth and twelfth centuries. Ibn al-'Arabi describes two meetings with him, one when ibn Rushd was dead and he transported his bones back to Spain – the corpse balanced with his books. And an earlier meeting when the younger man impressed ibn Rushd with his brilliance (Islamic philosophers are not famous for their modesty). These encounters are supposed to symbolise the victory of Sufism over the older form of philosophy, the sort of thinking represented by ibn Rushd himself. They were no doubt fictional but represent something that really happened, the eclipse for a long time of the sort of thought that ibn Rushd championed, in the Islamic world at least.

Ibn Rushd had a turbulent political career, and sometimes had to leave Cordoba, but this may well have had nothing to do with his philosophical ideas. He was a significant political and legal figure and it could well have been something in those areas of his career that led to his problems. On the other hand, his philosophical views are challenging and expressed quite frankly, and we do get the impression of a combative thinker. Ibn Rushd was a passionate defender of philosophy, not as just one among many paths to knowledge available to the Muslim thinker, but as the main technique, the way of doing things that represents the ultimate arbiter for theoretical problems. Philosophy has the leading role in the battle between the different factions in the Islamic intellectual world, the lawyers, theologians, grammarians, *muhadithun*, and so on, and in the demarcation disputes that had been running for centuries as to who had the leading role in the battle of ideas, ibn Rushd came down decisively on the side of philosophy.

We do not know how many, if any, of the stories that have come down to us about ibn Rushd are true. In particular, did the caliph really ask him to summarise the works of Aristotle, as is often suggested? Were this to have taken place it would certainly have validated his efforts, but it does not seem like a typical request for a ruler to a subject. Did ibn Tufayl (1105–1185), his friend and mentor, really decline this offer (perhaps rather prudently) and passed the poisoned chalice to the more incautious ibn Rushd? Did the latter really work every day of his life except the day his father died and the day he got married? That at least sounds quite likely, given what we know of his productivity. The dramatic context within which ibn Rushd worked has provided room for a romantic view of ibn Rushd at the hands of Ernest Renan (1823–1892) and Jorge Luis Borges (1899–1986), for example, and even Yusuf Chahine in his film *al-Masir* (1997). In this view we see the champion of reason, Averroes, confronting the forces of obscurantism and fundamentalism, first of all losing, but later on winning. There is a nice parallelism here with the debate with his predecessor al-Ghazali (1058–111) and the latter's attack on Islamic peripatetic philosophy and in particular on ibn Sina (980-1037) in his *Tahafut al-falasifah* (Refutation of the philosophers). Ibn Rushd's *Tahafut al-tahafut* (Refutation of the Refutation) had no visible impact in the Islamic world, but is often regarded as having answered al-Ghazali pretty definitively. Yet no-one seems to have noticed, at least none of the people he would have wanted to notice – his fellow Muslims. On the other hand, the debate was taken up by Jews and

Christians, where ibn Rushd's ideas were to flourish for several subsequent centuries. In fact, al-Ghazali's attack on philosophy is often taken to have destroyed it in the Arab world at least for a very long period, perhaps continuing to today, while ibn Rushd's response was largely ignored or dismissed.

The dramatic role that some have sought to establish for ibn Rushd is probably misplaced. He appears to have been personally a rather retiring individual and someone who couched his views in generally careful and cautious language. There is no evidence that he regarded his thought as radical, nor that he had any religious doubts or even heterodox views on Islam. On the contrary, as a Maliki lawyer his legal judgements portray a faithful and unoriginal approach based on the principles of that legal school. He was very much a member of the Andalusian establishment — his grandfather being a well-known lawyer, in fact better known than his grandson. The whole phenomenon of radical Averroism that was so significant in Christian Europe would have very much surprised him, and it is unlikely that he would have recognised himself in the film about him by Chahine, or even understood much of the dialogue, especially the Egyptian Arabic.

The issue of how radical ibn Rushd was has nothing to do with how radical he thought he was. The thought of significant philosophers has always burst its banks and ended up in surprising places, all of which does not mean that it did not have an original source with the philosopher himself. A source is just a starting place and cannot say where one has to stop.

What came to be known as Averroism is a mixture of doctrines. One of these is a sustained enthusiasm for Aristotle and what is taken to be Aristotelianism. It is not always easy to see what thinkers like ibn Rushd found exciting about Aristotle, since he is not the most thrilling of philosophers either in style or in doctrine. He comes over as middle-aged, cautious and restrained in his expression, by contrast with the more passionate Plato and the romantic story of the life and death of Socrates, often taken to be a mystic in Islamic philosophy. Aristotle survives largely through the lecture notes of his students, so much of his style must have disappeared in the process in any case. What made Aristotle exciting was not his style but what the main conclusions of his thought were taken to be, and these are both challenging to traditional religion and yet seemingly well-based. They include a theory of the creation of the world that has it as an eternal process, when combined with a form of neoplatonism, and great difficulties in the notion of a personal afterlife. What also made him exciting was the fact that his philosophical system was indeed a system, and could stand in opposition to other theoretical systems, those associated with traditional religion, and it could match the Islamic sciences in complexity and scope. In the Islamic world this is something that was noticed by the critics of philosophy, that philosophy's supporters often put their faith in philosophy just as uncritically as (some) people put their faith in religion. Al-Ghazali criticised *taqlid* (imitation) in all its forms. Philosophy comes to be an alternate way of understanding the world and our role in it, and as a plausible candidate here looks threatening to religion. When ibn Rushd argues in his *Fasl al-maqal* that many of the protracted disputes in Islamic theology can quite easily be resolved when they are examined philosophically he is advocating an entirely new approach to how to resolve difficulties that arise within Islam. His modesty here is disingenuous, since it is not just that according to him these protracted disputes rest on a slight difference in understanding the key terms of the dispute. In fact they are to be resolved by replacing the old methodology of the *kalam* with philosophy, the sort of philosophy that ibn Rushd developed, and that is because according to him the technique, *tariqa*, that he is offering is really powerful when compared with anything that Islamic theology can do.

The Link Between Philosophy and Religion

It might seem a strange claim that philosophy can replicate or even replace religion, especially as religion is much more of a system to help everyone understand the world than philosophy is. The relationship between philosophy and religion was much discussed in Islamic philosophy and a popular line ever since al-Farabi (872–950/51) was that they both express the same truth, while religion is more accessible to the public at large. Hence it is not so strange to see philosophy and religion as two ways of doing the same thing, as both presenting views of the world, and as requiring some theory to explain how they differ and how they are the same. Radical Averroism is often presented as arguing that philosophy and religion are both true but present incompatible propositions, which only have relevance in their own systems of discourse. Language does often ground the truth of a proposition within what we might call a particular language game. It is true within the normal practice of making knowledge claims, for instance, that as I make these remarks, if I am giving a lecture, I can claim to know I am awake, as Wittgenstein argued at some length in his *On Certainty*. Yet it is also possible that I am dreaming I am giving a talk, and so my knowledge claim is false. Wittgenstein would say that there are two different language games in operation here, the normal one of making knowledge claims and the very unusual one of trying to ground those claims in something rock solid. He suggested that although we can ground a claim made in a game according to the rules of the game, we cannot ground a game itself, and that seems right. After all, we cannot say that the rules of poker are good rules or bad rules, they are the rules of poker, and if someone wants to play a different game, that is fine, but they should not use that game to criticise another game. The 'should' here is not moral. It means that there is no point in criticising one game by contrast with another, unless we find somewhere outside of the games to provide us with criteria for such an approach.

This might seem to be a prevarication, since surely in the link between philosophy and religion we often have two claims made about the same thing that sometimes cannot both be true, and which cannot just be shrugged off as existing within different language games. For example, according to the Qur'an there is, after we die, judgement of us for our behaviour and punishment or reward for us in the next world. According to ibn Rushd, this cannot be true, since there is no 'us' after we die, just a blending of everyone into one mind, without a body, that sort of survives by thinking. But ibn Rushd does not say it in this way; he says it cannot be literally true, that we need to understand it as figurative language when looked at *sub specie aeternitatis*, under the aspect of eternity, as we ought to look at it. The Islamic philosophers had a theory of the links between different sorts of theoretical language which was shared by most of them. According to it, philosophy is deeper than religion, but accessible only to those capable of the sort of thinking it involves. So that the truths philosophers can grasp might be more widely dispersed among the general population, religions formulate those truths in more vivid and exciting ways than the philosophers can. A problem here though is that the religious statement may be implausible if not understood to be a more popular version of a more restricted truth. Why is this a problem? It suggests that those who are only able to access religion are obliged to travel second class, while the philosophers go first class. It suggests also that the latter try to hoodwink the former by hiding the real difference that may exist between their views. After all, there is a difference between second and first class which is different from the difference between poker and whist.

Here we need to be careful. There are two claims that could be made, and they are very different from each other. One is that religious and philosophical statements on the same topic are radically distinct in the sense that the former are false while the latter are true. Out of prudential reasons we would of course expect philosophers to clothe this harsh view in a sort of 'different but equal' theory. This was the sort of theory that prevailed under apartheid for instance to suggest that whites and the other races in South Africa were subject to different rules, yet despite this were all equal. We hear this today in countries which restrict women for religious reasons, they often say that men and women are treated equally, but differently. They are equal in the sense that they are treated in accordance with a theory that they have distinct interests and so different roles, and apart from these variations there is no basis to treat individuals unequally. The issue is not so much one of equality but rather of fairness. It is not fair to expect very different people to be treated the same. At an airport only those with physical problems should be transported in wheelchairs from plane to plane. It would be ridiculous for me to claim that I was treated unfairly if I was not similarly helped.

A milder distinction between religion and philosophy is to say that they both agree, but often seem not to, and this is a problem that can be clarified quite easily by some theory that shows how to get from one kind of language to another. Ibn Rushd defends the principle that it is philosophy that explains religion, and not the other way round, but as has already been pointed out, this is very much the standard view in *falsafa mashsha'i* (Peripatetic) philosophy. But the fact that it is the standard view does not mean that it is not radical. For one thing, it dethrones theology from its former role of superiority, and places hermeneutics at the behest of philosophy. It shifts the balance of power from religion to other ways of acquiring knowledge, it might be said, and this implies that religion is not the most important route to the truth.

On the other hand, religion is the most important route to the truth for most people. This is why ibn Rushd tells us that the Qur'an does not explain in more detail the various passages that refer to God in material language. Most people think in material terms and this is how they tend to think of God, in a way that strictly speaking is problematic. But it is not problematic for them, it is their way of understanding the truth. It is only problematic if they come to question it, because they will not be satisfied with the answer and do not have the right way of thinking to come to the right answer by themselves. If they listen to the explanations of the theologians they will become even more confused and perhaps end up doubting the main principles of religion. They will no longer be satisfied with their earlier unsophisticated take on the topic, and the suggestions of the theologians will be found to be entirely unsatisfactory. They will resemble medical patients who try to understand their disease and its treatment who then consider taking all manner of different measures as cures since they do not grasp how the cure really works. Their lack of knowledge may lead to a general scepticism about medicine which is unfounded and patients would be much better off just doing what they were told by those who know, 'those firmly grounded in knowledge' (Qur'an 3:7). For ibn Rushd this group of people who are well-grounded in knowledge are the philosophers, and it falls to them to interpret difficult passages, and for sick people they are the physicians. Every area has its experts and if we are wise we listen to them if we need to escape from some difficulty in which we find ourselves.

This reliance on experts goes against a great deal in modern culture that disapproves of paternalism, and also the elitism that this suggests. Cannot an ordinary person work out for himself or herself how to deal with at least some illnesses, for example, and also some theological problems? We tend to think now that illness does not have a clear cure in many cases and it is up to the patient to work out where to go for treatment, which treatment options to try, how to assess the evidence of their condition as relayed to them by the medical staff, and so on. Ibn Rushd, some would say like a typical authoritarian doctor, assumes that medicine has the answer and all the patient has to do is do what he or she is told, and then they will be cured. This is based on a view of science that identifies it with necessary connections and is far from our conception today. Although no doubt there is a well-established link between cause and event in medicine, and physicians know more about it than most other people, frequently decisions have to be made among alternative treatments, and there is little reason to think that only physicians have useful observations to make on this topic. On the contrary, ordinary people may develop a good insight in what works for them and what sort of treatment they would then like to try.

Ibn Rushd and Language

What is radical about Averroism is the idea that one form of language is better or more significant or stronger than the other, but this is not obviously the position of any of the major Muslim *falasifa*. To put it in the language of modern politics, it is radical to believe that one narrative is at odds with alternative narratives, because then one has to destroy or overcome the others. For example, it is important for many Armenians that the 1915 massacres of their countrymen in Turkey are classified as genocide. For many Turks this is entirely wrong, and although many Armenians were certainly killed, so were other national categories and it was in the middle of a war. It is not radical to accept a certain coming together of the narratives, in the sense that on major issues they can be seen to coincide. This is what happens when people in conflict become reconciled to each other, or when a situation that someone finds very difficult to accept becomes less traumatic. It is quite possible for those who regard the Armenian tragedy as genocide to find an acknowledgement of the suffering from Turkey in a form that respects the event, although perhaps not entirely in the terms that the Armenians find accurate. Although it is not unusual to consider Ibn Rushd as far more extreme and frank in his views than many of his predecessors, in fact this is hardly the case. He merely represents the tradition of linking and separating religion and philosophy that pervades the *mashsha'i* approach to the nature of language. Thinkers like `Abd al-Jabiri (1936–2010), the Moroccan philosopher, and Farah Antun (1874–1922), th Syrian secularist thinker, have interpreted him as doing something ver different from the *falsafa* tradition, but this is not an easy argument to make. To see him as a defender of secularism, or at least of the desirability of divorcing the state from religion is to fail to represent his views correctly. On the other hand, if it is thought that the use of reason will eventually overcome religion, then ibn Rushd is indeed an anti-religious thinker, since he does advocate and defend the significance of reason.

Where al-Jabiri is on more solid ground is in his suggestion that the whole philosophical tradition is just like a mirror image of the *salafi* position in religion, in that it bases itself on precedents, and in particular on what it takes to be the original and best thinkers. There is of course a criticism of reliance on reason that stems originally from Hegel and was emphasised by the Frankfurt School, and is based on the idea that there is nothing outside of reason to validate its use and significance. Aristotle and Muhammad have a similar role, it might well be argued, and just as Muhammad presents the message of God and recites it, so Aristotle receives the message of reason and passes it on. As al-Jabiri points out, there is certain dogmatism in this approach, since who would argue with God, from an Islamic point of view, or with reason, were one to be a philosopher? Yet philosophy does not consist just of answers, and it might well be said nor does religion; both are rich in questions and debates, and this is how a culture and society becomes revitalised and modern. Its citizens use their minds and do not just accept what they are told, however plausible it seems or powerful its backers. Even in the case of an individual, we tend to expect someone to have a lively mind and work out what he or she is going to do by themselves, whereas the sort of person who requires constant guidance and instruction is less impressive.

What the defenders of ibn Rushd as a radical thinker assume is that philosophy presents an alternative way of looking at the world compared to religion, and that once the former is introduced, the latter will barely survive in its shadow. This view fails to understand a really crucial aspect of ibn Rushd's system, the way in which every language game has its own rules and operates coherently within those rules. They do not require any further validation by looking for evidence outside of them, and they do not challenge any other language games, in just the same way that there is no criticism of cricket by people who play football. We can describe things in a variety of ways, and none is better than any other.

Yet it will be said that this might be true of games, but surely it cannot be true of things as important as religion and reason, where truth is at issue. After all, there is nothing true about a sport, it is just a sport. This does not present a problem for ibn Rushd, though, since he has a theory that both reason and religion are true, and point to the same truth, albeit in different ways. This theory, as we have argued, did not originate with him but was a staple of Islamic philosophy, and if it can be attributed to anyone originally it probably should be laid at the door of al-Farabi. The theory is plausible and it is not difficult to see how it works, and the more plausible it looks, the less radical it appears to be. This is because the challenging nature of the thesis is taken to be the attack on religion, or the attempt to replace religion with reason. This is not ibn Rushd's thesis at all, but does it follow from it?

Philosophy as Superior to Religion

In one final attempt at squeezing something radical out of ibn Rushd, what about the idea that the ultimate way of resolving theological issues is through philosophy, and not, say, the other way round? Surely this at least is to reduce the status of religion and elevate philosophy. What ibn Rushd claims is that philosophy is the ultimate guide to when we should interpret a religious claim literally or otherwise. If the religious claim makes no sense unless it is interpreted allegorically, then it should be interpreted allegorically. Is this not to demean religion, since religion might suggest that it should determine issues like allegory and literal meaning? But philosophy is the study of meanings in general, according to the *falsafa* tradition, so philosophy is in charge of deciding, as it were, how any language claim is to be understood. Criticising the use of philosophy here is a bit like criticising someone for opening a sticky door of a beautiful building with a humble but useful spanner. No-one would say that since tools create access to buildings, and indeed even buildings themselves, tools are more important than the buildings, nor that if language is important in prayer, then language is more important than prayer. This is a point that ibn Rushd himself uses in the *Decisive Treatise*, that an implement which is used for *halal* purposes itself become *halal*, although it is only an ordinary implement with nothing in any way different about it as compared with any other implement.

This is a plausible answer, but it fails to hide the fact that if Ibn Rushd is correct, then the balance of power in Islamic intellectual life will have to change. It will no longer be the theologians and those connected to them who have the ultimate expertise to decide controversial and difficult issues. They continue to have a role, but their role is a secondary one, and the main thinkers will be the philosophers, those who base their ideas on reason and not on religion. This is a radical doctrine, and however much ibn Rushd may have tried to sugar the pill, when it moved to the Christian and Jewish worlds its import became evident. While we may disagree with the rather naive enthusiasm of Renan and others for the Enlightenment and ibn Rushd's putative role in its Islamic version, the *Nahda*, the broad principle is correct. Ibn Rushd did have a challenging doctrine of the superiority of philosophy over the other Islamic sciences, not essentially a different theory from many of the other *falasifa*, but he describes it in starker terms than was common in the tradition, and perhaps his career in public life suffered as a result. He certainly had a tempestuous political life, but whether this had anything to do with his philosophical work cannot be said.

A Question of Methodology

We are going to have to conclude by reminding ourselves of an issue raised at the start. How far are we entitled to extend an author's views to explore what we take to be their logical implications, but not necessarily what the author himself took his views to be? Narrow historical concerns might tend to persuade us to restrict what we say about a thinker to precisely the views he would have identified with and leave it at that. I have argued here that this is misleading at least in philosophy, since philosophical ideas are not designed merely to deal with a specific issue but are taken to have much wider implications, and it is by no means misleading to connect a thinker with the drawn out consequences of his thought even if he himself would not have directly drawn those consequences. It is by no means inappropriate to identify with ibn Rushd the demand for a new balance of power in human thought between religion and reason, where the latter is given the leading role. This idea is pregnant with many other ideas, and came to have a revolutionary impact in the intellectual world, and that suggests that we should regard ibn Rushd, perhaps despite himself, as a radical thinker indeed.

AL-HALLAJ'S TRUTH, MASSIGNON'S FICTION

Robert Irwin

On the evening before his execution in Baghdad for heresy in 922, Husayn ibn Mansur al-Hallaj faced Mecca and, in a state of ecstasy, conversed with God. The following day he was dancing in his chains and laughing as he was taken to the place of execution and that laughter grew to a crescendo when he saw the gibbet. A large crowd had gathered to witness the Sufi's death and he told them that he would return in thirty days. Abu Bakr al-Shibli (861–946), a poet and friend, produced a prayer mat, and Hallaj performed his last prayer. Then, as he stood up, the executioner dealt him a blow that smashed his forehead. Shibli fainted. But Hallaj remained conscious while he was given one thousand lashes and then had his hands and feet cut off. His tongue was cut out. Then he was strapped to the gibbet and tar was applied to the stumps to stop him bleeding to death. On the gibbet he declared that 'My death will be the religion of the Cross'. As the day was ending, his head should have been cut off, but the officiating officer said it was late and this could wait until tomorrow. Hallaj was still conscious the following morning when he was lowered from the gibbet and placed on the executioner's leather mat. Disciples and friends continued to record Hallaj's last words. Shibli, who loved the martyred saint, threw him a rose. After Hallaj's beheading, his body, which was still seen to writhe, was wrapped in a naphtha-soaked mat and burnt, while the head was sent to a cupboard in the Caliph's palace which was used for storing severed heads. So ended the career of 'a highwayman on the route of desire' who had dared to declare his unity with God by declaring '*Ana al-Haqq*' (I am the Truth).

In the words of Louis Massignon, it was a 'death for love'. 'The huge gory setting of the gibbet execution: the explosion into ruins of the hoisted, tortured criminal, and his collapse, in the open air, the butt of everyone's sarcasms, mutilated, decapitated, burnt. His last words show his broken, yet so vital spirit filled with desire, aspiring after an even more piercing renunciation of himself, penetrating to the very solitude of God, even beyond death'. And: 'in the depths of the imperial harem, with daylight settling on the colonnades of date palms, their trunks inlaid with teakwood and copper, and over the solid pewter within its closed garden, the silence of the Queen Mother Shaghab ... to her would fall the preservation of certain relics (of Hallaj's head in the palace) ....'

The account of al-Hallaj's death is both theatrical and poetic. It is also to a significant degree fictional. The first edition of Massignon's *La Passion d'al-Hallaj* was published in 1922 and Massignon's steamy saga of blood and roses, of love and death, perhaps owed something to the popular culture of the time. Robert Hitchens's novel *The Garden of Allah* was published in 1904. Rudolf Valentino appeared in *The Sheikh* in 1921 and in *Blood and Sand* in 1922.

Louis Massignon, born in 1883, was one of the greatest orientalists of the twentieth century. As a young man he studied Arabic and Islam in Paris, Morocco and Cairo. In 1906 on a boat out from Marseille to Alexandria he encountered an aristocratic homosexual Spaniard, Luis de Cuadra, with whom he fell in love. De Cuadra was a convert to Islam and in Egypt he seems to have been influential in getting Massignon to turn his attention to al-Hallaj and Sufism. De Cuadra showed Massignon a quotation from the Persian Sufi poet Farid al-Din 'Attar: 'Two moments of adoration suffice in love, but the preliminary ablution must be made in blood.' In 1921 De Cuadra was to commit suicide in a Spanish prison. This tragedy marked Massignon deeply. An even more important experience had occurred in 1908 in Iraq where Massignon had gone to research the life of al-Hallaj. There he apparently fell under suspicion of being a spy and was threatened with death, but escaped and, while in the desert beside the ruins of a Sassanian palace, he experienced a mystical epiphany, as he heard the doves above him declare '*Haqq, haqq*' (truth, truth).

From 1907 until his death in 1962, he studied the life and works of Hallaj (though he claimed that it was not he who was studying Hallaj, but Hallaj who was studying him). A vastly expanded version of *La Passion d'al-Hallaj* was published posthumously in 1975 and an English translation of those four volumes was published in 1982. The English translator, Herbert Mason, appears to have had considerable difficulty in understanding what was before him and this is hardly surprising. For one thing, Massignon employed an intimidating vocabulary. My reading of the English translation enriched my vocabulary somewhat: méson, disarticulate, theopathic, dolorisme, claiaudience, genethlialogy, syneisaktism, illeity, hecceity, cynegetic, charism, heptacephalic, pernoctation, sosia, metasomatosis, intercision, arithmology, intersign, enchiridion, heterotrophy and many other lexical gems.

Massignon's methodology, insofar as it can be understood at all, seems eccentric and it carried him to very edge of sanity. It relied heavily on introspection (and he believed that this was al-Hallaj's own methodology). Rationality did not suffice to explain historical processes. According to Massignon:

We recall a man after his death, first of all, by intersigns. Which is to say, by unusual and unforeseen events of his life whose imprint we rediscover in ourselves through "correspondences". These "correspondences" are not rational normalisations that reduce individual existences to fortuitous series of analogous and impersonal components: they are shared anomalies. And instead of depicting individual lives as an infinity of segments of parallel straight lines, of commonplace probabilities computable by statistics, the philosophy of history must arrange them inwardly in curves, marking the nodes of realisation, the "points of osculation" through which they "communicate" where souls recognise each other outside the dimensions of time.

This way of doing historical research somewhat resembles a séance.

Massignon's arguments also relied heavily on philological minutiae and numerological connections. Though some of his prose is superbly eloquent, other parts of the book are in cryptic note form and it is as if a box of file cards has been emptied onto the floor. Reading *The Passion of al-Hallaj* is like getting lost in a vast ruined palace. The book bears comparison with other grand, literary enterprises conceived of by geniuses, but left unfinished, such as Walter Benjamin's *Arcades Project*, a work of cultural criticism that was centred on bourgeois life in nineteenth-century Paris, or Humphrey Jennings' *Pandaemonium*, a sprawling anthology that commemorated the impact of the Industrial Revolution on Britain.

Obviously some details in the account of Hallaj's execution are implausible. In the British Royal Navy a thousand lashes was deemed to be equivalent to a death sentence. Also how did Hallaj manage to say so much even after his tongue had been cut out? The portrait of Hallaj's death sketched above is a synthesis of many later and inconsistent sources – sources moreover which kept adding both to Hallaj's sufferings and to his last words. One of the broader problems with *The Passion*'s presentation of Hallaj was that the author was a fervent Catholic and the friend of such prominent Catholics as the desert hermit, Charles de Foucauld and the novelist, Paul Claudel. Massignon presented Hallaj as a saint and it is true that many Muslims have regarded him as one. But the Muslim concept of sainthood does not exactly coincide with the Christian one, since in Islam there is not a cut-off point at which a man or a woman, having been canonised by a high authority, becomes a saint. A Muslim saint's status rather depends on the consensus of the community. The Arabic for 'saint' is *wali*, but the more literal meaning is 'friend'. While many *walis* did do miracles, the performance of miracles was not and is not a necessary qualification for becoming a saint. But Massignon believed that Hallaj did actually perform miracles. He also selected and exaggerated dubious pieces of evidence to heighten the resemblance of Hallaj's execution to Christ's crucifixion and many Muslim writers have been critical of the way Massignon sought to Christianise the death of a Muslim mystic. It has even been condemned as a special form of cultural imperialism.

Not only was Massignon a Catholic, but he was an eccentric sort of Catholic. Massignon's father was a painter and a friend of the novelist Joris-Karl Huysmans (1848-1907). Huysmans had moved on from an early flirtation with Satanism to an impassioned version of Catholicism which placed great emphasis on the role of substitutes in taking on the suffering of others. Though this doctrine does feature in some of his later novels, it is most clearly expounded in his non-fictional study of the fifteenth-century Dutch saint Lydwine of Schiedam that he published in 1901. At the age of fifteen Lydwine had an ice-skating accident as a result of which she lost a rib and then took to her bed. Thereafter she was horribly afflicted with all sorts of ailments and her body fell apart. But she prayed to God that the sufferings that she experienced would be a substitute for the sufferings of others. Massignon, like Huysmans, came to believe in a chain of mystical substitutes throughout history. Hallaj was one of these witnesses who willingly embraced the sufferings of others. Joan of Arc and

Marie-Antoinette were also in this chain and it seems fairly clear that Massignon thought of himself as having the same status.

While it is true that the 'substitute' features in the Islamic spiritual tradition, it has a somewhat different resonance. According to Islamic lore there are forty *abdal*s, or 'substitutes', present in the world at any one time. But these *abdal*s are not intercessors and they do not take upon themselves anyone's suffering. Invisibly present in the Muslim lands, they perform good works which often go unnoticed, but they do not actually present themselves as candidates for mystical execution.

Furthermore, Massignon was obsessed with the homoerotic themes that he found in the story of Hallaj. According to Massignon, 'the unacknowledged ideal of Baghdadian high society' was the quest for the ecstasy that could be gained by gazing at a beautiful human body and certain mystics believed that it was possible to transmute uranism (homosexuality) into divine love. Consequently there were reports of Sufi sessions where the men sat gazing at naked youths and, in so doing, became witnesses to the beauty that was part of God's creation. This, Massignon thought was a narcissistic gaze into 'a cloudy mirror'. Certain Sufis taught 'that one must "sublimate" one's moody pleasure derived from contemplating masculine beauty (of novices) by a "uranian syneisaktism," penetrating through this tempting created beauty to the mysterious Face of the Divine Judge of the Judgement…' Massignon's fascination with the beauty of male youths may lead the reader of *The Passion* to forget that al-Hallaj was approximately sixty-five when he was executed.

The jurisprudent Ibn Dawud (c.868–910), the man who was ultimately responsible for the indictment of Hallaj, compiled a poetry anthology, the *Kitab al-Zahra*, the first half of which is devoted to love poetry. According to Massignon, Ibn Dawud, like al-Hallaj died for love: 'We glimpse the precious ordered setting of Ibn Dawud's death: still young, lavished with attentions and weary regrets, on a divan, between the light filtering in from outside through the *shahnishin* grating and the empty space that the *"tarma"* overlooks, before a cage that holds a blinded twittering nightingale … what was of concern to him was that he was allowed in this way to carry the mental conception of this forbidden pleasure intact, since it was unsatisfied to the paradise of the uranians'. But Ibn Dawud held that to love God was to fall victim to an anthropomorphic heresy. As for

Massignon, he became notorious for the lectures he gave in Paris in which he harped on the beauty of Joseph that is attested to in the Qur'an, yet, though he was obsessed with sex, he was most obsessed with sexual purity and he toyed with the notion that Hallaj's death was due to a single erotic glance of his at a woman.

The menace of Freemasonry and Communism was another obsession of Massignon's and he regarded both medieval Islamic guilds (for the existence of which there is little evidence) and Shi'ism as precursors of Freemasonry and Communism. Consequently he consistently minimised the influence of Shi'ism on Hallaj's teaching. Moreover, it remains uncertain whether Hallaj actually said 'Ana al-Haqq'. Massignon was enough of a conscientious scholar to muster the evidence that he did not say this and then enough of an intuitively guided mystic to decide that he did.

Hallaj was born in 857 in the Persian province of Fars. Though he was ethnically Persian, he spoke and wrote in Arabic. 'Hallaj' means wool carder and this was the profession of his father. The son studied in Basra and later in Baghdad gained the patronage of al-Junayd (830–910), the most famous Sufi of the age, though Junayd was later to criticise the manner in which Hallaj spoke so freely of his mystical states. Subsequently Hallaj travelled extensively. He made the hajj three times and he preached in Khurasan, Transoxania, India and elsewhere. In many of the places that he preached the crowds that assembled were unable to understand his Arabic, yet they were still moved by his speech. He acquired a devoted following, though his enemies accused him of using conjuring tricks to seduce the gullible.

In Hallaj's time it was common practice for Sufis to use conjuring tricks in order to impress their unsophisticated audiences. (In the nineteenth century the French government employed the famous conjuror Robert Houdin to tour North Africa and demonstrate to unsophisticated tribesmen that the French had a wonder worker who was up to all the tricks their Sufi sheikhs could muster and more.) Hallaj was widely accused of using sleight of hand and ingenious devices in order to draw people towards God. He studied the rope trick in India. He was supposed to have constructed a room with concealed pipes which pumped in air, thereby making his robes to billow out and seeming to show that his body had swelled to such extent that it filled the room. From the same room he produced a living lamb from a burning oven. In other rooms he had found ways of concealing foodstuffs which allowed him to masquerade as an ascetic who had not eaten for forty days. He claimed to produce fresh fruit from paradise and, when one critical observer noticed that the miraculous apple which Hallaj brandished appeared to have maggot holes in it, Hallaj responded 'How could it be otherwise? I plucked it from a tree in the Mansion of Eternity and brought it into the House of Decay and that is why it is touched with corruption!' His urine was alleged to have healing properties. Hostile critics (and they were many) recorded many examples of his alleged charlatanry.

By common consent Hallaj was the greatest medieval Arab Sufi poet. He was also perhaps the first to use the imagery of wine drinking in the service of Sufism, as in this verse which prefigures his death:

> My friend is not chargeable with any injustice;
> He invited me, and welcomed me as a host does a guest;
> But when the cup circulated, he called for the sword and the block:
> So it is with one who drinks wine with the dragon in summer.

Another of his poems opens with the lines:

> I saw my Lord with the eye of the heart.
> I said: "Who art thou?" He answered: "Thou."

Iblis, the Devil, featured prominently in Hallaj's mystical mythology, as he presented Iblis's estimable 'sin' as being his refusal to prostrate himself to anybody but God. For Hallaj's Iblis, God's transcendence was absolute and Iblis lamented that all but God was perishable. One of Hallaj's disciples reported that he was once walking with his master down an alleyway in Baghdad when they heard a flute which was so beautifully played that it made them weep with emotion. When the disciple asked 'What is this?' Hallaj replied 'This? It is Iblis who weeps over the loss of this world.' Hallaj, whose theological and literary works were highly sophisticated, was no kind of primitive rebel.

But Hallaj became increasingly involved in political and economic issues and in 895 he returned to Baghdad where, in alliance with prominent officials at the Abbasid court and with a lot of popular support, particularly among adherents of the Hanbali school of religious law, he campaigned against administrative corruption, fiscal abuses by tax farmers and the hoarding of grain by speculators. He has been compared to a torch which 'lighting up, suddenly reveals the casting shadow, the passions and crimes which make their way into the night'. He preached to the poor in the suburbs of Baghdad, as well as to nomads, robbers and bandits. After preaching to criminals, he was even alleged to have trimmed their hair and beards. But Hallaj also had influential supporters in the establishment and that was what made him dangerous. Prominent among them were members of the Caliph's family, notably the Caliph al-Muqtadir's (895–932) mother Shaghab, and the heir apparent, Prince Radi. One of Hallaj's wondrous feats was to resurrect the Prince's favourite parrot. Hallaj just put his sleeve over the bird and, when he withdrew it, the bird was alive again. When the Caliph related this miracle by Hallaj to his vizier, Hamid, he advised the Caliph to put Hallaj to death. Otherwise there would be a popular uprising.

Like the Arcades Project and Pandaemonium, *The Passion* combines cultural history with economic and social history. Massignon's work, which was primarily designed to present Hallaj's execution as an act of mystical substitution, nevertheless also presented plenty of evidence that the chief reason for killing him was political. Although Hallaj had powerful friends at court, unfortunately he had even more powerful enemies. The most noteworthy as well as the most colourful was the aforementioned Hamid Abu Muhammad ibn 'Abbas, a pedlar of spoiled pomegranates who rose to become an unscrupulous tax farmer and then rose yet further to become a corrupt vizier at the court of the Caliph al-Muqtadir. As vizier, he speculated in wheat and hoarded it in order to cause artificial famines and force prices up. Although he was a Sunni, he formed alliances with leading Shi'i financiers who hated Hallaj. Hamid was foulmouthed, wily and violent. Massignon evidently did not care for him, since he compared him to Petronius's Trimalchio and Alfred Jarry's Père Ubu, as well as to Pontius Pilate. A few years after the execution of Hallaj, in which Hamid had been the prime mover, he fell into the hands of one of his enemies, whereupon Hamid, who was by now very old, was flogged, made to dance about in a monkey suit and finally given a poisoned egg to eat.

Hallaj spent the last eight years of his life in prison during which time his enemies were unable to bring him to trial and his friends were unable to deliver him. The Caliph al-Muqtadir declared that the four pleasures of this world were 'contemplating beautiful faces, ridiculing dull minds, slapping fleshy fat necks and shaving long showy beards'. Consequently he took little interest in the intricacies of the proceedings against Hallaj. But eventually Hamid was able to persuade the Caliph that the trial should go ahead. As has been noted, the evidence for Hallaj having been executed for declaring that he was the truth is unconvincing. Officially he was found guilty of teaching that the hajj to Mecca was not necessary, since a Ka'bah could be constructed in one's own living room and round it one could circumambulate. (This was an extremely controversial doctrine at a time when the Qarmathian heretics were trying to destroy Mecca as a centre of pilgrimage.) But what Hallaj was really guilty of was social agitation. There are also indications that at times he posed as a sort of millennial redeemer and this attracted support among extremist Shi'is, but some Sunni critics identified him as the false prophet who is destined to appear at the end of time.

While, there were some Sufis, like Shibli, who venerated Hallaj even before his martyrdom, many Sufis at the time condemned Hallaj for a breach of decorum, since one simply did not make public statements about ecstasy and union with God and there were also Sufis who held that actual union with God was not possible, since that would deny his complete transcendence. The fourteenth-century philosopher and historian ibn Khaldun (almost certainly a Sufi himself) thought the execution justified, because Hallaj had divulged a mystical truth— something which the commonalty were not entitled to hear. Ibn al-'Arabi, the thirteenth-century Andalusian Sufi regarded Hallaj's alleged claim to be the Truth and other statements attributed to him as signs of shallowness and boasting. (Consequently Massignon formed an extremely poor opinion of ibn al-'Arabi and claimed that the decline of Sufism, which began after Hallaj, became worse as a result of the teaching of ibn al-'Arabi.) On the evidence so industriously accumulated by Massignon, the cult of Hallaj as mystic martyr was slow to develop over the centuries. As Massignon put it, 'A slow difficult work, taking many a century, it is carried out quietly in meditation by solitary spirits and chosen souls, while popular devotion, here and there, persists in associating his name with afflictions of newborn children, children's games, songs of beggars and predictions about the end of time.'

Many of the early orientalists guessed that Hallaj was a crypto-Christian. The orientalist Edward Granville-Browne (1862–1926), himself a notorious trouble maker and anti-establishment agitator, described Hallaj as 'a dangerous and able intriguer'. Ali Shariati (1933–1977), the distinguished Iranian social and religious thinker who studied with Massignon in Paris but also read Sartre, Guevara and Fanon, described Hallaj as someone drunk with the love of God, but as having no sense of social responsibility. Shariati went on: 'Hallaj was constantly immersed in the burning invocation of God, and this was a true source of exaltation for him. But imagine if Iranian society were to consist of twenty-five million Hallajs. It would be nothing but a vast lunatic asylum'. On the other hand, Muhammad Iqbal (1877–1938), who started out hostile, came to regard him as an authentic mystic engaged in a heroic struggle and he wanted the entire Muslim nation to be able to say 'Ana al-Haqq'.

AL-BIRUNI: AGAINST THE GRAIN

Bruce B Lawrence

Abu Rayhan Muhammad ibn Ahmad Al-Biruni liked school. No, he loved school. The challenge to read and recite, to count and to calculate was fun, but the real sport was to contest the ideas of others, to engage their motives and call into question their goals. A Muslim, he was also a Persian. And the Persian gene – some would call it 'genius' – was to argue, to debate, to advance through active exchange with the ideas of thoughtful others. Not everyone in his community was born thoughtful. Some never went to school. Some went to school and only memorised or repeated what others told them. He only did battle with equals, but he never ceased to find even his equals lacking.

Biruni was privileged to have a private tutor from a very early age. Born in 973, in the outskirts of Khwarizm (hence the name Al-Biruni, the outsider, or suburban), he may have lost one or both parents when he was very young. As a result, his academic tutor, Abu Nasr al-Mansur, also became his familial mentor. He made certain that Biruni learned all the basics of scientific inquiry in Arabic, and literary inquiry mostly in Persian. Abu Nasr also made it possible for his young protégé to undertake experiments on his own.

Biruni was impatient. A devout Muslim, he was also a sceptic about all received forms of knowledge. He was restless to know what the Author of the universe meant by the array of systems within the great system called the cosmos. He learned about distances, and loved geography. He excelled in mathematics, and delved into physics. He examined rocks and found their study, known as mineralogy, a constant fascination. He wondered about the nature of the earth and its component elements, their size, shapes and subfields, anticipating geodesy. Thinking about medicine, he explored the use, or misuse, of plants and their extracts for cures; he excelled in pharmacology. But above all, he looked to the stars, to their relationships, their movements, their influences, and so he delved deeply into astronomy.

Biruni made his first independent astronomical observations when he was 18 years of age, in 991. But he did not continue to work independently, or without interference. Though he had already developed strong views by the age of 20, and even engaged in correspondence with an older Iranian scholar, ibn Sina, while still in his 20s, he had no job security. It was a politically turbulent period of Iranian history. He found himself compelled to leave his native home of Khwarizm. For a brief time, he secured patronage with the Samanids, then rulers of Bukhara, but after they were conquered, he settled in another Central Asian court for perhaps a decade before it too fell to hostile forces during 1000. It was the Turkish ruler Mahmud of Ghazna (r. 998–1002) who captured the capital of Biruni's patron. His prize: to take hostage all the scholars of the defeated monarch and to employ them in his own expanded court.

Well, not quite all. There is a famous anecdote that depicts the defining moment of conquest and capture with a notable twist. Jealous of the splendour of his rival's court circle, Sultan Mahmud sent him an ultimatum demanding that all the leading scholars there be sent forthwith to Ghazna in order to adorn his own court. The story goes on to tell how the philosopher Ibn Sīnā escaped to the west, serving in the court of a Western Persian monarch, the Kakuyid ʿAlāʾ-al-Dawla Moḥammad in Isfahan, till his death there in 1037. But Biruni, along with others, went to Ghazna and entered Maḥmūd's service. Biruni then spent the remainder of his life, what must have been well over three decades, on the borders of India in present day Afghanistan, first with Maḥmūd, and then with his successors, notably Masʿūd and Mawdūd, till his own death in 1050.

None of these activities would have made Biruni a freethinker. He could have been, and was labelled, a great scientist. He was perhaps unique in his time in being a polymath. As one scholar noted, there were numerous notable Muslim scholars who were also exemplary scientists. In the eleventh century two stood out: Ibn Sina (980–1037) and Biruni. Yet Biruni 'surpassed ibn Sina both in the breadth and catholicity of his sceptical erudition in the fields of history and chronology, mathematics, astronomy, geography, pharmacology, mineralogy, history of religions and Indology.'

It is Biruni the precocious student who let his curiosity and intelligence take him down many paths we can justifiably described as a freethinker. He challenged not just his scientific predecessors but also his foremost contemporary scientific colleague, ibn Sina. Ibn Sina needs no introduction. He is, as Ahmad Dallal observed, 'the greatest and most influential Aristotelian philosopher in Islamic history.' But Biruni was his superior not just in the breadth of his knowledge but in the depth of his inquiry into the presuppositions of astronomy. Biruni challenges the Aristotelian cosmology. The mathematical astronomer, in his view, is not bound to any prior system. He must view the evidence with as much openness to observation as his instruments and his knowledge permit. Because ibn Sina had commented on the material nature of the universe, Biruni initiated a correspondence with him. He puts forth a number of questions that critique the presuppostions of Aristotelian physics. Bluntly, but also politely, he asks ibn Sina to respond to these questions, in effect, to justify his own predilection for, and reliance on, Aristotle.

Fascinated with the astrolabe, an instrument on which he relied and whose use he perfected, Biruni noted that one could pursue mathematical astronomy from either a geocentric or heliocentric perspective. It is not a matter of philosophical certainty but of experimental openness that is at stake. Like many scientists of his time, Biruni thought not only that the cosmos was shaped like a sphere and was made up of different regions but also that the earth was at the centre of the solar system. Yet he was also aware of the probability – though not the absolute certainty – of a sun-centred system. Instead of arguing for either theory, he, unlike ibn Sina, saw the scientific, psychological, and cultural importance of both models.

Indeed, one cannot understate the radical nature of Biruni's challenge to ibn Sina and so to Aristotle. Once it is possible to prove that some part of Aristotelian natural philosophy does not fit all the evidence, the entire system becomes suspect, its formulations unhinged. The stars and planets, that is, the heavenly bodies, are the subject on which Biruni begins his set of queries to ibn Sina. Some may sound obscure or overly technical to a non-scientist. For example: how do you explore and explain weight in space? How do you determine whether or not heavenly spheres are heavy or light? But one issue is germane to all physical and metaphysical reflection: are there other worlds than the cosmos as we know it from mathematical astronomy? For Aristotle, as for ibn Sina, the answer was no. For Biruni, the answer was maybe. Though we cannot prove the existence of other worlds, neither can we disprove their existence, he argues.

As fascinating as the correspondence and the debate between ibn Sina and Biruni – equivalent to the exchange between Einstein and Bergson on the theory of relativity or Einstein and Heisenberg on the uncertainty principle – are, they underscore how professional specialisation was already an issue in the eleventh century. Ibn Sina, in trying to counter/ refute the arguments of Biruni, often refers to his lack of knowledge in the mathematical sciences, where Biruni is expert, at the same time that he suggests Biruni does not have the credentials to venture into his field, which is natural philosophy. Biruni did not back down. As Dallal has acutely noted, 'he refused to concede the intellectual authority of systems of knowledge outside his own system'.

It would be hard to summarise his multiple accomplishments in the sciences. One writer has astutely observed that because he saw nature as a harmonious, self-regulating system, Biruni applied his philosophical observations of the world to his scientific studies of natural phenomena. But he did more than that. He used his powers of observation to describe the details of his environment, including birds, plants, minerals, and animals. While some of his theories about nature have been since disproved by modern biology, Biruni's studies of the natural world display his acute, unwavering reliance on empirical observations of natural phenomena.

Biruni was so successful in applying mathematics to his study of geography and the natural world that some consider him to be the founder of geodesy, the science of measuring the size and shape of the earth, mapping points on its surface, and studying its gravitational field. In *The Book on Astrolabe,* he considers how one can determine the circumference of the earth using geometry. His method involves climbing a mountain and using the horizon and the height of the mountain to create an equation. He attempted on different occasions to test this method, and used it successfully while travelling in India; his results do not differ significantly from those determined using modern methods.

As he did with his mountain experiment, Biruni sought to test many of his ideas with close observation, relentless logic, and repeated experimentation. In studying gems, for instance, Biruni used mathematics to arrive at the density of minerals. He began by using the weights of gold and the Oriental sapphire as a base for a variety of metals and gems. Through careful experimentation based on the displacement of water by the mineral substances, he was able to calculate the density of various minerals quite accurately.

A similar, radical empiricism characterised his study of geography. Biruni began with the ancient precept that the earth was divided into seven climatic zones. This idea was common to the Islamic world as well as in Greek, Zoroastrian, and ancient Babylonian beliefs, but Biruni was particularly concerned with understanding why certain portions of the earth were what he labelled 'uninhabitable,' while others were centres of civilisation and agriculture. His study of the earth's surface reflects both his work in astrology and his belief that the world exists according to a harmonious design.

There are few areas of the geographical sciences that Biruni did not explore. In addition to human geography, he analysed the weather, the climate, and landscape history. He took precise measurements of and mapped coordinates on the earth's surface. He also contributed knowledge about the effect of physical features such as rivers on the shaping of the landscape, and on the patterns of the monsoon in bringing rain to India. He developed an understanding of variations in the transference of the sun's energy to the earth at different times of year. Among his most important contributions to the study of the earth's physical features are theories about erosion and landform creation, conclusions about the force of gravity, the argument that the speed of light is faster than that of sound, discussions of the movement of the sun and the earth, and botanical observations.

Biruni's understanding of the plants and animals inhabiting different parts of the earth later helped him to build knowledge of the pharmacological properties of certain species. One of his most well-known works on pharmacology is the *Kitab al-Saydanah*. It is a lengthy text, bringing together a variety of information relating to medicine. The book provides information on drugs and other forms of therapy, including lists of medicinal herbs and their names in a number of languages. Much of the book reflects Biruni's interest in language and how the names of each drug were derived.

Biruni used both mathematics and visual observations of the heavens to study the universe. Among his accomplishments in astronomy were the calculation of the sizes of the planets and their orbits. He arrived at these figures using a Ptolemaic principle concerning the ratios of planetary distances. He also tried to explain planetary motion, planetary and solar positions, and the phenomenon of the equinox.

As a mathematician, Biruni translated the Hindu methods of mathematical notation. His abilities in geometry led to the term 'albirunic problems,' used to refer to the most difficult geometry problems of his time. He was able to create an accurate method for measuring latitude and longitude, and knew the trigonometric function of the law of sines. Working from Ptolemy's theory of the sine table, Biruni discovered a more direct way to derive basic trigonometric formulas; and succeeded in solving complex geometry problems, including the trisection of the angle. Much of his work in geometry and trigonometry involves theorems dealing with the chords in circles.

But Biruni's achievements in science only provide us with a limited understanding of his insatiable, free ranging mind. What bedevils us in exploring, revisiting and then reevaluating Biruni is the wreckage of time. Specifically, of the many, many books he wrote, only a very few have survived. We actually know how limited is our legacy of the preserved writings of Biruni from Biruni himself. In his autumn years, when he was perhaps 62–63 years of age, during 1035–36, Biruni catalogued both his own works and those of Razi. At the urging of a friend, he compiled an *Epistle concerning a list of the books of Moḥammad b. Ẕakarīyā' al-Rāzī* (d. 932). This consists of two parts. While the first is devoted to Rāzī and his works, the second provides Biruni's inventory of the books that he himself had authored up to that time. This sort of bibliographical treatment of an individual is modelled on those produced by Galen in antiquity and by the Syriac Christian scholar Ḥunayn ibn Isḥāq in the ninth century. Razi was (in)famous in his own circle as a freethinker, so much that Ibn Sina when struggling to refute Biruni in his correspondence, at one point opines that Biruni's objection to Aristotle must have been second hand, taken 'either from John the Grammarian, who wanted to mislead Christians by pretending that he disagrees with Aristotle ... or from Muhammad ibn Zakariya al-Razi, whose pretensions in meddling with metaphysics made him overestimate his abilities, which were limited to dressing wounds and testing urine and faeces.'

The actual catalogue of Razi's works, however, suggests that, *pace* ibn Sina, he did more than toilet sampling. In Biruni's estimate, there are no less than 184 titles divided into eleven categories: medicine; natural science; logic; mathematics and astronomy; commentaries, synopses, and extracts; philosophy and assessment; metaphysics; theology; alchemy; heretical; and miscellaneous. After it, Biruni presents a chronological table of Greek physicians from Asclepius to Galen followed by brief notes on the history of medicine that relate it to the labour of his scientific predecessor, al-Razi.

In comparison, Biruni's catalogue of his own literary production up to his sixty-third year, that is 1036, lists a mere 103 titles. They are divided into twelve categories: astronomy, mathematical geography, mathematics, astrological aspects and transits, astronomical instruments, chronology, comets, an untitled category, astrology, anecdotes, religion, and books of which he no longer possesses copies. After an account of the astrologers' predictions of the length of his life and of a dream he had a couple of years earlier, he adds ten more titles of his own works followed by twenty-five of those written in his name by other scholars. His own works, he says, he regards as his sons, and so also holds the same regard for those that were written in his name! We now know that Biruni composed at least 155 works. Some he wrote after he had finished his bibliography, others he simply forgot to include in it. But alas, perhaps five-sixths of the total number of 155 treatises are now irretrievably lost.

Of those that survived, two in particular demonstrate how radical a freethinker Biruni was, not only in his own epoch, but also across the ages, in all the annals of Islamic history extending to culture and religion as well as mathematics and astronomy. The first is *The Chronology of Ancient Nations*. The second is *Alberuni's India*.

The Chronology of Ancient Nations is interesting because it appeared so early in his career, when he was about twenty-seven years old, in 1000. It is peppered with charts, graphs and tables, but also interlinear descriptions of major non-Muslim religious groups whom he had observed in his day. Biruni never hesitates to compare non-Muslims with their Muslim counterparts. For instance, in his account of the life of Zoroaster, he discusses at length the eschatological expectations that Zoroastrian and Muslim sects attached to the 1,500th anniversary of the appearance of the Iranian prophet. Particularly valuable is his detailed description of the Zoroastrian feasts which contains much information on Zoroastrian beliefs, as well as on popular Persian superstitions of his day. And he shows deep respect for Mani, even while disagreeing with Manichaean dualism, not least for what he considers its lack of scientific verification. He even uses a Manichaean scripture to correct the chronology of the Arsacid kings, going out of his way to emphasise Mani's reliability: 'Mani is one of those who teach that the telling of lies is forbidden; besides he had no need to falsify history'. A fierce scavenger of primary sources, he found and used Arabic translations of the Old and New Testaments, but also other Jewish and Christian writings little known even within their own traditions. He devotes much space in *Chronology* to a description and critique of the Jewish calendar, concerning which his is apparently the oldest surviving source of any substance. Similarly, in his description of the celebrations of the Melkite (Greek Orthodox) Christians, he gives valuable bits of information about the Christians of eastern Iran, apparently supplied by Christian informants. When he can't find informants, he apologises for what he cannot say. Concerning the rites of Jacobite Christians, for instance, he is silent because 'we have not succeeded in finding anyone who belonged to their sect or knew their principles'.

As a scientific researcher and ethnographic observer, Biruni moves to a new level of sophistication when he undertakes to write about India. Had he followed ibn Sina and gone to western Iran, or had his royal patron offered him less freedom than he had with the restless but hands-off Sultan Mahmud of Ghazna, he might never have explored India, learned Sanskrit, and delved into matters relating to the Indic/Hindu tradition. He first translated some major texts, with assistance from scribes/informants captured by Mahmud during his plunders of Gujarat and Rajasthan. They included Samkhya texts and the Yogasutras of Patañjali. Biruni was aware of both the novelty and the precariousness of this undertaking:

Such is the state of things in India [he observes] that I found it very hard to work my way into the subject, although I have a great liking for it, in which respect I stand quite alone in my time, and although I do not spare either time or money in collecting Sanskrit books from places where I supposed they were likely to be found, and in procuring for myself, even from very remote places, Hindu scholars who understand them, and are able to teach me. What scholar, however, has the same favourable opportunities for studying this subject as I have? That would only be the case with one to whom the grace of God accords what it did not accord to me, a perfectly free disposal of his own doings and goings; for it has never fallen to my lot in my own doings and goings to be perfectly independent, nor to be invested with sufficient power to dispose and to order as I thought best. However, I thank God for that which he has bestowed upon me, and which must be considered as sufficient for the purpose.

It was sufficient to make Biruni not just the first but the unrivalled Muslim observer, commentator, and analyst of Hindu belief, thought and practice. Composed around 1030, while Biruni was at the height of his analytical powers, the *India* represents both a distillation and an extension of what had been broached in his earlier translation of the Yogasutras of Patañjali, *Kitāb Bātanjal*: to classify and evaluate the major categories of Hindu philosophy and religion. Nearly two-thirds of the *India* (48 of 80 chapters) reviews the achievement of Indian science in several fields. The *India* not only communicates but also evaluates the full range of Hindu thought and ritual. The initial twelve chapters provide a magisterial overview of Hindu notions of God, creation, metempsychosis (the passing of the soul at death into another body either human or animal), salvation, and idolatry. The Hindu approach to God, creation, and salvation is generously commended, bearing favourable comparison to reflections that emerged from ancient Greece and classical Islam. The same is not true for metempsychosis. While noting some parallels between it and the teachings of both Greek philosophers and Sufi masters, Biruni stresses the disjuncture between such notions and normative Muslim belief. He himself has memorialised the disjuncture by his oft-quoted remark: *al-tanāsukh ʿilm al-niḥla al-hindawīya* (metempsychosis is the password of Hindu belief). Nor is Biruni sympathetic to idol worship. He portrays it as class-specific, being the indulgence of uneducated, superstitious masses, rather than the preference of those literate Brahmins with whom he himself was in frequent contact.

It is in chapter seven of the *India* that we find Biruni's longest and best documented assessment of Hindu beliefs. If he is to be classed as a radical freethinker, it is perhaps at this moment of engaging the heart of Hindu metaphysical reflection with other traditions that he excels as a critical comparativist. He examines in detail the three paths to liberation, and in so doing, signals his preference for the teachings of Patañjali over the directives of other Indian scriptures, including the *Bhagavadgītā*. The contest is framed by the discipline of devotion (*bhakti-yoga*) and the pursuit of knowledge (*jñāna-yoga*). On the one hand, Biruni draws extensive attention to *bhakti-yoga*, especially in depicting ethical norms and drawing on parallel notions from the Sufi tradition. Many of the most extensive quotations illustrating the three-fold path to liberation derive from the *Bhagavadgītā*. On the other hand, however, the schematisation of these paths and the topical sentences for each are directly quoted or paraphrased from *Kitāb Bātanjal*. It is to *jñāna-yoga* that Biruni draws attention time and again. Salvation in his view is inseparable from self-cognition; in its most direct form, 'it is the return of the soul as a knowing being into its own nature', or as he states in the *India*, 'the soul distinguishes between things by defining them and so grasps its own essence (*'aqalat dhātahā*)'.

If Biruni seems to be an inadvertent theologian in the early chapters of the *India*, in the later chapters he assumes the role of a pre-modern anthropologist. Ten of the last seventeen chapters in the *India* address ritual practices, principally initiation and funerary ceremonies but also obligatory sacrifices and dietary rules, together with fasting, pilgrimage, and festival observances. Textual evidence is constantly checked off against the declarations of personal informants, nowhere more tellingly than in chapter seventy-one. Biruni begins by chronicling the mythical separation of scholars and warriors. The innate merit of the former failed because most Hindus, like most people elsewhere, were not philosophers, and so philosophers could not rule. Warriors filled the power vacuum. Becoming kings, they proved to be perverse purveyors of power: they exempted Brahmins from the death penalty but exempted themselves from the penalty of being blinded for theft. Hindu prisoners of war suffered the worst fate, however. According to canonical law (the *dharmaśāstras*), such prisoners could only achieve expiation by an elaborate rite requiring them to ingest *pancagavya*, the five products linked to the cow. While that requirement in itself seems extreme, even it is not adequate according to Biruni's Brahmin informants. In their view, no expiation is possible for

Hindu prisoners of war who return to India: they are never allowed to resume their former status.

Throughout the final chapters of the *India*, Biruni continues to display his penchant for comparing and evaluating. While he tries to offer his readers a compendium of Hindu religious lore, as he read, heard about, and observed it, he also hopes to appropriate the 'higher' truth of Indian philosophy, bracketing it with the Hellenistic corpus and integrating both into the worldview of educated Muslims. He cares little for the uneducated – whether Muslim or Hindu – and so the final chapters of the *India* that are devoted to Hindu rituals, appear as a kind of ethnographic afterthought. They lend an air of completeness to his massive tome without, however, burnishing his own credentials as a scientific explorer or achieving his primary goal: to pursue the Truth. In the final analysis, Biruni is better classified as an anthropological philosopher than a philosophical anthropologist.

Yet Biruni, the maverick thinker and dogged scientist, stands at the apex of Islamic scholarship on non-Muslim religious traditions. After him no one followed his lead as a dispassionate enquirer into the subtleties of Hindu thought until the late medieval–early modern period of Indo-Muslim history. It remained for nineteenth-century European scholars to spark an interest in further study along the lines he had initiated, among both educated Muslims and also Western scholars of Islam.

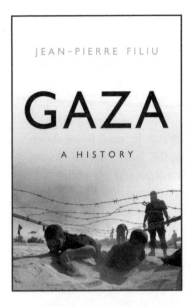

JEAN-PIERRE FILIU

GAZA

A HISTORY

ISBN: 9781849044011
£25.00 / Hardback / 424pp

GAZA
A HISTORY

JEAN-PIERRE FILIU

Through its millennium–long existence, Gaza has often been bitterly disputed while simultaneously and paradoxically enduring prolonged neglect. Jean-Pierre Filiu's book is the first comprehensive history of Gaza in any language.

Squeezed between the Negev and Sinai deserts on the one hand and the Mediterranean Sea on the other, Gaza was contested by the Pharaohs, the Persians, the Greeks, the Romans, the Byzantines, the Arabs, the Fatimids, the Mamluks, the Crusaders and the Ottomans. Napoleon had to secure it in 1799 to launch his failed campaign on Palestine. In 1917, the British Empire fought for months to conquer Gaza, before establishing its mandate on Palestine.

In 1948, 200,000 Palestinians sought refuge in Gaza, a marginal area neither Israel nor Egypt wanted. Palestinian nationalism grew there, and Gaza has since found itself at the heart of Palestinian history. It is in Gaza that the fedayeen movement arose from the ruins of Arab nationalism. It is in Gaza that the 1967 Israeli occupation was repeatedly challenged, until the outbreak of the 1987 intifada. And it is in Gaza, in 2007, that the dream of Palestinian statehood appeared to have been shattered by the split between Fatah and Hamas. The endurance of Gaza and the Palestinians make the publication of this history both timely and significant.

'A magnificent piece of historical writing: clear in its exposition, careful in its use of a treasure-trove of new sources and judicious in its analysis of competing political claims to this small and troubled strip of land. It is difficult to see how it will ever be rivalled in terms of scope, intensity and sympathetic understanding.' — **Roger Owen, Emeritus Professor of Middle East History, Harvard University**

WWW.HURSTPUBLISHERS.COM/BOOK/GAZA

41 GREAT RUSSELL ST, LONDON WC1B 3P
WWW.HURSTPUBLISHERS.COM
WWW.FBOOK.COM/HURSTPUBLISHERS
020 7255 2201

ABBASID CULTURE AND THE UNIVERSAL HISTORY OF FREETHINKING HUMANISM

Aziz al-Azmeh

On 13 July 1856, Charles Darwin wrote to Sir Joseph Hooker, Director of the Royal Botanical Gardens at Kew, wondering at 'what a book a Devil's chaplain might write on the clumsy, wasteful, blundering, low and horridly cruel works of nature.' Darwin was not predisposed by temperament to advocate the Devil's work, but he was nevertheless sufficiently sober-minded to engage, privately and to a considerable degree impelled by his knowledge of nature's cruel ways no less than by a private tragedy, with questions of theodicy and design that were all the rage among English scientists and theologians of his time. He was rather impelled to detect in claims for benign and intelligent design, or in the milder claims that this be the best of all possible worlds, an absurdity and a travesty.

In times more determinedly exercised by theological and dogmatic consideration, doubts expressed about theodicy were redacted otherwise than by sober musings over the results of research into natural history, or by their extension to the ethological, sociobiological and ethical study of homo sapiens inaugurated by Darwin himself in *The Descent of Man* (1871). A different redaction was required for doubts about the wisdom of a divinity creating a nature by nature messy and violent, and creating humanity by nature given to greed, aggression and injustice – doubts over claims for theodicy in the natural and human worlds equally characterised by 'clumsy, wasteful, blundering, low and horribly cruel works.' In these times past, the potential toxicity of creation's works, and the incongruity of any consequent notion of benign and firm stewardship, tended to be attributed to a pernicious, personified agency acting against the wholesome order of the divinity. The ways of nature were not so much hers as God's;

human disorder was generally attributed to the wiles of Satan and, when not, to divine retribution whose works in nature were legion.

A thousand years before Darwin, this bundle of themes was addressed in Abbasid domains in a variety of manners: in philosophical and theological works, in casual and sometimes exuberant blasphemy, by libertine literati, and in a variety of genres in which Abbasid freethinking was expressed. Before I come to this, I shall take up the bird's-eye view adopted by the historiographer and scholar of world religions al-Shahrastani (1086–1153). Wishing to account for the disorder that was, to him, right thinking and, by extension, of disorder in general, al-Shahrastani referred this back to an archetypical event, an aetiological legend standing alongside a myth of the creation of God's good order. In doing so, he has Satan cast aspersions on the consistency and wisdom of God's own works.

Satan appears as the Arch-Freethinker, an idea that occurs in a large number of other Arabic works. The Great Tempter is at the origin of what al-Shahrastani called *al-istibdad bi'l-ra'i*, wilful use of personal opinion and of the faculty of thought beyond limits prescribed by God. Iblis, al-Shahrastani held, 'relied solely on his own opinion and did not accept the authority of [God's] explicit command; ... he opted for vain notions, in opposition to the [divine] order ... because of his vanity.' Further, he was 'the first accursed one, for he imposed the government of reason on that which cannot be governed by reason.' In other words, the matter devolved upon the countermanding of reason by divine fiat called revelation.

Satan was complaining about God's inconstancy and inconsistency. The setting was the Garden of Eden where, according to the Qur'an, God created Adam and commanded the angels to prostrate themselves before him. Despite their warning God about the creation of Adam and setting him up as God's vicar forever, they did as commanded. All, that is, except Satan, who found himself banished after having protested that such a command subverted the hierarchy that God had willed himself. Al-Shahrastani put a series of questions into Iblis' mouth: 'Since God knew in advance what was to become of me, what was the wisdom behind Him creating me? Since He created me according to his wish and will, why did He command me to obey Him? What is the wisdom behind His Command since He neither benefits nor suffers from obedience and disobedience? Since He created me as I am, why did He drive me out of the Garden of

Eden? Why did He allow me to tempt Adam and Eve? Why does He allow me to pester and mislead humanity?' Finally, Satan wondered: 'Would it not have been better for Him to create a world free of evil?'

All these motifs representing Satan as a tragic figure rather than the figure of sheer evil, as an actor in a tragedy of Fate, caught up in an impossible and unjust situation of God's making, was a fairly standard motif attendant upon Abbasid discussions of theodicy in particular and of established religion in general. This was a universe of discourse in which the question of divine justice was a common topic in theological discussions. Satan was originally an archangel who refused to prostrate himself before Adam as God commanded him to – before Adam, who was made of a substance (clay) baser than Satan's (fire). This point was put into verse unforgettably by the blind, lecherous, and irrepressibly free-thinking poet Bashshar bin Burd (d. 784). The great antinomian mystic al-Hallaj (d. 922) stated the matter thus: God, he said, threw him into the sea, his hands bound, and warned him not get wet. More playfully put, by the libertine poet Abu Nuwas (d. 814), Adam was a confusing experience for Satan who received mixed signals from God, and therefore determined to act as a procurer to Adam's descendants. Much given to a jocular Satanism, Abu Nuwas inverted the Faustian scheme, the poet imposing himself compellingly and sarcastically upon Satan, whom he habitually and familiarly referred to as his uncle, and to whom he pandered, the two toying with each other in a tango of exquisite complicity.

It might be remembered that Satan's vexation reclaimed a number of themes and motifs addressed by Abbasid freethinkers. These were here, with al-Shahrastani, reclaimed systemically, and given aetiology. But the reality of Abbasid freethinking was not always so systematic, and it generally appealed to human reason rather than to a preternatural agency.

Satan as a tragic figure was a common motif to be added to others which made up the constellation of motifs of Abbasid freethinking and its later European legacy. It is likely that it was in the folds of Arabic anthologies and compilations translated into Latin and Romance languages during the Italian duecento, and filtered through Toledo and Palermo, perhaps also Bologna and other places of which Constantinople may well be the joker in the pack, that the motifs of Arabic freethinking were later to be made part of European freethinking, atheism and erudite libertinism of the seventeenth and eighteenth centuries: expressed first in a variety of clandestine texts of uncertain form and provenance circulated in manuscript, later in the rather desultory *De tribus impostoribus* ('Treatise of the Three Imposters') and finally in the firmly composed *Traité des trois importeurs* in the edition of the Baron d'Holbach (1768).

I shall come to this theme briefly later. But first, I should like to offer a general characterisation and description of the phenomenon of Abbasid freethinking in the period of roughly between the middle of the eighth and the eleventh centuries, in evidence most markedly in the cosmopolitan courtly and allied milieu of Baghdad, but in evidence elsewhere as well. Thereafter, and on present evidence, it persisted only in demotic form, in casual irreverence and blasphemy, sayings attributed to bawds, buffoons, fools and lunatics, in dialectal poetry and in shadow plays – but also in the works of certain mystics, and mysticism is the *locus classicus* for the tragic figure of Satan.

Let me be clear about the phenomenon I am endeavouring to characterise. I am speaking of freethinking, not of heresy: the latter is deviance within, the former is the repudiation of established religion in total, and in the process, the repudiation of claims for benign extra-terrestrial purpose. In this sense also I am speaking of humanism. For upon closer scrutiny, beyond emblematic and formulaic purposes, it might be proposed that humanism be seen as consisting of a number of possible categorical specifications: normative humanism expressed in philanthropy and the formation of character, roughly in terms of Cicero's counter-position of humanity and bestiality; anthropological and ethnological; and finally situational and historical. Abbasid freethinking would fall into the last category, being a humanism that engages the derogation of the human by the divine, the revaluation of human reason as against its derogation by commands and affabulations attributed to the divinity.

We should note that Abbasid freethinking, more common among Muslims than among Christians and Jews of the Abbasid era, might be characterised as having had two main registers. One is unstructured, playful, often frivolous, jocular impiety and blasphemy, often associated with libertine individuals and milieus of the courtly and literary elite (some radical fringes of the French Enlightenment, with the *roman du couvent*, and, somewhat earlier, the phenomenon of erudite libertines come immediately to mind). Abu Nuwas, for instance, related in highly elevated poetical register a risqué repartee between himself and a handsome youth he fancied, conducting the flirtation throughout by using Qur'anic quotations, in a sustained play of lewd double entendre, a mode continued much later, illustrated by anecdotal material in al-Tifashi's (d. 1253) medico-anecdotal compendium of erotica and in many picaresque works. This register, despite its playfulness, offered a generally fatalistic and wistfully pessimistic turn, sustained by an urbane scepticism of cultivated and sophisticated impious temperaments tending towards humanism, set against the *ulama*, the representatives of morbid and officious religiosity, with vituperative derision and pitiless satire. This was a register that was to persist throughout, and indeed until today, reflected in attitudes, jokes and proverbs. One may signal a large number of examples from poetry, anecdotes related in literary anthologies and books of erotica, and of course from what is known as popular culture: the *Thousand and One Nights* are of course well known; less well known are media such as shadow theatre. We have, for instance, the texts of shadow plays by Ibn Daniyal (d. 1320), one of which (*Tayf al-Khayal*) takes the form of a celebratory elegy for Satan, notwithstanding the fact that it ends with the repentance of the protagonist, once the point had been made.

This brings me to the other register of freethinking, one that is high-minded, serious, systematic, and theologically and philosophically engaged. Unlike the former register, being generally - but not entirely - sombre and humourless, scholars have generally found its representatives more congenial companions over years of research, and rather more presentable to the seminar room. What this second, more deliberative register does have in common with the more cavalier one I have spoken of are a number of shared motifs, especially the criticism of claims for theodicy, and the appeal to the human understanding in a manner reminiscent of al-Shahrastani's Satan.

On June 6, 1807, the German traveller Ulrich Jasper Seetzen recorded in his diary a conversation in a Cairo coffee-house during which anecdotes were related about a buffoon who quarrelled with God about the wisdom of His creation. The hero of the story was a certain al-Rewandi. What the German traveller was not aware of was that, 900 years earlier, a substantial theologian by the name of Ibn al-Rawandi (827–911) had produced a theological and social criticism of religion in terms of invective criticism of theodicy: God cannot be wise, as he created the world as it is, permeated by inequalities and injustices, and created, in addition, snakes, scorpions and other nasty creatures harmful to humanity, all of which cannot be seen as part of a grand design with benign intent.

Ibn al-Rawandi moved during the course of his life from inner-Muslim theological disputes, on to the criticism of theology overall, and finally on to the almost nihilistic scepticism recorded in his *Kitab al-Zumurrud* – *Book of the Emerald*, the title itself announcing a lacerating, corrosive intent: emeralds were then thought to have a blinding effect on snakes. The use of the snake metaphor for religion already announces his view that religion was a particularly harmful institution for human societies, a source of enmity and bloodshed, and a bane on the rationality inherent in cultivated humans.

I will mention only two other personalities, both of whom shared this view of religion as harmful at once to humanity and to the human intellect, and held that the works both of nature and of human society do not indicate benign design. The first is the polymath, natural scientist and physician Abu Bakr al-Razi (d. 925, perhaps a decade later), the second the poet and well-rounded litterateur Abul-'Ala' al Ma'arri (d. 1058), often described as the poet among philosophers and the philosopher among poets. Al-Razi applied to religion a naturalistic and inductive epistemology and a belief in the progress of science in the same way as he applied this to medicine, mineralogy, alchemy (bereft of occult elements) and magnetism; his critique of the Galenic traditions was built upon a physicalist physiology, in which humours were reduced to more elementary dynamics of purely physical interactive force between three-dimensional atoms of different shapes irrespective of the qualities of the five elementary substances, and vacuum (at once void and a medium where a force of attraction acted); his alchemy, bereft of occult elements, placed a premium on experimentation, as did his studies of magnetism and mineralogy. Al-Razi's ethical theory was Epicurean.

For his part, Al-Ma'arri – to whom John Milton bears comparison in many respects - had a most profound and bitter pessimism and bleakness of vision, doubly enfolded into his own blindness and his severe asceticism (this included abstinence from sex and a vegan diet). Both were made almost unbearable by the excesses of his archaising lexicon taken almost to the point of perversity, and he wavered continually between the desire for a morality which might gain sustenance from religion and an irrepressibl alertness to the absurdities of religious belief and practice, of obscuranti and self-interested clerics. He alternated continually between accents of faith and commendations of the simple piety of ritual observance on the one hand, and almost blasphemous statements, derision for ritual observance and parodies of religious feasts (including pilgrimage to Mecca) on the other. The spaces in between allowed him to develop an incipient deism shorn of theology and of organised religion and its desiderata, alongside a moralising sentiment, and a unfuse humanism continually frustrated by his vertiginous pessimism.

The three I mentioned by way of somewhat emblematic example were very different persons, and moved in different milieux. But their publics did cross, and they all contributed to a shared universe of debate, controversy and polemic: polemics between Muslim theological and denominational trends (and also between Karaites and Rabbinites, and between Christian denominations) vying for patronage and centrality as well as for political influence, polemics between Islam, Christianity, Judaism, Manicheanism and Zoroastrianism, elaborations of the heritage of antiquity and Late Antiquity including Oriental wisdom. Mention needs to be made here of heresiological and controversial literature, and of literature on all religion and indeed on religion as such – later, the Jewish author ibn Kammuna (d. 1284) of Baghdad was to compose a treatise detailing systematically the points held by the three monotheistic religions against each other. It should be added that, unlike Byzantium or the Latin West, the cosmopolitan realm of the Abbasids was multi-confessional, entailing the facility for comparing religions regarded as equally valid (but of unequal value) without necessarily regarding other religions as heresy or sheer unbelief and rank paganism, as had been the case with Christianity, a point already discerned by Ernest Renan in 1852.

For good measure, one might recall that in the time period under consideration there had not yet emerged a discernible regnant Muslim Orthodoxy despite short periods of official primacy for this group or that, according to Caliphal or Sultanic tastes and reasons of state; what primacy there was had been spasmodic, uncertain and contested, and there is no reason in historical fact for the common assumption that Muslim orthodoxy was a steady state, even a congenital predisposition rather than a developing process. Neither was there a properly crystallised and institutionalised, self-sustaining and self-reproducing clerical class – both developments were to come in gradually in the course of the later eleventh and the twelfth centuries, rendering an emergent Orthodoxy central and compelling enough to eradicate the others effectively. Yet, Abbasid freethinking has generally been regarded as a marginal phenomenon in modern scholarship. It will, I hope, be appreciated that this is an anachronistic position without firm empirical foundation, dependent upon an image of Abbasid society as theologocentric: wearisome and platitudinous as this image may be, it is nevertheless well-worn, familiar, predictable, formulaic and effortlessly repeatable: in other words, it has all the attributes that make for the popularity of lazy arguments.

In light of this absence of a regnant orthodoxy adopted by the state as its own, one needs to mention competition between socio-cultural milieu, between pietists and emergent traditionalists on the one hand, and those who cultivated *adab*, *paideia*, belles-lettres and courtly politesse on the other. The latter were much given to the cultivation both of Arabic letters and antiquarianism; they were given equally to the cultivation of exotic knowledge and tastes as a mark of social distinction, including the cultivation of ethnology and of orientalism, the image of the Orient sometimes emblematised in the figure of the Brahmin, whose primal sagacity and perennial wisdom was used as a foil against established religion – a similar fascination with India was to exercise German Romantics in the nineteenth century. This is much like Europeans of the Age of Reason and of the Enlightenment, Deists and others, who were to use Islam as a foil against the mysteries of Christianity and the against the established churches, and indeed as late Roman philosophers used Chaldean wisdom.

In this setting, the three personalities mentioned held a number of points in common with each other as well with a good number of other personalities, including theologians and philosophers such as al-Kindi (801–873) and al-Farabi (872–950/51). All three accepted religion on its own terms. This was unlike the earlier and more radical stance of Ibn al-Muqaffa' (d. 756), a prose stylist of prodigious talent and intelligence, and of great influence on Arabic letters, who had dismissed religion wholesale and regarded it from the outside, as rank unreason belonging wholly to the reason of state. Religion was, to this state secretary, a political artefact in the hands of the sovereign manipulating the rough and credulous demos. To him, the workings of religious sentiment could be explained in terms of almost Nietzschean accents, as driven primarily by resentment. Incidentally, given that we are dealing with societies that were severely stratified and hierarchical, it will come as no surprise that the idea was shared that the common mass of humans were an ingenuous lot, an excitable and ignorant herd that ibn al-Rawandi said was only technically human, it being in fact closer to apes. Whatever was said about the salience of Reason applies to the cultivated elite of cognoscenti only. The humanism I am speaking of was directed not to humanity as such but to human potential.

The points shared by our authors are many, and I shall highlight the most salient in the form of a number of theses. Let it also be repeated that theirs was a cosmopolite critique of all religion, and not of Islam only.

Thesis 1

Religion, at least organised religion, is not necessary, as a consequence of which prophecy is neither necessary nor credible. This is because humans are endowed by the Creator with natural reason which is the ultimate key at once to the secrets of nature and to the management of human sociality. The facts of nature, with its violence, and the facts of human history, 'clumsy, wasteful, blundering, low and horridly cruel,' both militate against presumptions of theodicy with a benign purpose and rational design. That which the prophets presume to bring to us is ultimately conjugated with the irrationality of religious dogmas and practices and the covetous and manipulative purpose of clerics. All this renders religion conducive to fanaticism, discord and war. Yet underlying all this chaos and disturbance is a diffuse divinity of Deistic description, which might, under conditions never specified, be conducive to human improvement. Al-Ma'arri presumed to correct God's own criteria of salvation and damnation, or perhaps sought to correct what established religion took for God's criteria: when his friend ibn al-Qarih told him he was about to die, and that he feared that he would go to hell, he composed the marvellous *Risalat al-Ghufran*, the *Epistle of Forgiveness*. This Epistle took ibn al-Qarih on a tour of heaven and hell, where, among other things, he was made to meet a large number of poets and engage them in discussion of poetry and philology; being more daring and less certain in his belief than Dante, al-Ma'arri populated paradise with rank unbelievers, even with poets belonging to the pre-Muslim era; only Bashshar bin Burd was to be found in hell.

Thesis 2

Prophets, including Muhammad, are imposters (al-Ma'arri excepted); what appear as miracles are slights of hand, using the laws of nature to their own purpose, just like wizards. Thus the Qur'an, which according to Muslim dogma is Muhammad's evidentiary miracle, is far from being miraculous and inimitable; it is more than matched in style by much Arabic poetry (thus ibn al-Rawandi), and in content by the writings of Ptolemy and others (thus al-Razi), and is more akin to the declamations of soothsayers (thus also al-Razi). We still have fragments of the *mu'aradat*, texts composed with the purpose of matching Qur'anic diction, rhythm, and vocabulary.

Thesis 3

Religions are self-contradictory, and contradict one another. Such multiplicity betokens confusion, not divine provenance. Thus al-Razi maintained that, among Muslims, some say the Qur'an is created in time, some argue the contrary, that it was co-eternal with God; some deny free will, others affirm it; some affirm anthropomorphism and others deny it; Jesus claimed he was the son of God, Moses claimed God had no son, and Muhammad claimed that Jesus was a man created like the rest of us. Mani and Zoroaster contradicted the three monotheistic prophets regarding God, the creation of the world and the reason for the existence of good and evil. The Jews (Torah) claim that God liked the smell of burnt flesh (this same point was made, at the same time, by Hiwi of Balkh in the ninth century) and portrayed him as an old man walking about in the Garden of Eden, and claimed that he demanded a finely-woven silken rug – these are the desires of someone who is needy rather than a self-sufficient and transcendent deity. For his part, ibn al-Rawandi, a highly accomplished dialectical theologian by formation, is reported to have written treatises intended to demonstrate both free-will and predestination.

In response to this situation, and as a polemical motif, our three authors had recourse, implicit or explicit, to the notion of *takafu' al-adilla*, the equipollence of proofs, what the ancient and late antique sceptical traditions termed *isosthéneia*, the idea that pro and contra arguments can be made on any point with equal plausibility. The perfectly reasonable conclusion was that no religion could claim, less so demonstrate, superiority over another. The same argument had been used by Shi'ite theologians in different settings and for different purposes.

One final observation: al-Razi, though a rationalist, was no sceptic. Unlike many others, he sought to think beyond the aporias of theological reason, and did not take cognitive dissonance between equally plausible yet mutually contradictory positions to be a charter for radical scepticism or its milder form of ambivalence and disorientation. He developed, in line with certain trends in Muslim theology, an atomistic physical theory, believed in metempsychosis, and proposed that the cosmos be composed of what he called the Five Eternals: God, the Spirit, matter, space and time. Though averse to religious myth, he proposed his own cosmogonic myth: the Spirit desired matter, and God allowed it to couple with it, as a pedagogical exercise which will end with the Spirit learning that such coupling can yield only the desire for liberation from matter – al-Razi composed a commentary on Plato's *Timaeus*, and another on Plutarch's commentary on the *Timaeus*; neither is extant.

Thesis 4

Religions are full of absurdities insulting to sound reason. Beginning with Ibn al-Muqaffa', all freethinkers paid special attention to religious rites, which they considered to be absurd. To what purpose, it is continually asked, do Muslims on pilgrimage at Mecca circumambulate a dumb black stone, and scurry between the hills of al-Marwa and al-Safa? There were anthropological explanations advanced by Muslim jurisprudence, as arbitrary ritual practices instilling a habitus, and this point had been a staple of anti-Muslim polemics by Jews and Christians charging Muslims with paganism. Further: can the Muslim paradise, so asked ibn al-Rawandi in a satirical turn, be pleasing to anyone but a rustic? Why did the Heavenly Host of avenging angels help Muhammad's army at the Battle of Badr, while at the Battle of Uhud they stood by as onlookers? Do the doctrine of the Trinity, the status of Jesus as increate, agennetos, and the Chalcedonian notion of a double nature and one hypostasis, square up with a rigorous conception of monotheism (so al-Razi and Abu 'Isa al-Warraq, Ibn al-Rawandi's sometime associate and the most formidable technical critic of Christian theology, whose works on the Trinity and the Incarnation are available in English translation, and of Manichaeanism and religion overall)? More radically: is the very concept of monotheism not structurally dependent upon an implicit dualism involving the play of God and Satan (so ibn al-Muqaffa')? And, apart from what is said by clerics who, on account of their cultivation of long beards, are satirised by al-Razi as goats, why does Qur'anic myth pretend to be history? Is Qur'anic myth any less absurd than Zoroastrian myth? In all, we find here a view of myth that rejects it entirely, at once simpler and more decided than Greek and Roman elite views of myth as amenable to rationalising allegorical Euhemeristic interpretation, which of course was also cultivated in the Abbasid period.

Such were the main points made by Abbasid freethinkers, and such were ideas that received elaboration, but were also in common currency in more casual settings. One does not discern atheism in these propositions, but a notion of divinity as a *deus otiosus*, belonging more to natural philosophy than to religion. In a way, this is akin to Varro's gods of the philosophers, as distinct from gods of the poets and that the magistrates, much decried by our thinkers. Addressing the title of this essay, with its reference to a universal history of humanism, one must say that there is much continuity with Euhemerus, Lucretius, Cicero and other antique thinkers, including sceptics. One finds in the critique of Christianity specifically many of the motifs of Porphyry, Celsus and of the Emperor Julian, and of Rabbinic propositions as well. The critique of Judaism is inspired by Christian polemics, as is to a considerable extent the critique of Islam.

We can trace certain textual filiations to these motifemic and argumentative concordances. But this is, to my mind, an unsafe option which risks infinite regress and plentiful over-interpretation. It would be far better to take a less tractable but nevertheless more plausible and historically more verisimilar procedure. This would postulate and search for the circulation of critical motifs from a variety of provenances, in a variety of textual locations certainly not confined to formal treatises, consistent arguments, and other forms of formal expression, and to look into the reclamation of such motifs in appropriate contexts, again not confined necessarily to genres bearing the formal and systematic expression of such motifs – motifs travel well; think only of Plutarch's satirical reference to beards in relation to a certain type of late antique philosopher, and al-Razi's use of a comparable image. This use of discrete motifs, as suggested, is less readily tractable, as it would require a far larger body of texts and the consideration of a broader swathe of genres, media and milieu, as well as mechanisms and pathways of circulation apart from the scholar's desk. This seems to be an equally serviceable procedure - now facilitated by the possibilities of digital technology - when we turn to look at the Fortleben of the four major theses I sketched above, and theses connected to them, that we find resurfacing in the Age of Reason and in the Radical Enlightenment. Looking both backwards and forwards of Abbasid freethinking, we might thereby be able to consider the circulation of motifs, arguments and concepts, and not only the circulation of specific books, as the contexts of persistence and transmission across time, space and languages.

There will be some resistance to the notion of continuities between Abbasid freethinking and modern European ideas, much less so for an argument of continuity with antique and late antique traditions. My view is that this has little justification apart from academic institutional habits and boundaries, and their anxieties of influence allied to ideological criteria of admissibility. The transmission of Arabic philosophy and natural science is well known. Medieval Arabic criticisms of religion, including criticism of the Old and New Testaments, has recently been seen as having had determinate pathways to Spinoza's *Tractatus Theologico-Politicus*. Institutional reticence notwithstanding, the correlative question of Arabic literary forms and moods, especially the lyric, in connection with Romance literatures, including Dante, have been succinctly explored in erudite manner recently. What remains for me to do before I conclude is say a few words about the criticism of religion overall in connection with

Deism, atheism, Reason, and the Radical Enlightenment, theses and motifs that resurfaced in European history under the signature of *De tribus impostoribus*, whose existence as a book prior to its publication has been regarded by many as a fiction.

A work of this description had been attributed to the 'baptised Sultan' of Palermo, the Holy Roman Emperor Friederick II and to his aide Pierre des Vignes (Petrus of Vinea) by Pope Gregory IX in 1293. In ensuing centuries the title was bandied about by a variety of persons and ecclesiastical authorities, and attributed to a number of authors, including Machiavelli, Giordano Bruno, Guillaume Postel, Jean Bodin, Pierre Bayle, Hobbes and, of course, Spinoza. Texts finally emerged and were put in circulation, the edition of d'Holbach having the distinction of being placed on the Index on more than one occasion.

The nature of the texts in circulation in the centuries prior to publication and attestable circulation still escape us, and we shall for the moment have to be content with the assumption that motifs were in circulation in a variety of ascertainable contexts. What is interesting is that we find the four theses that I outlined systematically connected in the two types of work published, first in Holland, under the title of *La vie et l'esprit de M. Benoit Spinoza* and the *Traite des Trois imposteurs*, and in English and German versions. This, as might be expected, was a materialist treatise – none of the Abbasid personalities mentioned was a materialist as such, but at least two held the world to be eternal, which is tantamount to materialism according to their adversaries.

This treatise also recapitulated in systematic compass the world of ideas and the polemical motifs I have outlined. Thus God appears as a vengeful being, creating evil in order for humans to succumb to it, and fully complicit in the evils that Darwin would regard as being grist to the mill of a Devil's chaplain. We find the Bible to be a bundle of self-contradictory fables, and religions to be based upon imposture, falsehood and violence, designed to empower the clergy who manipulate sentiments of elemental fear on the part of the mob. We find, finally, prophets to be impostors: Moses was something of a magician much under the influence of Egyptian wizards; Jesus preached a false message of hope, contrary to nature, and preached it to idiots. He was a human made to pass for a god by St. Paul (this is a persistent and not implausible motif in Muslim polemics), creating a religion whose claims to truth are vitiated by its very many divisions. Muhammad was fair game to the author as he was to most Europeans of the time, including Cantemir, in spite of philo-Islamic positions expressed by certain anti-Trinitarian, Unitarian Protestants, Deists, and Freethinkers.

All of this, and emphasis on human reason, is familiar from the Abbasid ideas and motifs that I outlined. That these circulated persistently in a variety of ways is evident. Renan had already made this connection with regard to Latin Averroism. In 1920, Louis Massignon postulated some form of transmission of similar ideas propounded by Muslim Qarmatians in the tenth century. This is somewhat implausible as it is, and it succumbs to the all-too-common tick the conflating concordance of ideas with influences and origins. There is no need to assume that, apart from his medical works, al-Razi was read in Europe in the Age of Reason, or that Ibn Kammuna was known (though Spinoza might have had access to this in some form or another). But in the perspective of the approach I am suggesting, this hardly matters. The context of interpretation is not so much a linear sequence of intertextual relations between formally-constituted texts as much as contexts of circulation and deployment of ideas and motifs.

I wish to conclude by suggesting that the capillary pathways to which I referred be properly investigated in a manner more creative than that involving the normal philological search for intertextual evidence. These are the capillary pathways of motifemic, argumentative and conceptual concordances, echoed in a variety of settings, my assumption being that an echo is as good as a quotation for this purpose, and that quotations might indeed be regarded as more of the nature of echoes than as calques or simple transpositions. In doing so, we might be able to reconstruct a forgotten chapter in a universal history of freethinking Humanism to which the Abbasid contribution was crucial: crucial, in that it was a moment during which all the threads were brought in together, as they were to be brought together in the seventeenth and eighteenth centuries. We would thereby have a history shaped somewhat like two connected hour-glasses: the diffuse sceptical and Euhemeristic heritage of antiquity and late antiquity gaining a textured consistency during the cosmopolitan era of the Abbasids, loosening out its critical mass to a diffuse circulation in a variety of genres and milieu over a number of centuries before, again, its motifemic and other elements were recombined into another consistent, internally articulated critical mass with an identifiable texture, textual as well as social, during the Radical Enlightenment.

Finally, I should say that my purpose in this essay is entirely cognitive. I am not in the business of bridging cultural divides, nor of the post-colonialist or post-modernist advocacy of restitutive justice. My impulse – perhaps not my sole impulse – is the curiosity of a natural historian and of a reader of historical thrillers and crime fiction, alert to interesting signals and clues.

ADONIS' HERESY

Stefan Weidner

The notion of 'modernity' has been used to cover a multitude of complex, often very different phenomena over the last two hundred years. It has been applied for such divergent purposes that it has probably become more misleading than helpful, and we should be careful not to regard it as a criterion for distinguishing between positive and negative developments. One of the phenomena usually linked with modernity in the cultural sphere is the crisis of religions and growing scepticism towards the theological foundations of belief in God. Even if the questioning of traditional religious beliefs has never been as widespread as the social or technological phenomena of modernity, it has nonetheless been one of the most decisive factors of twentieth century intellectual life, not only in the West but also, albeit to a lesser degree, in the Islamic world. It is in this context that the work of Ali Ahmad Said Esber, known by the pen name Adonis, a naturalised Lebanese citizen born in the coastal region of northern Syria in 1930 and one of the Arab world's most prominent poets, needs to be seen. Hardly any other modern Arab author tackles the crisis of the Divine as forthrightly as Adonis, who seeks to resolve the dilemmas spawned by this crisis through the means of poetry.

Although Adonis' preoccupation with the Divine can be traced back to the early 1950s, it became the main thematic issue of his poetry in his famous collection *The Songs of Mihyar the Damascene*, published in Beirut in 1961. Expressed fifty-three times according to my count, the word Allah (and its derivations including *rabb*, Lord) is the most used proper noun in the volume.

The importance of the Divine and the superhuman is obvious from the opening pages. The protagonist, introduced in the grammatical third person but not yet named, is presented in the introductory *Psalm* – the title itself, of course, already hints at the religious dimension of this prose poem – in terms of qualities and characteristics which transcend the human. He is not only said to encompass opposites (*he is the reality and its contrary, he is the life and its other*), thereby escaping any definition, but has neither a bodily outward appearance (*he has the shape of the wind*) nor an ancestry (*he has no ancestor and his roots are in his footsteps*). Furthermore, he has abilities which are marked by power over life and death: *He fills life and no one sees him. He whips it into foam and drowns in it*, and, *he scares and vivifies (...) he peels man like an onion.*

The character described here shares many of the attributes the Islamic theological tradition ascribes to God. According to this theology, God's main characteristics are his indefinability and his being uncreated, meaning that he has no predecessors. Other features also seem to imply that a God-like character is presented here. For instance, it is said that *he creates his kinds starting from himself*, an idea close to the creation of man as depicted in Genesis 1:26/27, although at the same time this seems to contradict the aforementioned traditional Islamic notion of God who is not supposed to create his own kind because He is uncreated. Moreover, when he is said *to have the shape of the wind*, (wind, *rih*, being the last word of the psalm), one is reminded of the conception of God as *pneuma*, or of the 'spirit' of God as being comparable to the 'wind' in the Biblical tradition. The etymological link of *rih* (wind) and *ruh* (spirit) with the *ruakh* (spirit) of the Hebrew Bible further stresses this idea. In the literary tradition, both Western and Eastern, only gods have been said to have 'the shape of the wind'.

Quite obviously, however, it is not a God who is presented here. The subject of the poetic speech displays traits decisively contradictory to the notion. He is, thoroughly inconceivably for a God, *dancing for the mud so that it yawns and to the tree so that it falls asleep.* More importantly, he shows signs of being *at a loss*, as if he were lacking something. It is said that, after having turned 'the morrow into game', he runs after it *in despair.* His words *are chiselled into the direction of loss,* and *perplexity* (a well-known mystical term denoting a degree in the Sufi spiritual states) *is his homeland.* The protagonist thus appears as a god-like creature, a demigod, or someone who, despite all his divine attributes and elusive sense of omnipotence, is not without needs and is certainly familiar with distress. He represents the sphere of the human and the profane as much as the Divine.

The collection's second poem 'He is not a star' brings the reader closer to the protagonist, once again depicted in terms usually associated with the religious sphere. However, his divine character is now explicitly denied: *He is not a star, not the inspiration of a prophet*. The distance between the protagonist and the traditional notion of the Divine is further widened and stressed by an imputing simile: *he is coming like a heathen spear, invading the earth of the letters*. It is only in the third poem of the volume that the protagonist is finally named, and with the naming given a status: he is called 'King Mihyar'. The domain of this king is not real however, but symbolic – he shares his domain with the poet; his castle is the dream; he lives in the kingdom of the wind and rules in the country of secrets. The figure of Mihyar has been compared to the ancient Persian God Mithra. The name Mihyar therefore bears, albeit in a rather remote way, divine connotations.

The whole range of transformations and aspects of the person of Mihyar cannot be explained here. It should be noted however that while he possesses a considerable array of Divine traits, he is by no means impervious. In his figure the Divine is mingled with the human. Indeed, a subsequent poem makes it clear that the 'heathen spear' is directed most forcefully against the Divine in the traditional Islamic sense: Mihyar is said to transgress 'the frontiers of the Caliphate' and 'to reject the Imamat', thus expressing his disregard for the worldly order of Islam (both Sunni and Shia).

This 'transgression' of the religious order and value system is elaborated and illustrated in several other poems. The titles of poems like 'The Holy Barbarian', 'The New Noah', or 'Shaddad' (the name of a legendary person) already indicate a heretical tendency. In 'The Holy Barbarian' Mihyar is presented with attributes of sainthood as well as paganism: *This is Mihyar, your holy barbarian [...]/He is the suffering creator*. As a creator he belongs to the sphere of the Divine, but he also suffers and thus belongs to the human.

In the poem 'Shaddad' the heresy is more deeply rooted in the Arabic-Islamic tradition. The poem alludes to the myth of 'The many columned city of Iram', mentioned in the Qur'an (89:6–7) as having ignored the orders of God. In its very first line the poem tells us that Shaddad, the ruler over Iram 'has come back'. An age of rebellion against the orders of God, the reader is led to conclude, has begun anew. According to the poetic persona, the city of Iram, condemned by God in the Qur'an, is 'the homeland of those who are desperate and those who refuse'. This would seem to be the same refusal associated with the character of Mihyar in the earlier poems, marked by the same desperation and the same perplexity. The inhabitants of Iram are blithely careless as to their salvation and ignore the menace of God. Whereas in the Qur'an the Lord unleashed 'a scourge of punishment' on the city and its inhabitants, in the poem 'Shaddad' the city is presented as a home for all those who condone and share the poetic persona's attitude of refusal. The final two verses underline this affiliation, for the poetic persona now switches to the first-person plural, 'we', merging with those he has previously addressed and designating Iram as *our land and our only heritage*.

In the following and final line, he goes on to say: *We are its sons who are reprieved until the day of resurrection*. The full meaning of this line only becomes clear by tracing its Qur'anic reference. In the Qur'an (for example 15:37-38) it is Satan who is said to be among the reprieved: *You [Satan] have respite [...] until the Day of Appointed Time*. Employing the first-person plural as in *we (...) are reprieved until the day of resurrection* thus creates a parallel to Satan: the poem's final line tells us that we, like Satan, are condemned and will be subjected to the punishment of God on the Day of Judgment. It is only until then that we are reprieved. Although this is stated somewhat neutrally as a simple fact in the poem, when read in conjunction with the preceding poems it becomes clear that the poet regards our state of being in reprieve as a *conditio humana*, and accepts it as such.

Heresy and the longing for a new worldly or religious order also emerge clearly in the poem 'The New Noah'. In Islamic tradition Noah is one of the first and most important prophets of the monotheistic God. Here this Islamic Noah is replaced by a new Noah, the speaker of the poem. Towards the end of the poem, this new Noah says that he does not listen to the words of God, but *long[s] for another, for a new Lord*. Although once again the heretic impact of the poem is quite obvious, it is remarkable that the notion of God is not completely dismissed; rather, there is a longing to replace the traditional God with a new one, and the new Noah's most important role is to be one of his prophets. While the meaning of God and Noah as well as the worldview they convey may have changed, what we may call the divine structure remains: there is still a god and there are still prophets – they are, however, to symbolise new values.

At first glance, another highly interesting poem for our purposes is the homage to one of the most venerated persons of early Islam, 'Elegy to Umar ibn al-Khattab'. At the same time though, it is somewhat obscure, for it refers to a story told in Abul-Faraj al-Isfahani's *Book of Songs* which might not be recognised by every reader. The story in the *Book of Songs* relates the encounter between Umar and Jabala (the latter is rendered as Jibilla in the poem for reasons of rhyme). Jabala is a Byzantine nobleman and leader who has converted to Islam and performed his visit of duty to the caliph and the holy places in Mecca. During the circumambulation of the Kaaba, a Bedouin inadvertently tears Jabala's robe. Upset, Jabala beats the man. As a result of the assault, Umar allows the Bedouin to ask for satisfaction or to take revenge, justifying this decision to the surprised Jabala by telling him that everybody is equal in Islam. Jabala responds by claiming that under these conditions he would prefer to return to the Christian faith, exacerbating the situation: as an apostate, he is now threatened by death. Umar, however, tolerates Jabala's leaving, probably fearing a clash between his adherents and those of Jabala.

The poem's meaning becomes apparent when read against this backdrop: a 'voice' poses the question *when are you beaten, o Jibilla?* enabling an interpretation based on the story in the *Book of Songs*. Jabala has not yet been beaten, but he should have been if the promise of Islam to treat every Muslim equally regardless of his origin had been kept. It is this promise which is alluded to in the last two lines: *And we are waiting / for your promise which comes from heaven.* As pronounced by Islam, the promise is of Divine origin. But it has remained unfulfilled until now; justice has not been done. The striking feature of this poem is that this failure is attributed to such a venerated figure as Umar. It was his task (and opportunity) to see that this promise was fulfilled, but he preferred a more diplomatic solution. The reader is thus witness to how the poem deconstructs the myth of the so-called rightly guided caliphs from the Golden Age of Islam, and thus one of the most popular of all Muslim creeds. (It should be pointed out here that Adonis is by background an Alawi, a Shia-offshoot sect, and that the Shia do not share the Sunni's veneration of the first Caliphs.)

The destruction or deconstruction of established religious orders and creeds is not the only direction in the *Songs of Mihyar*. In most cases, the impulse of destruction is matched or accompanied by a creative act or an establishment of positive values. The poem about Umar is thus of course not only a deconstruction of the myth of early Islam, but also the acknowledgement of the value of equality among men regardless of their origin.

The dialectic of destruction and creation is also at work in the short poem *Death*, which opens with the lines: *We die, if we do not create gods / We die if we do not kill gods*. By talking of gods and their creation by men, the poem immediately takes up a position beyond the sphere of the Islamic or Christian conceptions of the Divine. The constant creation and destruction of gods as well as all that they entail, i.e. the accompanying worldly and religious order, is presented as the *conditio sine qua non* of life. While this is quite obvious, the last of the poem's three lines is comparably obscure: an apostrophe addresses the *Kingdom of the straying rock*, whereby straying forms a significant rhyme with 'Gods', a clear echo of Matthew 16:18–19.

The rock is a symbol of stability. Whatever is built on rock will last forever, remain where it is, and stay what it is. The notion of a 'straying' rock is thus paradoxical. As I see it, this poem is the quintessence of how the Divine and God are represented in *The Songs of Mihyar*, encapsulating the worldview of this whole divan. As we will see, it is also a key to understanding the later works of Adonis.

The metaphysical security guaranteed by the rock is only that of a fragile equilibrium. It is the equilibrium between creating and killing gods. We still need gods, the poem tells us, and we still need the kingdom, the worldly order created by God. However, as a very condition of our life (that is, of the *conditio humana* in modernity) this order is no longer built on stable grounds. Moreover, the poem seems to imply that the function of the Divine is more important than its particular form, its realisation in a specific religion. Although the latter, together with the belief in a particular God, may or indeed must differ and change, there always has to be a power comparable to the Divine which 'produces' a religion and a 'kingdom', and it is this power that is posited as an anthropological necessity. In this way, the poem expresses a Copernican Revolution in the field of the Divine: the Divine moves.

Although there is a danger of reading too much into such a short poem, I feel that this interpretation is more than justifiable given how the notions of God or the Divine are by no means dismissed out of hand, but are rather 'reworked' or 'reconstructed'. As we have also seen, the notions of particular gods in the traditional sense or of traditional world orders are dismantled and demystified. This short poem is thus a microcosm of *The Songs of Mihyar* as a whole: gods are destroyed and created.

The Book of Transformations and of Emigration in the Regions of Day and Night, the volume of poetry written after *The Songs of Mihyar*, also betrays an obsession with the Divine. Of particular interest for our theme is the treatment of the Divine in the section entitled *The Transformations of the Lover*. Here, for the first time in Adonis' poetry, the body shifts to the centre of the poet's attention; on the surface at least, the Divine seems to be completely absent. However, a closer analysis of the language and ideas in this poem reveals that the Divine remains important.

To a great extent, the thirty-page poem is a collage. As far as I am aware, not all of Adonis' sources have been traced; nonetheless, the most salient ones have been identified by Arab scholars. The collage technique Adonis uses is rather simple: taking a classical text with a certain religious meaning, he then transposes the text into a profane context, whereby – and this is the decisive transforming moment inherent to the collage approach – he changes precisely those words and expressions which denote the former religious context. The religious is thus erased and replaced by locutions connected to the body or sexuality. The following three examples provide perhaps the clearest testimony of this supplanting of the religious.

In the first example, Adonis changes a text by al-Asma'i. Instead of a pilgrimage *to the holy house of God via Syria*, Adonis talks about a journey to a woman, while the rest of the story is, more or less, identical. Another striking example is based on a saying by al-Niffari. In *al-Mukhatabat* 57.9 al-Niffari says: *The Lord stayed me, and said to me: Say to the Sun, O thou that was written by the Pen of the Lord*. In Adonis's version, it is not the Lord (*al-rabb*) who says this, but *assayyid al-jasad*, 'Mister Body'. Instead of the sun, the beloved is addressed, and she is not, like the sun, written by the pen of the Lord, but by the pen of the lover. One need not to be an adherent of the psychoanalytic school of literary analysis to see that here the highly venerated Qur'anic *qalam* ('pen', e.g. in Qur'an 96:4) is nothing but another name for the phallus. The heretical impact of this reinterpretation of the Divine is unsurpassable.

The third example of an allusion to a Qur'anic expression is somewhat more subtle and may pass unnoticed. Describing the act of lovemaking, Adonis writes: *I am torn while descending into the depths of the body which are filled with creatures burning, dying down, moaning and wailing.* In the Qur'an (11:106) *sighing and groaning* is used to describe the cries of those cast into the fires of Hell. In Adonis's version, these cries become part of the sexual act. By incorporating these words into a description of lovemaking, however, Adonis simultaneously revives another meaning of these words: *shahiq* and *zafir* also mean the cries of rutting donkeys. Again, we cannot know if Adonis has used this expression consciously. Those Arab readers who know the Qur'an well are most likely to be reminded of how the words are employed in the holy text. And we may interpret Adonis's provocative appropriation of Qur'anic language so: that heaven and hell are located in the body, not in a transcendental sphere.

The Divine is thus literally replaced by the profane, the traditional notion of God by an adoration of the body. As simple as it is, this method appears even more striking when we realise that the Divine, as a function or system of thought and approach to the world, is largely retained. Although now founded on the body instead of God, it still functions as if there were a God. There is still a pilgrimage, we are led to conclude, but it leads to the other gender, to women. There is still a mystical experience, but instead of being concerned with God, it is rooted in sexuality (a shift which is, by the way, the inversion of the Sufi technique, which consists of using the profane terminology of love to describe love of God). There is even a direct and explicit adoration of specific gods. Several times in the poem the poet says 'Liber, Libera, Phallus', thus invoking the ancient pagan gods Liber and Libera, who, according to Augustine in his *De civitate dei* (Book 7, chapter 21), were celebrated in processions exposing giant Phalli. Fortunately for the poet, this subtext has largely gone unnoticed.

To summarise, we may say that the internal structure of the Divine is kept while its traditional outward shape is replaced by the notion of the body. The *Transformations of the Lover* therefore represents Adonis' first decisive attempt to 'create' or determine a new God from the profane and to use the tradition to bestow it with divine traits. Whereas the demigod Mihyar was a rather diffuse, intangible figure and at times interchangeable with the poetic persona or other figures like Odysseus, the body is now presented as the rightful successor to the Divine – and the poet is its herald. From now on, the body remains at the centre of the poet's attention and is, in some poems more, in some less, bestowed with divine attributes.

Some poems written during the Lebanese civil war lend the relationship between the body and the Divine a new quality. To explicate this enrichment I would like to briefly analyse two poems written in 1977 and 1982 respectively. From the outset, the *Unintended Worship Ritual* is clearly recognisable as a follow-up to *The Transformations of the Lover*: *And thus, she was an unintended worship ritual*. Instead of God, the worship ritual is directed towards a woman. As the poem unfolds, however, it turns out that it is not a woman who is portrayed, but the city of Damascus, where the poet lives. The city is described in terms of a body and throughout the text the city is rendered in terms largely synonymous with a woman. Several times the poet calls on and evokes his beloved 'woman-city'. Making love and writing, i.e. finding the right words and the language to express his love, are also paralleled: *Her body being his language by which he spoke / he listened to her body speak about a travel between ink and paper / between member and member.* Moreover, Damascus here is not only an image of the beloved, but the symbol of the Arab world, the political division of which becomes apparent in the Lebanese civil war. The poet regards it as his task to heal the Arab nation through his poetry and the beloved through his body. This redemptive task is expressed quite clearly in the last part of the poem: *your [i.e. Damascus'] name is being doubled now / and, by the glory of your other name, / it is now poetry / that recasts you letter by letter / in order that you will be in people's reach, / in order that you will be at hand so long as there is poetry.* In short, the task of poetry is to reconcile and to heal the Arab nation from its wounds and defects. And this task is rooted in an almost religious conception of poetry. The model character of the religious in the poet's struggle becomes obvious when he calls his act of love *i'jaz* (miracle): *I exclude you [the beloved] from how, why, and where, and I practice my inimitable miracle.*

The transcendental poetical power of the Qur'an, laid down as a dogma in the term *i'jaz*, is, by using this term for the sexual act, now projected onto the body, the powers of which are said to be as miraculous as the Qur'anic verses. The body of the poet thus becomes the symbol for the powers of poetry, which now seems even to compete with the Qur'an in its promise to heal and redeem, in short, to exercise its divine powers.

As it was in *The Transformations of the Lover* and *The Songs of Mihyar*, the traditional religious conception of Islam or any other religion is discarded. In a frank admission, the poet says that he is 'embraced by heresy'. Yet still the main characteristics of the religious are maintained and transposed onto the poet, his body and his language. The Divine as a system of thought or the fount of alleged powers remains, as in the former poems.

Written in response to the Israeli siege of Beirut in 1982, *The Time* (*al-Waqt*) displays a pattern comparable to *Unintended Worship Ritual*. The poet overcomes the vicissitudes of the war and the omnipresent destruction by exercising his magic poetical powers. In contrast to his age, marked by destructive forces, the poet embodies the reconciling forces of poetical language, stressed in the last lines of the poem: *My skin is not a cavern of thoughts, [...] / my weddings the grafting of two poles; this epoch is mine / the dead God, the blind machine — [...] / I am the Alpha of water and the Omega of fire — the mad lover of life.*

The religious dimension of the last phrase is obvious; by calling himself 'the Alpha and the Omega,' the poet identifies himself with what was formerly the Divine, the only difference being that here the Divine is not located in the other world, is not transcendental but tellurian, elemental. As in *Unintended Worship Ritual*, the definition of the Divine has obviously changed, but nonetheless the stance of the Divine is again adopted. The poet has, so to speak, usurped the Divine.

Naturally enough, the credibility of such a stance, as well as its acceptance amongst readers, is a question that needs to be probed. We can enjoy the poem aesthetically — I consider it be one of the most perfect of Adonis' later poems — and admire the poet's determination to fight war by means of poetry. The impact of the poem is another matter however: to my mind its textual perfection is tarnished by the pathos-laden, hubristic claim put forward by the poet, and moreover, it is certainly unclear as to how poetry could ever manage to overcome war and put an end to its divisiveness (or, as in *Unintended Worship Ritual*, reconcile the Arab nation).

In assessing these problematic traits, we need to keep the following in mind: while modernity has brought about a crisis in religious beliefs and notions, impressively mirrored in Adonis's *The Songs of Mihyar*, this crisis is most certainly not limited to a specific religious system, but has undermined the Divine itself, or more specifically the pattern or system of thought organising and guaranteeing the credibility of the Divine. It is such a system which makes dogmas such as the *i'jaz* or phrases like *I am the Alpha and the Omega* (as the word of God in the Apocalypse) truths beyond doubt and discussion. Such truths have however been the subject of rigorous scrutiny from the end of the nineteenth century up to the present day. This questioning has probed religious thought per se, shaken belief in the Divine as a whole, and has not been restricted to a particular dogma in a particular religion. While leading people to question dogmas, this same impulse also nourishes our incredulity and scepticism whenever a figure with a prophetic voice, no matter how grandiose an artist or poet they may be, confronts us with an unfounded claim and seeks to garner our belief. The problem resides less in what the poet asks us to accept than in the circumstance that the poet asks us to now give up precisely our scepticism, to place our trust in him and follow his path in the attempt to change the world by means of poetry. Only to a public of disbelievers can a poet say that his body performs the *i'jaz* or that he is the Alpha and the Omega of the elements; but, strangely enough, the same public of disbelievers is asked then to accept that a poet re-establishes the Divine. Maybe the poet has reckoned with a different audience, i.e. a public for whom this remains unnoticed or is unproblematic, and not with sceptical Orientalists who do not share his belief in the magical healing powers of poetry. In any case, the Divine is not only one of the main themes broached by Adonis's poetry, it is its main problem, the unresolved centre of the poet's preoccupation and one of his main motivations in writing. The twofold question which haunts this poetry, already detectable in *The Songs of Mihyar*, is how to represent and to found the Divine anew, giving it a new form while ensuring that it does not suffer the same fate as the established religions. For Adonis, poetry is the means of introducing this new type of the Divine and to grant it the necessary credibility.

One of the most gifted poets of the Arab world invests all his powers of expression in the attempt to save the Divine – by reconfiguring for it for the modern age and so making it once again acceptable. Although this Divine has lost most of its traditional appearance, its most important functions are retained. We may regard this as an impressive attempt to fuse modernity and tradition. We might read it as a first-hand testament as to how the Divine is still rooted in Middle Eastern societies, represented here by one of its foremost and most libertine intellectuals. Both, I think, are true. Whether we want to or not, we have to accept that even the most perfect poetry is sometimes subjected to contradicting forces which multiply its meanings and possible readings. The treatment of the Divine in Adonis' poetry is one of the best examples of this. And last but not least, it is an invitation to debate.

THE NEO-MODERNITY
OF SOROUSH

Mohammed Moussa

Paradoxes are the hammers and chisels used to sculpt the life of the mind. Among contemporary Muslim thinkers and scholars, Abdolkarim Soroush, the *nom de plume* of Hussein Haj Faraj Dabbagh, has best personified this modus vivendi of the intellectual. Provocative to say the least, the forward thrust of Soroush's ideas have acquired a robust quality of deconstruction of the Islamic tradition. However, pulling the figurative rug under the feet of his critics has also consisted of proposing an alternative space for faith, knowledge and politics. Two key dimensions stamp Soroush's venture of reform which is located within, for the lack of a better term, an Islamic 'neo-modernism': deconstruction and reconstruction. Thus, a dialectic ensues between tradition and modernity. His thought explores three key recurring themes: the intellectual as critic, Islam and modernity; and the Qur'an as both the word of Muhammad and the word of God. These themes require a journey of reflection on the part of both the writer and the reader lest their central significance is somehow missed.

Soroush strikes a figure at once possessing a modest demeanour and a prodigious intellect. His intellectual journey took an everlasting turn in the 1970s when he left his native Iran to study the philosophy of science. A doctorate in this area exposed him to the works of Karl Popper, the renowned philosopher of science and impassioned champion of liberalism, which would later form a major plank in Soroush's project for the deconstruction and reconstruction of knowledge in an Islamic context. By the end of the decade, Soroush found himself back in an Iran turned upside down, with the Shah overthrown in a popular revolution. The return of Ayatollah Khomeini after a decade and a half in exile ushered a new order and brought high hopes for a country hitherto under the iron fist of the Shah and the security apparatus of the notorious SAVAK. An Islamic republic was announced after a referendum and Khomeini emerged as its head in the role of *rahbar* (Supreme Leader). Tumultuous change was still gripping Iran when Khomeini appointed Soroush to the seven-member Cultural Revolution Institute tasked to re-open the country's universities and implement an Islamisation programme of higher education. But Soroush resigned in 1983, signalling the end of his fleeting career in political officialdom. He subsequently migrated onto a path of intellectual activism outside of the realm of the state.

Public debates on a whole plethora of issues dominated the 1980s. One particular debate centred on a clash between Soroush and Reza Davari-Ardakani pitting 'Popperians' against 'Heideggerians', with an accent on the nature of epistemology and the fate of the West. Davari-Ardakani was a philosopher and self-confessed follower of Martin Heidegger. He argued, contrary to Soroush's positions, that science was an integral element of the West, which was distinguished by a single 'essence'. And moreover, argued Davari-Ardakani, the pernicious cultural phenomenon of *Gharbzadegi* (Westoxication), rooted in the godless conception of individuality, posed a threat to the very essence of Islamic Iran. Soroush had no time for a putative fixed and single essence. He promoted transcultural encounters and was concerned that official politics and intellectual thought in post-revolutionary Iran had converged to mistakenly privilege the discourse on cultural authenticity.

Soroush's intellectual pursuits in the late 1980s and the early 1990s led him to arrive at the distinction between religion and religious knowledge. While the former was transcendental and fixed, the latter was immanent and mutable. Absolute religious truth was beyond the understanding of human beings and as a logical corollary all political claims based on religious authority were redundant. New horizons were explored in the pages of the magazine *Kayhan-i Farhangi* (Cultural Universe), where he published some of his important essays. After the magazine was closed down, Soroush and his cohorts founded *Kiyan* (Source) in 1991 and remained energetically prolific in sharing their ideas with the Iranian public, much to the chagrin of an influential section of the political and religious establishment. Although Soroush was still teaching at the University of Tehran and lecturing to audiences in Qom and elsewhere, his activities were gradually curtailed.

From regime-insider to dissident, the meandering career of Soroush provides an illustrative example of the contested boundaries of political authority and religious orthodoxy in Iran and the rest of the Muslim world. The publication of *The Expansion of the Prophetic Experience* immediately prior to the millennium angered his opponents in Iran. It explored the taboo subject of the subjective elements of revelation, particularly the Qur'an. Shortly afterwards, Soroush was forced into exile and left Iran for Europe and then the USA. Abbas Milani, a fellow Iranian academic who was subject to the displeasure of both the Pahlavi regime and post-revolutionary Iran, observes that exile is a longstanding tradition among Iranian intellectuals leading many to the soul-searching needed to re-imagine the seeming irrevocability of the status quo in one's homeland. I would add that exile for Soroush brought opportunities to engage with a wider network of interlocutors outside of Iran from the late Nasr Hamid Abou Zayd, a scholarly giant in Islamic hermeneutics, in the Netherlands, to the pioneering sociologist of religion José Casanova in the USA.

The Intellectual as Critic

The idea of the intellectual, for Soroush, is premised upon a clear division of labour in society. Whereas the intellectual is primarily driven to innovate and produce ideas, the politician is concerned with the mundane affairs of running the state. Interestingly, the invoking of the case of Karl Marx the 'theoretician' and Vladimir Lenin the theoretician's 'handyman' by Soroush, citing Karl Popper, further affirms the primary distinguishing characteristic of these two vocations. Two different manifestations of power emerge in a contentious milieu pitting the ever unruly intellectual against the conservative-minded politician. Proximity to the corridors of political power is thus not part of the criteria which defines and animates the life of intellectuals in their daily existence. One can and ought to participate in society in a fashion which introduces a creative dynamic into its public life but to reap the material rewards of one's labour is ruled out. Politics is seen by Soroush to undermine the objectivity of intellectuals in the effort to rethink ideas, values, practices and institutions. G.W.F. Hegel and Martin Heidegger provide Soroush with instructive examples of the ruinous consequences of the relationship between intellectuals and politicians. Heidegger's membership of the Nazi Party and his thought appear to have been commensurate with fascism, especially the cynicism exhibited towards reason.

Difference of opinion is a hallmark feature among intellectuals with rationality wedded to individualism. Inevitably, rationality engenders different interpretations of reality on the plane of ideas. No single orthodoxy dominates the life of the mind with pluralism, a *sine qua non* for any kind of deliberation involving reason and its discontents. The role of the intellectual has an innate power thereby rendering superfluous the pursuit of politics. Ideas are not merely abstract entities: they possess a tour de force of their own in being able to unsettle the foundations of social and cultural norms and it is in this sense the intellectual intervenes in politics. Speaking truth to power is imperative and is the modern equivalent of the classical Islamic norm of 'enjoining the good and forbidding the bad'. For Soroush, criticism is the lifeblood of the intellectual and decisive interventions in public life express the adage, coined by him, 'criticising is the piety of politics'.

The intellectual, according to Soroush, emerges from modernity, which has ushered far-reaching changes throughout the world. Rupture and transition have shaken societies from the slumber of tradition to the vibrancy of modernity. Thus, the intellectual as a vocation was born. Implicit in this view of modernity and the concomitant rise of the intellectual is the acceptance of modernisation which deems tradition to be an unwanted historical legacy. Soroush sees the evolution from tradition to modernity in Muslim societies as a transition from equilibrium to disequilibrium. And it is this disequilibrium that has generated the conditions needed for the emergence of the intellectual. Various spheres of life from the economy to science to philosophy to religion no longer resonate with one another. Discordant strings hold together society with unease.

The crucial function of the intellectual in the Muslim world is to act as midwife to modernity in the quest to transcend the existing disequilibrium and establish a new equilibrium in society. The religious intellectual in Soroush's thinking occupies a vantage point which is essentially holistic. Continuity and change are the pressing issues to be addressed in a variety of binaries: old and new, sacred and mundane, essential and accidental, fundamental and peripheral, kernel and husk, and religion and rationality.

From tradition to modernity, the well-trodden path of the West illuminates the stages of change for the rest of the world. Modernity is the hard-won prize for the intellectual, as well as for his or her society, who must strive, in the face of fierce opposition, to formulate ideas that are able to effect social change.

Post-revolutionary Iran is not only the formative experience responsible for Soroush's insights on a variety of themes but it also furnishes examples in his discussion of these themes. Take the distinction made by Soroush between the intellectual and the cleric. The unsettling effects of modernity have churned out a wide, yet not unbridgeable, gulf between these two vocations. Ali Shariati, the doyen of Shi'i Islamic modernists, and Khomeini belonged to modernity and tradition respectively. For Shariati, a revival of Islam involved its recasting in a modern mould. Mysticism infused with jurisprudence shaped Khomeini's indebtedness to tradition entirely shorn of the repertoire of modernity. The birth of the intellectual marks a departure from the dual functions of the cleric: preaching and guidance. And moreover, the defining attribute of the intellectual is criticism which locates him or her in direct opposition to the cleric's enterprise of exegesis. A clash of interests is the inevitable product of the primacy of the material interests of the clergy over the spiritual life of the Muslim faithful. Religious intellectuals, on the contrary, are not party to this dismal state of affairs. They distance themselves from the practice of profiteering from Islam thereby safeguarding their moral autonomy. Criticism and innovation are primarily motivated by the desire to bring together religion and modernity.

Islamic orthodoxy within Shi'ism has taken many twists and turns since the self-conscious symbolism of the twelve imams was elaborated into a coherent theological and judicial system over a millennium. A ubiquitous presence in local communities and the exercise of reason, both mediated by jurisprudence, were established norms for Shi'ite jurists after the Usuli school of thought, champions of *ijtihad* (independent reasoning), won the argument for a greater role for their corporate institution at the end of the eighteenth century against their scripturalist Akhbari counterparts who advocated little or no resort to reason. As a result, a religious hierarchy composed of formal investiture was strengthened and acquired greater clout in social matters. Ayatollah and Hojjat al-Islam were among the titles bestowed after a considerable number of years studying the Islamic religious science in religious seminaries. Shepherd to the flock of the faithful, these religious scholars guided the conscience of the lay believer and instructed the rituals to be observed. Occupation of the highest offices of the state, however, would have to wait until the emergence of Khomeini and his theory of *Wilayat al-faqih* (Sovereignty of the Jurist). Soroush is highly critical of the political status quo, conflating politics and religion, in today's Iran. Previously separate, the religious seminaries and the state are in a marriage with the former holding the upper hand. According to Soroush, the satirical poetry of Hafez, the renowned fourteenth century Persian poet who expressed the perennial trope of ridiculing the relations between the learned and the powerful, supplies pertinent reminders of this scenario:

Behold, the town Sufi gorges on many a dubious morsel
May the rump of this craving beast remain ample';
and I am no Judge, professor, picket or jurisconsult
Why should I interfere with the drunkards' cult'.

Religion in the Age of Modernity

Islam's fate in the age of modernity is contemplated in light of the past. For Soroush, early modern Europe is the most significant example for the route, similar to that of Christianity and Judaism, Islam must take. Modern science and philosophy have changed the epistemological foundations of knowledge and religion in particular. Soroush's article 'The Theoretical Contraction and Expansion of the Shari'a' is perhaps the quintessential expression of the dialectic between the deconstruction and reconstruction of religious interpretations. No longer guarded by the certainties of the past, Islam urgently requires a rethinking in the here-and-now which would entail nothing less than a return to the original purpose of religion: a spiritual encounter between man and God. Christianity and Judaism have already arrived at this critical juncture in a sequence of transformations. Modernity has wrought a more circumscribed role for religion and humbled, in a constructive sense, the influence it formerly possessed to make way for science to be the arbiter of knowledge. Reason and revelation in Europe equally benefited from their conflict with one another. Islamic revelation escaped this process, and as a result, has remained untested in its relationship with reason, especially empirical reason.

Soroush identifies four sequences waiting to prepare Islam to be better suited for the raison d'etre of religion: the deconstruction of religion, the emergence of new interpretations, an adverse reaction in the form of 'traditionalism', and the appearance of heterodoxies and heresies. The first stage witnesses the various contents of modernity wreaking havoc with religious dogma and experience thereby weakening its power in a thorough-going deconstruction. New interpretations in stage two are primarily concerned with building a bridge between religion and contemporary knowledge, perhaps exemplified in the inception of Islamic modernity at the turn of the twentieth century, using *ijtihad* for this purpose. The third stage could be aptly described to be a return to tradition in rejection of modernity, celebrating the past centred upon a lost identity: fundamentalism is also considered to be an integral and aggressive expression of this phenomenon. Finally, the intersection between religion and modernity produces the fruit of heresy at stage four with the contemporary experience of Islam not entirely dissimilar from that of Christianity's. Revival of tradition is tantamount to pursuing an imaginary goal. Soroush argues that the absence of the elements of knowledge and modernity lead to the deleterious effects of treating Islam as an identity which takes it towards fundamentalism. Knowledge is unequivocally the proper field for the reform of Islam.

Deconstruction of the dominant interpretations of Islam is implicated in a broader web of disciplines and fields of inquiry. Relationships among ideas point to the dynamic nature of knowledge. Soroush draws a clear and substantial demarcation between religion and religious interpretation. Continuity is elevated to the level of the transcendental in direct contrast to the humanly-conceived changes in religious interpretations and other branches of human knowledge. Furthermore, human beings occupy the role of interpreters rather than lawgivers in a post-prophetic period. Epistemology is the contested terrain for Soroush's forays into the Islamic tradition. Religious interpretations are continually evolving with other disciplines which determine the state of knowledge in a particular time and place. These interpretations of religion are, by their very nature, stamped with incompleteness and the intellectual baggage of individuals invariably weighs heavily on how the scriptural texts of Islam are understood. The line between the sacred and the mundane is drawn ever larger to endow human agency with the ability to deconstruct the received wisdom of religious authorities and subsequently to construct the edifice of religion anew in accordance to the critical knowledge of the age.

Although Soroush appears to give weak authoritative value to the Islamic tradition, he traces the roots of his intellectual venture to the classical schools of the Mutazilites and the Asharites. Each one of these schools of thought looks at the world with its own particular prism with decisive implications for the interpretation of Islam. Soroush identifies himself as a 'neo-Mutazilite'. The Mutalizites' emphasis on the independence of reason from revelation equips and emboldens Soroush with a method to discover moral values. Reconciling these two opposing views involves the elaboration of a rational conception of morality firmly ensconced in experience which does not invoke revelation. Morality and ethics join science and politics in their detachment from religion thereby restricting the scope of Islam to meaningfully engage with and in the world. Furthermore, the body of knowledge on philosophy, ethics and law contained in the Islamic tradition is more or less relegated to the intellectual margins. Such a dismissal of the legacy of Muslim scholarship is premised on the position that the tradition inspired by Islam is a static entity without any real hope of renewal.

Prophecy and Islamic Law

In Soroush's writings, the context of the Qur'an plays an overwhelming role in determining the meaning and relevance of the text. Such an approach runs the risk of severely restricting the scope of the constant or universal applicability of passages which would be able to speak to a higher plane. These passages are, instead, located on the ground of specificity. Generally, the divine, Soroush appears to argue, has very little to say about other ages which do not fall within the grasp of the Prophet Muhammad's own immediate experience. Certain qualifications indeed do exist. The dialectic between continuity and change for Soroush acquires a robust character in the discussion of the Qur'an as simultaneously the word of

Muhammad and the word of God with echoes of the medieval Islamic past. Several themes are raised by Soroush in his formulation of the notion of the 'prophetic experience'. The interpretation of the Qur'an and the illustration of its context proceed from the framing of the relationship between the supernatural and the natural.

It was the Mutazilites who first explored the worldly dimensions of revelation. All creation, subsuming the incidences of revelation, they argued, was willed by a transcendental God without any attributes to speak of. Thus, the Qur'an could not, against the concept of the uncreated Qur'an of the theologians and the later Asharites, be other than the created word of God which does not partake of His divine nature. This position on the nature of revelation strikes an important cord with Soroush's scriptural agenda.

But this position is not unique to the Mutazilites. Classical Shi'ite theologians were also predisposed to this notion but added a few revisions aiming to include the existence of attributes, albeit, on a lower scale of importance than their fellow Sunni colleagues. Plenty of illustrative examples, past and present, can be found for rethinking the status of the Qur'an. For example, the polymath and philosopher, ibn Sina (980-1037), wrote extensively on prophecy emphasising the subjective personality of the recipient. For ibn Sina, the imaginative faculty of the prophet, once perfection has been attained, gives a visual and acoustic form, including the manifestation of angels, to the inspiration it receives without a concomitant external reality. Almost a thousand years later, the noted scholar of Islam, Fazlur Rahman (1919–1998), put forward a radical conception of how the Qur'an was revealed. Muhammad undoubtedly received inspiration or *wahy* from 'the Other' whereupon the idea-words from the divine become sound-words in his consciousness. Islamic 'orthodoxy', writes Rahman, 'lacked the necessary intellectual tools to combine in its formulation of dogma the otherness and verbal character of the Revelation on the one hand, and its intimate connection with the work and the religious personality of the Prophet on the other, i.e. it lacked the intellectual capacity to say both that the Qur'an is entirely the word of God and, in an ordinary sense, also entirely the word of Muhammad'. No external agent, an angel, is presumed to have delivered the Qur'an and the orthodox postulate is merely an embellishment, reflecting its time, on an otherwise profound, at times intense, subjective encounter of the heart with God.

Neither ibn Sina nor Rahman are cited by Soroush. He sidesteps them in order to invoke the Mutazilites and introduce his critical hermeneutics. However, stark similarities with both scholars are clearly present in Soroush's ruminations on prophecy as a mental phenomenon which is not external to Muhammad. Instead, one of the grand figures of the Islamic tradition whom Soroush quotes to support his position of the dual natures of the Qur'an is none other than Rumi: the heart duly receives divine inspiration with all the veils of intermediaries falling away. The name of Ibn Sina, however, appears fleetingly in a letter by Soroush to one of his detractors, Ayatollah Jafar Sobhani, to validate his position that the imagination does play a necessary role in the reception of revelation.

The omnipresence of God provides Soroush with the foundations to elaborate a theory of revelation aiming to reconcile the supernatural and the natural worlds. There is no recognition of the boundaries between these worlds in the metaphysical realm. Everything is equidistant to the metaphysical thus precluding the elevated proximity of one of God's creation over others. Angels form part of this intertwined tapestry of being and the experiences of Muhammad and Mary, mother of Jesus, are exclusively on the plane of consciousness. The modes by which God communicates with humanity are identified in the Qur'an, 52:51: 'it is not granted to any mortal that God should speak to him except through revelation or from behind a veil, or by sending a messenger to reveal by His command what He will'. For Soroush, these modes are perceived to be largely immaterial to the actual substance of revelation. Under God's guidance, Muhammad 'discovered' the truths revealed onto him. Rumi's poetry affords an eloquent defence and expression for Soroush's position:

I need no intermediary or wet nurse to give me the kindness of God
For, Moses-like, my wet nurse and my mother are one and the same.

And once again, the ideas of Rumi are interpreted to lend a mystical quality to the adaptation of the supernatural to the natural. However, Soroush attributes the origin of his understanding of prophecy to Charles Darwin's theory of evolution. Rumi and Darwin sit side-by-side as unlikely passengers in a journey of interpretation centred on the Qur'an's text. Muhammad Iqbal's own efforts in the reconstruction of Islamic thought proposed hope from the wisdom of Rumi to be the panacea for the pessimism engendered by Darwin's theory of evolution in a univers where creativity is neither predetermined nor acquires finality.

The awing presence of Rumi allows Soroush to refer to revelation as a sea which, of necessity, complies with a jug which is a metaphor for Muhammad and his environment. Darwin in the hands of Soroush is used to build the theoretical scaffolding to make the case for a dynamic conception of history. Many ideas from a variety of sources are held together in Soroush's contextualism thanks, in part, to the elevation of the environment, broadly defined, of seventh century Arabia. The environment, for Soroush, are 'the events that took place in Arab society at the time; the development of the Prophet's personality; occurrences in the course of the Prophet's life and the political and social conflicts that he encountered; the language spoken in the Prophet's society; and so on'. Context subsumes the text and the latter is a mirror of the former. Ultimately, revelation is in keeping with the Prophet's environment. This is how, according to Soroush, the supernatural enters the natural in nature and society bound by their laws.

Soroush discerns the beginning of the tale of the 'Prophetic discovery' in the Qur'anic verses of 97:1-5: 'We sent it down on the Night of Glory. What will explain to you what that Night of Glory is? The Night of Glory is better than a thousand months, on that night angels and the Spirit descend again and again with their Lord's permission on every task; [there is] peace that night until the break of dawn'. This night is rich with symbolism, rather than literal significance, for the virtue of being the occasion when Muhammad became a prophet in his reception of what would be the first of such revelations for the following twenty-two years. A night of union commences the mission of prophecy, embodying the ideal abode or station of the Sufi path, when the veils hitherto obscuring God fall. The Night of Glory is thus a synecdoche for the entire process of revelation: transforming Muhammad into a Qur'anic personality in this particular event. The relationship between Soroush and Sufism appears to colour his venture of reform in a variety of ways, namely recurring throughout his writings to reveal a mystical bent of mind.

Change is frequently contrasted with continuity in Soroush's thought. Nowhere is this creative thrust, entailing both deconstruction and reconstruction, more evident than in his taxonomy of the three layers of Islam: beliefs and worldview, morality, and law. Each layer pertains to the very identity of Islam whereupon the distinction between the essential and the accidental arises: the pearl to be protected by the shell. In Soroush's demarcation of the categories of continuity and change, morality and law are excluded from the essential with the express desire to subject these two areas of religious life to new interpretations that serve to protect the pearl. The existence of the essential is unambiguously sanctioned by the Qur'an itself: 'this day I have perfected your religion for you, completed My blessings upon you, and chosen as your religion Islam' (5:3). Perfection, however, is bestowed upon the design of religion. Neither the particular Prophetic rulings and norms nor a putative all-encompassing Islam benefit from this divine dispensation in Soroush's thought.

According to Soroush, 99 per cent of Qur'anic rulings were already current during the life of the Prophet Muhammad and only one percent is of a novel character. God simply endorsed the law-making efforts of the Prophet. And more importantly, the customs and practices engendered as a result are not necessarily the best contained in history with the critical implication that better methods can be found or invented. Injunctions of a legal import found in the passages of the Qur'an are, in the first instance, to be assumed to be temporary unless their universal relevance can be established. Although the inversion of the universal and the particular within Islamic law by Soroush is peculiar to his deliberations on the accidental facets of Islam, it is part of a wider recognition on the part of contemporary Muslim reformers and thinkers who argue for a fresh reading of the Qur'an. Rahman, for example, points out that the Qur'an, chiefly containing religious and moral norms, accepted the society of the Prophet Muhammad as a frame of reference. Freedom and responsibility in a variety of areas from women and slavery point to a yet unfinished moral endeavour to be pursued further by Muslims in both the present and the future. While Rahman provides an astute account of the historical status of the injunctions present in the Qur'an and manages to endow them with a forward-looking spirit, Soroush aims to discard its ethical and religious basis for any future legal thinking within an Islamic framework.

Soroush's efforts to rethink of Islam have led to a new binary categorisation substituting the classical broad divisions of *ibadah* (worship) and *mu'amalat* (social transactions) with the supplementary category of *siyasah* (politics). Acts of worship and justice and injustice compose the primary categories in Soroush's binary. A subtle recasting by Soroush of jurisprudential scholarship indicates a certain degree of continuity with the Islamic tradition. The classification of the acts of worship appears to be a conventional account of the practices and rituals observed by the Prophet Muhammad in his life. Hidden benefits fill the acts of worship. For Soroush, however, the states of excellence of the Prophet led to the discovery of the precise forms of rituals. What is now incumbent upon Muslims is the performance of the rituals of worship to attain the states of excellence which produced, in the case of Muhammad, these forms. Perhaps in no other area of Islam, according to Soroush, is the Prophet to be faithfully emulated without question. Genuine spiritual contemplation requires a state of mind caught in the absorbing acts of worship to the exclusion of the distractions of the world.

The juristic category of justice and injustice embraces a vast range of issues from women rights to inheritance to politics to divorce law. Soroush applies the tool of *ijtihad* for the purpose of formulating new rules. The Prophet Muhammad is the model to be emulated, rather than imitated, in this creative venture. He brought the people of his period from what was then considered to be injustice to justice but the latter cannot be construed to be ahistorical justice. The task of *ijtihad* for our times is similar in scope: to bring about a change from this period's injustice to today's justice. An act of cultural translation from the past to the present is required of the essentials, the Lawmaker's intentions, and the accidentals. Imitation, even of Muhammad, is ruled out and a changing new set of laws for the category of justice and injustice involves an escapable moral negotiation on the part of Soroush with the text of the Qur'an. While *ijtihad*'s creative capacity can push the boundaries of the given arena of thought such as solving new problems, it does not possess any revolutionary implications for *fiqh* or Islamic jurisprudence as a discipline.

Deconstruction of the Islamic tradition is the trademark feature of Abdolkarim Soroush's Islamic neo-modernist venture. His formulation of the contraction and expansion of religious interpretation can perhaps be better described as the deconstruction and reconstruction of the man-made knowledge of and about Islam. What is of serious concern in his thought is a rather uncritical embrace of modernity in its entirety; Islam must follow the trajectory of the Western civilisation, the apex of human achievement. No genuine engagement with the intricacies of the Islamic tradition is made by Soroush which could lead to a creative rethinking of its elements unhindered by either the totalising effects of an unmediated modernity or a conservative disposition towards all things Islamic. Interestingly, a secular conception of Islam appears to emerge from Soroush's writings predicated on the idea of a 'minimalist religion' as an essentially spiritual experience of God within the individual.

However, Soroush the iconoclast continues to stoke the embers of controversy even when in exile in a tussle with official Iranian discourses on religious authority (read political power) and cultural authenticity. A single theoretical thread ties his ideas to give them a sharp edge: history as a constant movement or adaptation. This is conspicuous in Soroush's naturalistic formulation of the creation of the Qur'an: revelation adapts to the environment and henceforth is in keeping with the Prophet Muhammad and his immediate cultural world. Soroush's inversion of the universal and the particular in Islamic law is a simultaneous break with the classical body of jurisprudence and other notable efforts of reform among his contemporaries who have sought to preserve the ethical and legal spirit of Islam without sacrificing it at the altar of modernity.

MAHMOUD TAHA: HERESY AND MARTYRDOM

Abdelwahab El-Affendi

The lowest point for the regime of former Sudanese President Gaafar Nimeiri (1969–1985), if not for the whole of modern Sudanese history, came on the morning of Friday 18 January 1985. At that fateful hour (around 10am), a seventy-seven-year-old man was dragged in chains to the gallows, with tens of thousands of people watching, most of them cheering with glee. The courtyard of the main prison in Khartoum, the Kober prison, was full to capacity, and the masses were queuing for miles around in the vain hope of catching a glimpse of the spectacle. Just before being dispatched, the hood covering the convict's face was removed so that he could behold the hate and condemnation in the eyes of the crowd.

To the astonishment of all watching, there was a confident and benign smile on that well-known face, with its traditional parallel scars on both cheeks. Just at that moment, the hundreds of political prisoners housed in that jail shouted in unison a slogan calling for the downfall of the regime. His smile broadened slightly as he acknowledged the implied support. His face was covered again, and he was promptly hanged. His body was then winched in a helicopter and taken to an anonymous burial spot on the edge of the desert. His grave remains unknown to his family and friends to this day.

The condemned man was Mahmoud Muhammad Taha, at the time an established religious thinker with a small but dedicated band of followers, mainly among the educated youth. He was relatively unknown outside Sudan, and was shunned by the established religious mainstream. Already a Shari'a court had condemned him in 1968 as an apostate. But since Shari'a courts, a remnant of the days of British rule, had no jurisdiction beyond personal affairs, that was more of a *fatwa* than a judicial decision.

However, after Nimeiri announced sweeping 'Islamic' legislation in September 1983, things began to change.

In 1984, frustrated with the mounting opposition to his measures and the reluctance of the judiciary to cooperate, Nimeiri established a tier of courts dubbed the 'Prompt Justice Courts', operating under emergency regulations. These courts were manned by zealots from both Nimeiri's core support among minor Sufi groups, plus an assortment of Islamists. The courts adopted a cavalier attitude towards procedures, and scores of summary harsh sentences were meted out every week and were publicised in the media. Some of the trials were televised.

In January 1985, Taha was hauled with four of his followers in front of one of these courts. He had been arrested in December 1984, having been released from nineteen months of detention earlier that month, on charges of sedition for distributing leaflets condemning Nimeiri's anti-Islamic laws. Criminal Court no. 4 in Omdurman happened to be manned by a young judge adhering to a small Sufi sect headed by Nimeiri's key adviser on Islamic law at the time. The charges against the accused were, ironically, under secular law: they were accused of sedition and 'inciting hatred against the state'. After just two days of trial, the five accused were sentenced to death on 8 January. The Appeals Court, within the same Prompt Justice Courts system, not only affirmed the sentence but added the charge of apostasy, citing the 1968 court decision and a statement by the Muslim World League, also in 1968, declaring Taha's ideas contrary to Islam. In its ruling issued on 15 January, the accused were given three days to repent or face execution. The four other accused decided to recant and were reprieved. President Nimeiri endorsed Taha's sentence; and it was carried out.

The speed with which the trial was conducted sent shock waves through the Sudanese intellectual and political scenes. There were wide condemnations from trade unions, lawyers and academic bodies, and the process which led to Nimeir's toppling from power in a popular revolution three months later was set in motion. In February 1986, the Appeals Court quashed the ruling retrospectively.

A Turbulent Life

Mahmoud Muhammad Taha (1909–1985) first came to national prominence in September 1946 when he led a demonstration that stormed the prison in the provincial town of Rufa'a to free three women imprisoned under a law which banned Female Genital Mutilation (FGM). The British colonial authorities had passed the FGM ban a year earlier and the women included the mother of a little girl and the midwife who performed the operation. Taha and his followers forced the release of the women, and entered into further confrontations with the police when the mother was re-arrested. Taha argued that he was not in favour of FGM, but resented colonial interference in local customs. The women were freed, but Taha himself was arrested and sentenced to two years in prison.

That was his second stint in jail that year. Earlier in the year, and a few months after setting up the Republican Party in October 1945, he was detained by the authorities and sentenced to one year in prison for sedition. But he was released after less than two months due to popular pressure. However, in the Rufa'a protest case, he was forced to serve his full term. It proved a turning point in his life.

In prison, Taha, an engineer by profession, found religion. Prior to that episode, his rhetoric was largely secular, with a focus on opposition to the traditional 'sectarian' parties. However, following his detention, he began a period of deep reflection on religious issues. Emerging from jail two years later, he went into voluntary seclusion for three more years. When he emerged, he was a new man. His 'republican' party became a religious cult centred around his mystical vision. He still maintained a liberal outlook, prioritising individual freedom and the anti-colonial struggle. But this time, he used the term 'jihad' as a rallying cry. Many of his colleagues left to join other parties, and he had to make do with a small ever-growing circle of disciples.

His full vision was not coherently developed until the mid-1960s. But in the meantime, he began to campaign on a number of issues. In the run-up to independence in 1956, the main Islamist movement, the Muslim Brotherhood, emerged on the scene and managed to put the question of the 'Islamic Constitution' on the agenda. Taha vehemently opposed this call, and later resigned from the Constitutional Commission in protest at its domination by what he saw as 'sectarian' parties. He wrote one of his first pamphlets, *Usus Dustur al-Sudan* (the Fundamentals of Sudan's Constitution, 1955), in which he outlined his vision for Sudan as a decentralised presidential republic. Already, however, we can discern here some of his future core ideas, such as arguing that 'absolute freedom' for the individual should be the goal of the political system, but citizens need to be educated to deserve it; and part of the education is political empowerment. He also argued that the Qur'an should be the basis of the constitution, adding a 'cosmopolitan' flavour to his prescription by arguing both that the future of humanity requires a proper understanding of Islam, but also that Sudan should orient itself to become part of a world order based on peace and equality. He also advocated some form of welfare state.

The democracy in Sudan did not survive long, and Taha was quick to write to the generals who took power in 1958, beseeching them to implement his vision of a 'socialist, federalist, democratic system'. The request was completely ignored. But it set a precedent that would prove problematic, and ultimately disastrous, in days to come: pinning the hope on a dictator to realise a vision of ultra-liberal democracy. Taha had a problem with actual democracy in a context like Sudan, where he detested the main political actors, blaming them for misguiding the masses into adhering to reactionary visions.

It was under the military regime, however, that Taha encountered his first serious setback. In 1960, three of his disciples were expelled from the Ma'had al-'Ilmi, the highest institution of religious learning in Sudan. They were accused of propagating Taha's ideas, in particular his views that the obligatory daily prayers need not be performed by one like him, who had achieved an elevated spiritual rank. Taha tried to negotiate the students' reinstitution, and when he failed, he wrote one of his first major works, *Al-Islam*, in which he summed up his reform vision.

His problems got much worse once democracy was restored after the popular uprising which swept the military away in October 1964. He revived the Republican Party again and plunged headlong into the politics of the day. His first major clash with the establishment came in 1965, when parliament decided, by an overwhelming majority, to ban the Sudanese Communist Party (SCP) and dismiss its eleven MPs. This came after a young man who claimed to be a member of the party launched a public attack on the Prophet Muhammad and his family, provoking public protests. The Communist Party denied the man was a member and distanced itself from his remarks. But its opponents decided to exploit the popular backlash and banned it anyway. When the Supreme Court declared the measures were unconstitutional, the government and parliament defiantly refused to abide by the ruling, causing the Chief Justice to resign in protest.

Hassan Turabi, the leader of the Muslim Brotherhood and at the time the country's leading constitutional lawyer, produced a booklet supporting the ban. His argument was that ultimate sovereignty rested with parliament, which was the source of law. Therefore, no other authority, including the courts, had the power or right to challenge the parliament. Taha produced a scathing counter-attack, questioning Turabi's Islamic credentials (he scarcely produced Islamic arguments to support his case) and his legal competence and understanding of democracy.

In 1967, he launched into another battle, this time targeting Arab leaders following the catastrophic defeat against Israel in June that year, challenging them to recognise Israel and accept a peace deal with it on the basis of the Partition Decision of 1947. He had been engaged for years prior to that in a crusade against Egypt's Gamal Abd al-Nasir (Nasser). He had sent him letters (in September 1955 and again in August 1958) urging him to espouse Islam as a basis of his rule, and chastising him for his populist anti-Western policies, which he deemed demagogic and irresponsible. Taha was deeply hostile to pan-Arab nationalism, which he branded as 'racist'; he argued that Arabs have only entered history as Muslims, and that is the way they will do so again. Like Sudan's generals, Nasser did not bother to reply to his messages.

In 1966, Taha gave up his job as an engineer and dedicated himself fully to his mission. Over the next two years, he published some of his most important works, including his magnum opus, *Al-Risala al-Thaniya fi'il-Islam* (The Second Message of Islam, hereafter *RTI*, January 1967). This landed him into big trouble. Shortly after the second edition of *RTI* was published in April 1968, some clerics lodged a complaint against him in one of the Shari'a courts, accusing him of apostasy. These courts had no real powers, and no jurisdiction. Taha boycotted the proceedings, and treated the court with disdain. Nevertheless, the court held a trial in his absence and declared him an apostate on 18 November 1968, after just three hours of deliberation.

Taha and his followers saw this as the culmination of a long struggle with the traditional religious establishment, and in their riposte, condemned the *ulama* as hypocrites who were not qualified to judge Taha, being themselves a creation of the colonial order and having a history of serving colonial rule and all variety of authoritarian regimes. Interestingly, they also accused Nasser of instigating the court procedures against him in a 'conspiracy' to silence him and avenge his vocal criticisms of Nasser.

It was a poignant irony, therefore, that when Nimeiri took power in a bloodless military coup in May 1969, Taha offered enthusiastic support to the new regime, even though it was supported by Nasser and the SCP. Even when Nimeiri engaged in massacres against the Mahdists and later against his own Communist allies, Taha maintained his support. Nimeiri banned all political parties, so Taha's movement changed its name to the Republican Brothers and continued to operate with tacit regime approval. This remains one of the most controversial positions of the Republicans, given their principled support for freedom and their blanket condemnations of dictatorships elsewhere. The justifications offered for this position tend to compound the problem, since it reiterates the unprincipled claim that the 'reactionary' sectarian parties and Islamists were a worse alternative. Expressing the hope that Nimeiri's rule would 'liquidate' the sectarian parties and suppress the Islamists, as well as eliminating the Communists, thus permitting a period of 'enlightenment' and change, is apparently an overt endorsement of repressive violence. However, not only did Nimeiri fail to eradicate sectarians and Islamists, but he later allied himself with them. Further on, he declared himself an 'imam' in his own right and became Taha's worst nightmare: a zealot religious dictator. That is when he decided to oppose him, and paid with his life.

The Core Theory

It is not easy to pin down the essence of Taha's innovative thought, but two interconnected strands pervade his discourse: a commitment to liberal individualism and a mystical inclination. It is also not clear which came first, given his trajectory. It is also problematic that he combines his almost dogmatic liberalism with socialist notions. In this sense, at times one discerns that the liberalism frames the mysticism, while at others, it looks as if it was the mysticism which framed the liberalism. But there is no doubt that it was his mystical certainties which sustained him through his turbulent times.

The way he expresses his hopes and analyses also indicates an evolutionary vision which operates at multiple levels: biological, historical, social, political and spiritual. He combines the traditional creation story with conventional Darwinism by arguing that when Adam was banished from Heaven, he was banished into almost nothingness, and had to be created anew along the lines suggested by Darwinism: life emerged like a spark from sheer matter, then evolved until man came into being. This was the tortuous path through which Adam became human again and was forgiven. Human society also evolved from a primitive state of superstition and barbarism to civilisation. Social evolution was also paralleled with spiritual evolution: from primitive paganism, to advanced paganism, to monotheism. This was also a kind of objective process, like the biological evolution: as humanity evolved and became more mature, it became deserving of a higher level of spiritualism. Within monotheism itself, there was an evolution that could be described as the 'Islamic Trinity': Judaism was strictly regulatory in its prescriptions, while Christianity swung like a pendulum in the other direction, concentrating on spirituality rather than behaviour. Then Islam came to restore the balance to the middle, between the arbitrary strictness suitable for primitive societies, and the idealist spiritualism which borders on permissiveness.

On the basis of this analysis, Taha builds his core theory of individual spiritual evolution. And here, his mystical inclinations come into their element. He begins by arguing that man is not only a divine creation, but essentially divine. The verse which states that 'O Mankind, be conscious of your Sustainer who created you out of one living entity (*nafs*)' (4: 1), is interpreted to mean that you have been created out of God himself. Having been banished into oblivion, this *nafs* (soul, self) then evolves back into humanity, and through Shari'a could be restored back to its divine status and absolute freedom.

Thus in political society as in religious law, the absolute freedom of the individual is the most fundamental principle. In Islam, the individual is the basic unit of accountability, and each individual confronts God on his/her own. But to be exercised, freedom needs to be earned and deserved. Those incapable of respecting the freedom of others must be restrained through 'constitutional law' and chastised until they reach the requisite level of maturity. The whole objective of Shari'a is to attain this end of absolute freedom. This includes the harsh provisions, such as 'an eye for an eye', since these are primary educational tools. The main reason for aggression by man against his fellow man is a 'lack of imagination'. But when an aggressor is made to suffer the same harm he had perpetrated on a fellow human being, his eye is then opened and he realises the enormity of what he had done. The 'Law of Compensation' is thus a fundamental law of the creation. As well as being a legislative provision, it is a cosmic law (for the universe has come into existence through truth and justice *b'il-Haq*). Through this law, man draws nearer to God through will and freedom, while the rest of the inanimate universe obeys God's will through coercion. However, this difference is only apparent, since man's will is only apparent. The naïve individual may imagine that he/she has a will and can control his/her action. But a truly knowledgeable individual would realise that this is mere illusion. In reality, both the unbeliever and believer obey God and prostrate to His will. Only the true believer does this willingly and knowingly, while the unbeliever does so without knowing it. The whole objective of religion is to help attain this stage of awareness of obedience.

To attain this condition of genuine freedom and knowledge, the individual can choose to elevate himself/herself to a higher degree of obedience through strict training, beginning by shunning sins of action, then sins of speech, and finally sins of thought and even of the 'unconscious'. The realisation that there is no will but God's is attained through strenuous exercises of fasting, prayer and charity. It also reflects itself in moving beyond justice and retaliation to forgiveness of those who wrong you, and then caring and loving them. At the level of realisation of complete absence of will and compete submission to God, the soul attains absolute peace and identity with self, and then free will again:

> Here, the heart bows, forever, at the threshold of the first stage of servitude. Then the servant is no longer in the complete grip of fate, but with complete free will; that is because complete obedience to God has raised him to a status of nobility, handing him over to the freedom of choice; he has obeyed God until God obeyed him in compensation. He becomes alive though God's life, and in possession of God's knowledge, God's will and God's power. He becomes God.

When a person ascends to this level, religious laws no longer apply to him/her. This is the level of 'individual Shari'a', where every person follows norms appropriate to that level, up to level of 'absolute individual freedom':

> And as the conscience becomes progressively more purified, the conduct becomes more correct and the circle of prohibitions narrows, while the circle of permitted things widens… When the journey reaches its ultimate end, with a completely pure heart, all sensible things revert to their original status permissibility.

Islam, New and Old

It is within this overall evolutionary theory of life that Taha proposes his vision of the 'Second Message of Islam'. According to Taha, this 'second message' was in fact the first one, revealed in Mecca but rejected by the Quraysh. Therefore, the message was diluted because humanity was not at that time capable of shouldering it. Only the Prophet observed the dictates of this message in his personal conduct. The second message thus involves reviving the Prophet's 'Sunna' and generalising it to become the conduct of everyone.

The Shari'a, as it was revealed and applied in the seventh century, was suitable for that period, but totally incapable of addressing the challenges of the twentieth. But if we say that the Shari'a is to be suitable for every time and place, this can be only because it is a living and evolving system. To launch the second message of Islam, we need to go back to the Qur'an and read it in a new way. We need a new messenger to receive the new revelation. This revelation comes directly from God, without the mediation of the Angel Gabriel, through reading the Qur'an. The new messenger is someone whom God has endowed with the appropriate level of comprehension and given permission to speak. And as Christ said, 'by their fruits you will know them'.

In reality, Taha argues, the second message of Islam is the only genuine Islam. He bases this on a rather significant reversal of the accepted hierarchy between *iman* (faith, belief) and Islam. Traditionally, it has been accepted, based on very clear Qur'anic and *hadith* injunctions, that Islam is the bare minimum and formal acceptance of the faith, which is followed by *iman*, is backed up by dedicated action. Above *iman*, we find *ihsan* (perfection), which is to worship God as if feeling His actual presence. Taha overrides this hierarchy by postulating two levels of religious experience, the first (inferior one) is the level of faith, and the second is the level of knowledge (*'ilm*) and truth (*haqiqat*). In the first level, Islam is indeed the lowest rung, followed by *iman* and then *ihsan*. At the level of *'ilm,* however, we start with *'ilm al-yaqeen* (knowledge of certainty), followed by *'ilm 'ayn al-yaqeen* (knowledge of the very certainty), and then *ilm haqq al-yaqeen* (knowledge of true certainty). Islam is the level beyond that third phase.

At this level, Islam was in the past available only to prophets and exceptional individuals. However, now that humanity has evolved sufficiently to qualify for accepting this level of Islam, it is time for the emergence of the first and true Muslim community. Humanity is now ready for the message because it is sufficiently advanced socially, intellectually and economically, but impoverished spiritually. This combination of material advancement and spiritual impoverishment is the sign that a new dispensation is needed, and only Islam can provide this dimension.

But Islam provides this in its second message, not in the first. In its new mission, the norms of Islam in the areas of worship (except for *zakah*, or charity) and the areas of justice (including the *hudood* punishments) need not be revised, but social and political norms and practices should be. For example, jihad is not a fundamental precept of Islam, since the original and fundamental norm is that of individual freedom, so coercion is not admissible. However, since at that early stage, coercion was appropriate, jihad was permitted. Similarly, enslavement of individuals was permitted as a consequence of jihad, and as a concession to prevalent norms. By the same token, 'capitalism' and private property, inequality between men and women, divorce, *hijab* and the segregation of men and women, were all permitted as interim measures, since the societies of the early Islamic era would not have been able to handle the true injunctions. For example, the Prophet did not retain any property above his most basic needs, giving away everything beyond absolute necessity. In this regard, the provisions of *zakah*, as the obligatory allocation of a portion (between 2.5% and 10%) of one's assets or income to charity, is not the true Islamic norm. In reality, the true Islamic society is a 'democratic socialist' system, where social equality is the norm, and where individual control of means of production must not be permitted.

If the believers observe these norms of true Islam, they will achieve on this earth the paradise described in the Qur'an. That divine promise is 'only a miniature model for the greater paradise, which will be realised on this earth on which we live today, when it is filled with justice after having been filled with injustice':

This is the dream entertained by Marx, but which he has completely missed, lapsing into error. It will not be realised, however, except by the Muslims, who have not yet appeared. When they do, part of what God foretold in the verse: 'Verily, the God-fearing [shall find themselves in the hereafter] amidst gardens and springs; [having been received with the greeting,] "Enter here in peace, secure!"; And [by then] We shall have removed whatever unworthy thoughts or feelings may have been [lingering] in their breasts, [and they shall rest] as brethren, facing one another [in love] upon thrones of happiness; No weariness shall ever touch them in this [state of bliss], and never shall they have to forego it.' This aspect is the communism which will be achieved by Islam the moment the Muslim umma appears. At that moment, 'the earth will shine bright with her Sustainer's light', and God's grace will fully encompass its inhabitance, and peace will prevail all over and love will triumph.

Evaluation and Critiques

It is clear from the preceding that there are many aspects of Taha's thought which the orthodox will find troubling, beginning with the last point where paradise is not an alternative to earthly life but a continuation of it. Then, there is his claim that not only can man become one with God, but he can become God, and therefore become a law unto himself, with no need to observe any religious prohibitions or taboos. Such views were naturally found outrageous by the orthodox, including the Sufis, some of whom could have become his allies.

The secular components of his theses, including his critiques of Western civilisation, are not without problems either. This is not least because such points are often offered in a few paragraphs, and with such generalisations as 'man and the universe in philosophical thought', without citing a single philosopher. His followers complained that Taha had been systematically ignored by the intellectuals. This might have been out of deference, since the secular intellectuals would have to criticise his rather maverick ideas, which they did not want to do, happy to have him as an ally against the Islamists and conservatives.

Islamists also ignored Taha's ideas, concentrating instead on condemning him as a heretic and attacking him for his alliance with the Nimeiri dictatorship. In another irony, Nimeiri in fact pursued the policy of previous regimes of depriving Taha and his followers of any access to the media. To circumvent this obstacle, the group relied on innovative methods, such as conducting regular daily debates in universities and some public squares, in addition to members volunteering as itinerant sales people to distribute their literature. These tactics, and the deep isolation nationally and regionally (surrounding Arab countries were not that receptive either), ensured the membership remained small, but cohesive.

The main critiques of Taha came from the religious establishment, which built what one of his supporters described as a 'broad Islamic alliance', made up of the religious establishments in Sudan, Saudi Arabia and Egypt, backed up by some Islamic movements and a wide array of religious functionaries (imams, ulama associations, etc.). This alliance succeeded, as al-Bashir notes, in 'misleading the peoples of Sudan and peoples of Islam' through their anti-Taha propaganda.

Taha's confrontations with the orthodox religious establishment was a straightforward issue: the traditionalists rejected his claim of authority to override accepted dogma and practice on the basis of personal communion with God, for that amounted to declaring oneself a prophet. But his conflict with the Sufis, including the group which masterminded his demise, was more complex. For Sufism does accept the possibility of direct communion with God, and many renowned Sudanese Sufis had regularly challenged the authority of the ulama, including a sixteenth-century ancestor of Taha, Sheikh Muhammad al-Hamim, who defied the judge of the day by marrying two sisters and exceeding the limit of four wives. However, Sudanese Sufis also consistently rejected 'radical' claims, such as those of the Sudanese Mahdi (d. 1885), who claimed communion with heaven through visions of the Prophet. The judge who tried Taha also reiterated claims citing Al-Ghazali (d. 1111) that mystical knowledge is personal and privileged, and should not be shared or used as a basis of public claims.

Secular critiques, which were rare, centred more on the man's obscurantism, his hold on his followers and his 'reactionary' views. His support for the Nimeiri military dictatorship also remained an unresolved issue. An additional problem is that Taha (and some of his followers, such the human rights advocate Abdullahi An-Na'im), tend to offer the most restrictive interpretation of Shari'a (such as that it is lawful to use violence to force people to accept Islam) in order to justify their arguments that it should be transcended.

The group now receives little criticism, except from hard-line Islamists, most probably because it is not seen as threatening. Since the demise of its charismatic leader, the movement's already low profile has receded further into the background. According to the movement's own adherents, the membership of the group never exceeded one thousand followers. However, the movement has witnessed a minor revival recently, in terms of political and media presence, if not in membership. In 2010, Taha's former modest home in Omadurman became the locus of the most appropriate tribute to the departed thinker: the Ustaz Mahmoud Muhammad Taha Cultural Centre. Earlier this year, the group applied for a registration as a political party in Sudan, but its application was rejected in May 2014 after a challenge from a group of *ulama*. The issue is currently being hotly debated, and the Parliament has intervened by summoning the independent Parties' Registrar for questioning on the constitutionality of this rejection.

Conclusion

Taha was no doubt a charismatic and very interesting person, with very deep conviction. His instincts – if not his practice – were liberal. His attempt to combine a deep spiritual commitment with similarly strong liberal convictions is rather unique. His notion of the need for a radical rethinking of Islamic norms by deepening understanding of its fundamental values through a process of reflection and rethinking cannot be disputed. His visions of democracy, including his critiques of Islamist political leader, Hassan Turabi, are pointers in the right direction.

However, his vision suffers from three main problems: theoretical, ethical and spiritual. Theoretically, his views are based on a hotchpotch of amateur physics, amateur anthropology, amateur philosophy and amateur economics, among others. In his writings, he makes sweeping claims about the findings of whole disciplines without quoting a single reference or even mentioning a name. At times, the sources quoted are secondary translated newspaper or magazine articles. This is deeply problematic, since he often builds the whole edifice of his theory on such casual claims (as in his 1960 book *Al-Islam*, where his proposed 'spiritual experimentation' is entirely premised on the claim that the whole physical universe is reducible to –and could be explained in reference to – energy). Similarly, his theories of biological and social human evolution take for granted Western modernity's claims about being the most advanced in all aspects, including ethically, in human history, a questionable proposition, to put it mildly.

Ethically, Taha faces the dilemma of all modern Muslim 'liberals', who cannot accept the right of Muslim societies to govern themselves, and advocate what I have elsewhere called the 'guardianship of the liberal' (in contrast to *wilayat al-faqih*, the guardianship of the religious scholars). This leads to some stark self-contradictions. For example, Taha rightly and courageously challenged the decision by Parliament to ban the Communist Party in 1965, and cited this in supporting Nimeiri's coup against what he termed 'civilian dictatorship'. However, when Nimeiri banned all political parties, including the Communist Party and Taha's own party, the arch-liberal did not utter a single word of protest. Nimeiri was not satisfied by just banning parties, but imprisoned hundreds of opponents, and massacred Mahdists and Communists. He also eliminated media freedom and judicial autonomy. The democratic system Taha defied did not imprison the Communists, nor did it interfere with the media or freedom of speech. But Taha was content to support a regime which perpetrated far worse transgressions than the ones he had so vehemently decried. In fact, the Republicans continued to support the dictatorship, issuing a pamphlet as late as 1979 justifying this position.

Spiritually and theologically, Taha's position poses the most serious problem. His notion that the believer, by immersing himself in the Qur'an and engaging in spiritual exercises of fasting and seclusion, could receive 'revelation' poses a serious challenge about what happens if different individuals receive conflicting revelations. More fundamentally, what is the mechanism of determining when a revelation is authentic as opposed to a mere hallucination? This is not just a theoretical problem, since throughout Islamic (and Sudanese) history, many claimants of 'Mahdist' and other missions have emerged. Some, like the Sudanese Mahdi, have demonstrated deep convictions and admirable selflessness. But does that guarantee authenticity?

In any case, the spiritual dimension is not Taha's most enduring legacy, since the mystical experience he advocates is by nature not communicable or replicable. None of his followers had claimed to have attained his level of perfection, as far as we know. His legacy has thus restricted itself to three areas: a cultural and intellectual dimension of diffuse liberalism, propagated by the Taha Cultural Centre and in the writings of select followers; a political dimension, also disseminated through the activism of the writings of his remaining followers; and a legal dimension propagated, almost single-handedly, by Emory University's Abdullahi An-Na'im, and becoming more and more detached from the original mystical foundation, and tending to be plain liberal and secular.

In a characteristic statement made by Taha when he was condemned by the first 'Apostasy Court' in 1968, he said that he did not blame his adversaries, who believed that Shari'a as they understood it was the last word in matters of Islam, for not understanding him. 'If they were sincere in their own sphere [of understanding], then even if they condemn us as apostates and decree our death, they could be considered Mujahids and we become martyrs if they succeed in killing us. But if they are not sincere, then their acts are rather trivial. And we know that they are not sincere in their own sphere, since they have always been tools in the hands of authorities'.

The same test of sincerity could be applied to Taha and his followers. But sincerity in itself is no guarantee of validity or truthfulness.

THE DEVIL'S INTERPRETER?

Nazry Bahrawi

He does not come across as your run-of-the-mill infidel. In an interview just before his untimely death, widely available on YouTube, Nasr Hamid Abu Zayd (1943–2010) sports an affable smile. He is mild-mannered and erudite. One would be hard-pressed to imagine how such a genial man can be deemed devilish rather than a dervish. Then, about halfway through the interview, while talking about his scholarly work, he declares: 'it was surprising and shocking in the meantime to find how the meaning of the Qur'an was subject to manipulation by different theological schools. And they (the commentators) wrote about this, about their strategy of getting what (they) want from the Qur'an, not really looking (at) what the Qur'an signifies'. Thus, the accusations hurled at him are revealed.

A 'good' Muslim hearing these words would react instinctively; and pronounce Abu Zayd an apostate, an act known as *takfir*. Yet there is a sense of ambiguity about the man and his thought. His mannerisms may be highly respectful, but his discourse is not so. It is in fact ambiguity that fuels the late thinker's most renowned idea: a method of reading the Qur'an known as 'humanistic hermeneutics'. And it is through the virtues of ambiguity that we must reclaim the good name of Abu Zayd – the Devil's interpreter to some, but God's advocate to others.

How did Abu Zayd morph into Abu Lahab, the strident enemy of the Prophet Muhammad denounced in the Qur'an? Given his bold proclamations against normative Islamic practices, it is easy for Abu Zayd's detractors to dismiss him as the quintessential Muslim apostate. He described the Shari'a, which many Muslims hold as divine, as artificial and arbitrary. 'The whole body of Shari'a literature as expressed in the four major sunni schools', he wrote, 'is a man-made production; nothing is divine about it'. This is a statement that would rile most conservative scholars, likes the religious elites in oil-rich Brunei, where the full force of the Shari'a – including flogging for adulterers and death by stoning – is to be implemented in phases starting from May 2014.

Yet, this is hardly a radical view. Critical scholars such as Ziauddin Sardar and Abdolkarim Soroush have been making such declarations for decades. In his 1985 book, *Islamic Futures*, Sardar declared that the Shari'a has become an instrument of 'oppression and despotism', that 'the legalistic rulings of the classical Imams, and their associated schools of thought… were space and time bound', and that the Shari'a had no 'contemporary relevance'. The project of re-examining the objectives of the Shari'a, or *maqasid al-shari'ah*, has re-entered the contemporary lexicon of Islamic thought through the works of mainstream Muslim scholars associated with the International Institute of Islamic Thought (IIIT), such as Mohammad Hashim Kamali.

In his 1999 essay *Maqasid al-Shari'ah: The Objectives of Islamic Law*, Kamali explained the notion of *maqasid al-shari'ah* with these words: 'by comparison to the legal theory of the sources, the *Usul al-Fiqh*, the *maqasid al-Shari'ah* are not burdened with methodological technicalities and literalist reading of the text. As such the *maqasid* integrates a degree of versatility and comprehension into the reading of the Shari'a that is, in many ways, unique and rises from the vicissitudes of time and circumstance'. Thus, Abu Zayd's provocation, 'Shari'a is man-made', does not look as unpalatable as it initially sounds.

Amidst the murkiness of Kamali's prose, one can suss out the astute voice of Abu Zayd. Hashim's invocation of such phrases like 'methodological technicalities' and 'literalist reading' imply that much of our understanding of Islamic law smacks of human, not divine, intervention. The Qur'an has been done unto. God's words have been manipulated. And the culprit was not the Devil, *Iblis*, but man himself. If we have done unto ourselves this injustice, we can also undo it. This is the thrust of Kamali's second sentence when he speaks of transcending 'the vicissitudes of time and circumstance' – in essence, traversing the confines of human meddling as these are tied to their contexts. Read this way, Abu Zayd's description of the much respected field of Islamic law and jurisprudence (*usul al-fiqh*) was meek compared to that of Hashim; and the much harsher words, expressed in his later writings, of Sardar. The Egyptian thinker merely called it 'a system of induction and deduction' built by jurists. It is therefore odd that the reception of both scholars in their respective communities and the wider Muslim world differed gravely even though both are seeking and engaging in *ijtihad*, or sustained reasoning, one of the pillars of Islamic law.

Herein lies a tale of two critics. Educated in his native Afghanistan and the UK, Kamali found his intellectual fortune best served in Malaysia where he first became head of the International Institute of Islamic Thought and Civilisation (ISTAC), a faculty member of the International Islamic University of Malaysia (IIUM), and finally the chief executive officer of the nation's International Institute of Advanced Islamic Studies (IAIS). Abu Zayd, on the other hand, tilled and toiled the cerebral sphere of his native land only to face a series of persecutions. He was first refused tenure at Cairo University in 1992 for 'clear affronts to the Islamic faith', though he was later promoted. Shortly after, in 1995, Abu Zayd was instructed to divorce his wife when the Egyptian appeals court ruled in favour of a plaintiff who accused Abu Zayd of apostasy, thereby rendering his marriage to a Muslim woman null and void. But the seminal event of his life took place a little later, in the same year, when Ayman al-Zawahiri (yes, he of the Al-Qaeda notoriety) called for Abu Zayd's assassination for his alleged apostasy. Facing the double threat of divorce and death, Abu Zayd was left with little choice but to leave Egypt. He eventually settled in the Netherlands where he was appointed visiting professor at Leiden University.

Abu Zayd's endeavour to re-read the Qur'an is symptomatic of this background as well as his material condition. 'My primary question was about the meaning of the Qur'an', he says in the interview. 'How far the meaning of the Qur'an could be manipulated. This is annoying for me. I believe in the message of Islam as a message of equality and justice. ... As someone from an ordinary, poor family, I needed this'. Here, Abu Zayd implies that some Qur'anic exegetes, or *mufassirun*, have interpreted Islam's sacred scripture to maintain a power hierarchy. This is certainly the case with patriarchy, if one considers the rise of feminist interpretations of the Qur'an such as those of Moroccan thinker Fatima Mernissi and the American scholar and activist Amina Wadud. But Abu Zayd's also draws our attention to the divide between the rich and poor: his 'humanistic hermeneutics' is motivated by a need to overcome that gap. Through 'humanistic hermeneutics' he wants to revolutionise the way Islamic societies view wealth distribution. That is to say, his treatise is designed to lay down the foundation for an Islamic liberation theology. Abu Zayd is certainly not the only Muslim intellectual thinking about or engaging in this exercise. The Iranian sociologist Ali Shariati is motivated by the same revolutionary zeal when he makes a distinction between 'Black Shi'ism' and 'Red Shi'ism' – the former acting to entrench the power of the monarchy and clergy, whereas the latter is built on the virtues of social justice for the common man. Then there is the fellow Egyptian thinker Hassan Hanafi, who speaks of the Islamic Left and suggests that:

The task of the Islamic left is to uncover the revolutionary elements inherit [sic] in religion, or, if you wish, to show the common grounds of one and the other; that is, interpret religion as revolution. Religion is the gift of our heritage and revolution is the acquisition of this age .... This is not an external and forced reconciliation, for religion is in essence a revolution, and prophets were reformers, innovators and revolutionaries .... The historical record of prophethood in the Qur'an depicts it as a revolution against social and moral decay.

Here, Hanafi's emphasis on *ijtihad* for social betterment ('interpret religion as revolution') may appear to be more blatant than Abu Zayd's 'humanistic hermeneutics', but the two ideas resonate with each other. In Abu Zayd's 'humanistic hermeneutics', we find seeds of struggle from literalism, patriarchy and class war.

At the heart of humanistic hermeneutics is the idea of context. For Abu Zayd, Qur'anic exegesis was fossilised as dogma because the commentators and interpreters did not fully account for the historical elements of the Qur'an, leading them to interpret the holy book in a literal manner. Considering that the Qur'an was not designed as a linear text in the style of the other two Abrahamic scriptures, the Torah and the Bible, this ahistoricist mode of reading does not make much sense. In his seminal essay, 'The "Others" in the Qur'an', Abu Zayd writes:

Without an understanding of the entire Qur'an as an historical phenomenon, one cannot make a sensible distinction between the parts of the Qur'an that still have the same literal meaning today, those that have acquired metaphorical and allegorical interpretation in the developing cultural context, and those that are limited to a particular historical situation. This is a pre-condition not only for the appropriate understanding of the Qur'an but for the understanding of any writing.

In his more famous work *Rethinking the Qur'an*, Abu Zayd outlines several instances whereby a contextual interpretation of the Qur'an can offer us new perspectives about prevailing ideas on Islam and its history. Abu Zayd's charge of human intrusion was not just levelled at the Shari'a but also at the Qur'an - a litigious charge in the eyes of many Muslims. Here, he makes the novel gesture of differentiating between two Qur'ans. The first is the idea of the sacred scripture as 'text' or *mushaf*, God's words as codified by the third caliph Uthman ibn 'Affan. The second is the notion of the Qur'an as 'discourse', a living tradition that is defined by its believers across time. Underlying this distinction is something quite fundamental, and this is the practice of how meaning is derived, what is known as hermeneutics.

Abu Zayd demonstrates their difference by referring to an episode in Islamic history, the battle of Siffin between the fourth caliph Ali ibn Talib, and the governor of Syria, Mu'awiyyah ibn 'Abi Sufyan in 657. As Muawiyyah's army was losing, his army signalled for arbitration by hoisting copies of the Qur'an on their lances. Weary of battle, 'Ali agreed to the mediation. Both figures agreed to appoint non-partisan memorisers of the Qur'an to search through the holy book for instructions of how to settle this discord. But a segment of Ali's supporters argued against this human intervention by pointing to 49:9: 'if two parties of the Believers fight with one another, make peace between them, but if one rebels against the other, then fight against the one which rebels until it returns its obedience to God'. This group argued that 'Ali had a duty to obliterate Mu'awiyyah's rebel forces if this verse is to be read literally as divine instruction. Disagreeing, Ali responded to them by way of an analogy: the Qur'an as a codified text is akin to the notes of a musical score, whereas the Qur'an as a living tradition is like the orchestra performing that score. For Abu Zayd, Ali was making a case for recognising multiple interpretations of the Qur'an. If Abu Zayd's reading of this episode can be surmised as an epigram, then we could say: 'Ali's law of interpretation states that the Qur'an is not anchored by a fixed meaning for all time and cultures; rather, meaning in the Qur'an is anchored in a fixed time and culture'. However, Ali's insistence that the Qur'an is pregnant with multifarious meanings led to his eventual assassination at the hands of the Kharijites, those very dissenters who insisted on a literal interpretation of the Qur'an. Once firm supporters of Ali, the Kharijites retracted their backing and declared Ali an apostate who is to be assassinated for betraying Islam - the same charge that was levelled at Abu Zayd centuries later. Seen this way, Ali can be seen as the first critical interpreter, a precursor to Abu Zayd.

Heresy may invite death but it is also empowering if practised as humanistic hermeneutics. This is most evident in Abu Zayd's reading of the so-called 'satanic verses', or the lines (italicised below) that came after 53:19-20, but which were later removed. Evidence of their existence can be traced to the *hadith* literature compiled by several familiar Islamic figures and the classical biographies of the Prophet by Ibn Ishaq and al-Tabari, though numerous Muslim scholars have denied their existence on the charge of polytheism. Following Yusuf Ali's translation of the Qur'an, the entirety of the Satanic verses would have read something like this:

Have ye seen Lat, and 'Uzza,
And another, the third (goddess), Manat?
They are the high-flying cranes (ghanariq),
Whose intercession (with God) is hoped for.

While Abu Zayd did not make it explicit, his writing suggests that Muslims are losing out by seeing these verses as contradictory to the monotheistic message of Islam. By doing so, the classical commentators are befuddling Muslims from seeing these verses as outlining an aspect of the Qur'an that is under-explored – its dialogic form. He reminds us of the genealogy of interfaith relations between Muslims and polytheists in Mecca: one that 'started calm and soft, but gradually was hardened'. If we accept this rubric, then the satanic verses can be read in context as having been revealed to Muhammad during the early years of his prophethood when Muslims needed to negotiate with the ruling pagan powers to accept their deities in exchange for them accepting Allah, the One God, says Abu Zayd.

So all-encompassing is the dialogic nature of the Qur'an that this pervades not just the book's content but also its form. Abu Zayd demonstrates the latter again by referring to the satanic verses, wherein an internal dialogue can be gleaned, one that would irate the deniers of the verses' existence. Here, he points to 22: 52:

Never did We send an apostle or a prophet before thee, but, when he framed a desire, Satan threw some (vanity) into his desire: but God will cancel anything (vain) that Satan throws in, and God will confirm (and establish) His Signs: for God is full of knowledge and wisdom.

Abu Zayd considers this verse to be a response to the Satanic verses, dismissing the latter as Satan literally putting words into Muhammad's mouth, or as he writes, 'an intrusion to be deleted'. Through this injunction to banish the controversial verses, 22:52 also acknowledges their presence. Thus, a dialogue has occurred between two verses, one that is mired in irony. There is yet another level at which the dialogic nature of the Qur'an occurs – and that is without. Here, Abu Zayd points to the opening chapter of the Qur'an, Surah Al-Fatiha, which anchors the five daily prayers as the core recitation:

Praise be to Allah the Lord of the Worlds.
The Compassionate, the Merciful.
Master of the Day of Judgment.
It is You whom we worship and it is You from whom we seek help.
Guide us to the right course,
The course of those whom You blessed,
Not the course of whom provoked Your anger neither those who got astray.
(1:1-7)

This prayer, aptly translated as 'The Opening', is an invocation of the highest order. It seeks God's intercession, and begets a response, says Abu Zayd. The response, suggests Abu Zayd, can be gleaned from a *hadith qudsi* – that is, a sacred saying of the Prophet Muhammad which is regarded as the words of God though not included in the Qur'an. The line-for-line answer has God replying such:

Prayer is divided between Me and My servants in equal shares
When he says, praise be to God, the Lord of the whole world,
I say, My servant praised Me;
When he says, the Compassionate, the Merciful,
I say, My servant exalted me;
When he says, the Master of the Day of Judgment,
I say, My servant glorified me,
When he says, It is You whom we worship and it is You from whom we seek help

I say this is between Me and My servant; all what My servant asked for is
guaranteed;
When he says, guide us to the right course, the course of those whom You blessed,
not the course of whom provoked Your anger neither those who got astray,
I say, these are for My servant and all are guaranteed for him.

Paired together, the two accentuate a sense of God as something other than
the unyielding judge, jury and executioner as portrayed by religious scholars,
past and present. Paired together, the two speak of a God who is not too
bothered about the nitty-gritty of human conduct, a God that is not always
waiting to pounce on a sinner, a God who is not too keen on demanding
Muslims obey His Shari'a to the letter. Rather, by way of His reassurances in
the *hadith*, we are presented with a view of God who listens more than pon-
tificates, a God who helps a person in need. Put simply, we get a sense of a
cosmopolitan God.

How can we figure Nasr Hamid Abu Zayd within the bigger scheme of
things Islamic? To answer this question, we need an honest review of the
impact of his scholarship. Perhaps the most balanced review of his work is
provided by the Sudanese scholar Mohamed Mahmoud. He regards Abu
Zayd's scholarship as important and brave. In a review of Abu Zayd's *The
Concept of the Text*, Mahmoud notes that 'though his polemical tone at some
points may mar his treatment, this should, nevertheless, be viewed against
the backdrop of the current state of intellectual malaise and intimidation
that prevails in the Arab and Islamic world'.

Mahmoud identifies several flaws in *The Concept of the Text*, including Abu
Zayd's bid to downplay the influence of Judaism and Christianity on
Muhammad's prophethood as well as a failure to comprehend the
ideological milieu that governed classical scholars debating *tanjim*, or the
phased revelations of the Qur'an. Mahmoud argues that Abu Zayd is too
quick to dismiss classical scholars' proposal of getting around the early
Meccans' scepticism to *tanjim*, for they believed that the Qur'an must be
revealed at once. In doing so, Abu Zayd misses out on the ingenuity of
certain juristic (*fiqhi*) principles such as the doctrine of 'the generality of
the utterance and the specificity of the circumstance', says Mahmoud. This
is a fair and astute critique of Abu Zayd. The idea that some kind of
generality, even ethics, can be derived from an exact historical instance can

be a powerful interpretive strategy in making the Qur'an relevant for all times. It is, in fact, an appeal to understanding the spirit behind the text, thus justifying the practice of *maqasid al-Shari'ah*.

In Abu Zayd's defence, *The Concept of the Text* can be seen as an early experiment of his idea of humanistic hermeneutics. The book examines historicist reading in the form of *asbab al-nuzul*, or the science of abrogating Qur'anic verses by way of context, at length. Yet the development of literary theory in the West should make us think twice about historicist reading. Since the 1980s, a movement among literary theorists to understand the cultural practices of a text by reading into its wider context has been gaining ground – what is widely known as the New Historicism School of literary interpretation. Much of its principles are attuned to Abu Zayd's humanistic hermeneutics - both methods place literary and non-literary text on equal footing, focus on the material life outside the text, and make the case that a text captures the intellectual and ideological currents when it was produced. Given their similarities, humanistic hermeneutics is just as vulnerable to the critique levelled at New Historicism. It is best expressed by the noted literary critic, Harold Bloom, who describes New Historicists as belonging to the 'School of Resentment', for failing to recognise the aesthetics element of literature, and for reducing the likes of Shakespeare and Dante to their context, as if their works are mere footnotes to history.

While the Qur'an is not exactly literature in the strictest sense of the word, there exists a hermeneutical tradition emphasising the Qur'an's formalistic aspects. It has been articulated by such classical commentators as Abu Bakr al-Baqilani (850–1013) and the Persian grammarian of Arabic language Abd al-Qahir al-Jurjani (d.1078). That school of thought is collectively known as *i'jaz al-Qur'an*, built on the idea that the holy text is inimitable, an idea that was justified using several verses scattered throughout the Qur'an in which Muslims were challenged to produce something similar. Some point to 17:88 which reads: 'if men and jinn banded together to produce the like of this Qur'an they would never produce anything like it, even though they backed one another'. Another more direct challenge can be found in 11:13: 'Say, Bring you then ten chapters like unto it, and call whomsoever you can, other than God, if you speak the truth!'. Normative Islamic history has it that none of those aware of the Qur'an's literary merits were able to meet the challenge. This is a significant development, considering that the Arabs were a literary lot given to poetry slams in the *souq* and that Muhammad was unlettered. It has led to the idea the Qur'an was hailed as a miracle because of its inimitable form.

We must not think that Abu Zayd was just an indiscreet advocate of contextual reading. In *The Concept of the Text,* he speaks of the *i'jaz* tradition by stressing the Qur'an's poetic form. A more detailed reading can be found in his *The Rational Trend in Qur'anic Exegesis*. Here, he dwells into the debate about the use of figurative language in the Qur'an that divided the rationalistic Mu'tazilites and the traditionalists of their time. He argued that this debate constitutes 'the first hermeneutical principle as the dichotomy between clarity and ambiguity'. This debate, he wrote in *Rethinking the Qur'an*, feeds into his notion of the dialogic Qur'an, wherein the Qur'an's poetic nature — its use of metaphors — becomes a way for Muhammad to convince a literarily inclined group of sceptics as to the divine stature of his revelations.

There is much that Abu Zayd has contributed to Islamic scholarship. His humanistic hermeneutics exposes the weaknesses of centuries of Islamic exegesis that tends towards the idea of singular meaning. He emphasises the importance of the Method over the Message, the journey over the destination, the know-hows over the know-it-all. For his innovative and bold scholarship, Abu Zayd is doubtlessly the archetypal maverick. The wise man who once said no one likes a maverick has obviously not encountered Abu Zayd.

THE USE OF THE PEN

Johan Siebers

'Who taught the use of the pen – taught man that what he did not know.'

(The Qur'an, 96: 4-5)

Why is the pen more than anything else the instrument of the dangerous freethinker? Plato, in his dialogue *Phaedrus*, set the tone for the complicated relation to the written word that has determined much of the intellectual history of the cultural traditions that have been decisively influenced by the Greeks: the West and Islamic culture. The transmission and development of ideas grew incomparably after the invention of writing, but writing is colored by the hue of mediation. The author, whose words, thoughts and ideas the text contains, is absent from it once the text has been published, or even merely written. Plato tells the story of the invention of writing in a myth. The Egyptian god Theuth showed his invention to king Thamus, as a way to help people store their knowledge and to learn. But the king was not impressed. In his opinion, writing things down would only make people's memory lazy and, what is more, a text is never unambiguously clear, it always needs the help of its author to bring across what the author wanted to say or defend it against criticism. Plato sums up the problem with the written word by saying that it does not speak when asked something, it remains silent. A text is not a dialogue. The only use of a text is as entertainment or as a reminder of things that are already known by the reader and that have been transmitted in oral, face to face, teaching. Only that kind of embodied togetherness can communicate the seeds of genuine knowing; the spectre of the direct interpersonal communication has continued to haunt the attitude towards writing. We feel that the living word, the spoken exchange, gives the transmission of knowledge a contextual immediacy and intimacy without which the content of ideas becomes abstract. The words we speak not only signify abstract ideas or

meanings, they arise out of a welter or organic knowing, a dimension of
feeling or pathos, that is always there and without which it becomes
unclear very quickly what is being said. Language is embodied. Especially
in philosophy it is often uncanny to experience the difference between
reading a text by a philosopher and hearing her speak, in an interview,
lecture or sound recording. 'Oh, now I understand what she is getting at!'
– an experience we often have in such a situation. And so writing does not
leave the context of the spoken word as its background. But it does blow
it open like nothing else: otherwise we would probably never have listened
to the interview, or lecture or recording in the first place.

Many thinkers of the last fifty years have been critical of these traditional
assumptions about the relation between speaking and writing. We have
come to see the centrality of the spoken word (Derrida called it the
'logocentrism' of European philosophy) as a kind of medial hegemony,
ingrained over centuries of ideological thinking. The idea that the word is
the outer sign of an inward intention, that has to be represented,
communicated and replicated as perfectly as possible in the mind of the
receiver, ignores the multiplicity of meaning that lies within all utterances
and it ignores also the freedom of response of the receiver. It ignores that
meaning in interaction is a joint creation of the participants in the
interaction. A communication is always a precarious endeavour, a free
meeting of minds. If it is not, it is not a communication in the sense of a
mutual recognition, but a coordination, transmission of information or
some other form of equalisation. The possibility to be understood
differently from how you wanted to be understood, the possibility even of
being misunderstood, is an essential condition of all communication; the
French psychoanalyst Jacques Lacan even went so far as to say that all
communication is miscommunication; a poignant formulation of the
paradox of communication. The written word merely augments this
possibility as compared to the spoken word, makes it all the more clear
and present. The fact that the text is on its own once it has been published,
that it can be picked up and read by anyone in any context whatsoever,
shows that our language is never simply our own. But already at the point
of writing, and even in the moment that we speak, this alienation to our
words occurs. We think we know what we are saying, but we may
communicate other things, or be understood in another way. And we have

to use the words that are available to us. We speak the language, the language speaks us.

The dominance of identity thinking, of one single meaning that prevail: or one truth or authority to which we all must bow – this image of what truth is, is indeed challenged most directly by the written word. That is why the written word has always been kept in check, closely guarded, the privilege of those in power and their scribes, the instruments of power. Without the written word it is nearly impossible to install and maintain an imperial regime – politically but also ideologically. However, writing is also a dangerous tool; more dangerous than free speech – which, let us be clear, hegemonic rulers have never favoured – is free writing. For speech is evanescent, it is momentary and tied to place and time. On the other hand, the written word flies. It is not for nothing that it is the king, in Plato's dialogue, who does not like writing. Writing democratises; it is a product and a cause of the freedom of the urban space, away from the controlling immediacy of social relations in the tribe or the village. And so writing has two sides: on one hand it can be used as an instrument to fix meanings, to spread a power structure to imperial proportions; on the other writing unhinges meaning, sets it free and spreads this freedom of thought much faster than free speech on its own ever could. In between these poles of consolidation of ideology on one hand and the contention of meaning on the other, the cultural function of writing has moved and continues to move today.

In the religions of the book we see the problematic nature of writing in many ways. God reveals himself to human beings in many ways, but in Judaism, Christianity and Islam writing has a special place. The holy texts in these religions are the word of God himself – from the stone tables of the Torah to the word that became flesh of the Gospels to the 'the use of the pen' the Qu'ran speaks about. The distinction between the letter of scripture and the spirit of scripture, its need for interpretation, is a reminder of the awareness of the space of uncertainty opened up by writing. A literalising tendency can be seen in almost all religions that have a text as their medium of revelation; as if its readers thought like Plato's king Thamus, and took the written word for a record or representation of the spoken, living word of God, rather than take the text *as text* as the divine revelation. Instead, in the religions of the book, the holiness of scripture has often been a way of avoiding or oppressing the multiplicity of responses that the written word solicits. God writes, we don't. We read and recite, at most copy, sometimes without understanding. Even reading was for long periods in history confined to a special class or caste who guarded the authoritative interpretations of the scriptures. And yet, in their nature as text and in their content as demanding justice for all, the holy texts of the religions of the book contained the kernel of freedom of thought, of change from below, of a new heaven – and a new earth.

The use of the pen, taught to us, in Plato's story, by an Egyptian god at the disapproval of a monarch, set off on a path through history on which it had to fight canonisation, appropriation by authority, oppression and regulation in the name of dominant ideologies and identities. Nevertheless it kept open the gap in meaning in which each one of us lives, the gap that makes change possible. It made that gap stronger, it spread an awareness of it, it made for human beings who want to think freely, write freely, speak freely. The British philosopher A N Whitehead thought that the term 'subject' is not quite right as a name for individual conscious human existence. It suggests something lying underneath; it is also a monarchic term. Better to speak of the human being who creates himself or herself freely in the practices of speaking and writing with others as a 'superject', throwing themselves up out of the welter of language in what is ultimately a spontaneous, free act, it is the moment in which we live authentically. The superject lives into the new, bringing about what was not there before. In this sense, too, the use of the pen teaches us something we did not know before and creates selves that were not there before. Only the use of the pen creates the distance that is needed to see that what goes on in speaking also shares in the paradox of communication.

Has the oppression of the written word in the name of canonical meaning stopped? By no means. We know about the many places on our planet where free speech and freedom of writing are by no means guaranteed. But also in less obviously political ways we are still subjects of language more often than superjects of language.

Today there is a stylistic uniformity that dominates our global culture, from journalism to academic writing, education and even literature, which acts in more or less the same way as the old structures that dominated the written word.

In a beautiful study on the meaning of lines, anthropologist Tim Ingold considers the difference between handwriting and typing on a keyboard. He associates the keyboard with a chunking of meaning that resembles a changed understanding of lines in the modern era, away from the line as a pathway along which we move or travel, towards an understanding of the line as a connection between a series of dots, each immovable in their place. The series of dots are like the keys on a keyboard, stepping stones that we connect into the prose line on the page. This way of writing almost automatically leads to a concentration of the experience of the written word in the abstract meaning of it, rather than in its nature as an inscription, a trace of a moving hand on a material reality. This is the sense in which writing is embodied, like speaking but in a different way. Writing as a material trace stands to the typed text as the fluent line to the series of connected points. In the contemporary stylistic canon, the connected points, luminous in their clarity, are favoured exclusively over the contours and fluency of the continuous line. Think of the rule of the bullet point in many professional cultures, the chunking of paragraphs in journalism and online writing, the inane and anaemic voice of reason that dominates academic writing and makes every article and book that passes through our peer review system sound as if it is written – by the same editor. Typewritten text displays a uniformity, it is somehow already depersonalised in the moment of writing, especially when the demands or even the affordances of the technical medium determine the act of writing itself, as is so often the case today. The difficult, long-winded or meandering text along whose roads and by-roads so much can be discovered and experienced, has long since fallen out of grace. The discontinuities in that form of written text (which set the reader off in unexpected directions and make the unity of the text an elusive and joint creation, not something simply to be found) are not the same as the discontinuities of typewriting, which are merely the gaps between the immovable stations of the type.

With Ingold we might well urge for a return of handwriting. We might well sensitise ourselves to the difference between writing by hand and typewriting, and come to appreciate the fluency of the handwritten text, the concentration in the single tip of the pen that traces flowing lines on the page, traversing a landscape and opening it up to the freedom of the gap between speech and writing. The freedom of thought and the concentration of writing in the hand that moves across the page have something to do with each other. We relate differently to the way we put words on paper with a pen and the way we put words in a computer memory on a computer. The first is a personal trace along which we can travel, concrete and embodied, the second is a web of abstract meaning. Perhaps freedom of thought needs the double step of writing by hand and then entering the text written in that way into the memory banks of the computer where that original trace can be worked on, promulgated, distributed, but without losing its origin in the act of inscribing, the true calligraphy ('beautiful writing') and use of the pen. The full impact of the democracy of writing perhaps needs it that everyone is taught how to write by hand: a technique and also a mentality. Beyond the canons of revelation and high literature there is a whole uncharted future for a writing humanity, which is a free humanity, that we have barely begun to explore.

But there are always more ways that lead to Rome, or for that matter Mecca (a Rome or Mecca that does not yet exist in the free process of creativity, but which nevertheless orientates us). The crucial moment in the writing process is the moment of the now, when the next word emerges. That point, which remains almost invisibly modest in the use of the pen – it is slightly more than the momentary hovering of the tip of over the page – becomes the more demanding blinking cursor on the computer screen. But the moment does not change that much. It disrupts a pre-existing continuity that aims to project itself into the future, as in the continuous line, but it also disrupts the typeline as a connection between motionless points. What comes next is not yet there, not-yet: fore-felt, intuited or experimented. There is an orientation towards it, even if we cannot say it exists as a goal that we might connect to. This is the moment of creativity and, again, it is a moment where we meet freedom. Freedom of thought happens at this front moment in the process of realisation, of ourselves as superjects or of the text we are writing. It is a moment of improvisation, no matter how strictly the form of writing we are engaged in is being enforced. Without the recognition of this moment of improvisation, no free relation to thoughts, ideas, actions or language can arise. I claim it is absolutely fundamental in understanding what makes our existence human. We are speaking animals, yes; thinking animals, yes; sons and daughters of the divine, yes: but first and foremost we are the improvising animal. No time, no novelty, no communication, no self, no freethinkers without living in the moment of improvisation, at the tip of the pen of time: what is 'danger' in the realm of thought other than this moment, where things are as yet uncertain and something has to be done without full knowledge, where life is made in the living?

But this moment exists in handwriting as much as in typewriting. And we can even come to understand it better by looking at the typewriter and how a writer might relate to it. When American novelist Truman Capote, who used to write his novels by pencil while lying in a lounge chair ('I am a strictly horizontal author'), read beat writer Jack Kerouac's *On the Road*, he said 'this is not writing, this is typing'. And he was right. The novel had been written in three weeks in April 1951, on a typewriter that was fed paper on a long scroll so Kerouac would not have to stop writing to change the sheet of paper: a bit like a computer today, where the page break also does not necessitate an interruption of the flow of typing. Within the possibilities of the machinery, Kerouac had reconstituted flow, recreated the conditions that would allow improvisation to keep going. In this way he created for himself a new relation to the typewriter, no longer the instrument that chunks what was a flowing line before, as in Ingold's reconstruction of the move from handwriting to typing, but as an instrument resembling more a musical instrument than a substitute for a pen. The writer becomes the musician of the typewriter. When typing in this uninterrupted manner, the writer moves into the zone of writing, in which he or she has access to a deeper level of consciousness that allows personal meaning and understanding to be expressed. In Kerouac's thoughts about the act of writing this level of consciousness is central, and musical metaphors abound to describe the process of activating it: 'Time being of the essence in the purity of speech, sketching language is undisturbed flow from the mind of personal secret idea-words, blowing (as per jazz musician) on subject of image'; 'no periods separating sentence structures already arbitrarily riddled by false colons and timid usually needless commas – but the vigorous space dash separating rhetorical breathing (as jazz musician drawing breath between outblown phrases); 'measured pauses which are the essentials of our speech'; 'divisions of the sounds we hear'; 'time and how to note it down'. Allan Ginsberg,

Kerouac's close friend, summed up the spirit of improvisation: 'First thought best thought'. We see the emphasis on spontaneity, improvisation, the musical practice of the jazz musician, the dislike of the canonical and the access to a personal encounter with truth: 'write as deeply, fish as far down as you want, satisfy yourself first, then reader cannot fail to receive telepathic shock and meaning-excitement by same laws operating in his own human mind'. Rather than asking how to bring the message across to his readership, rather than worrying about how to communicate with his audience, the writer has to follow his own path which will then be automatically communicable by recognition. Finally, Kerouac includes in his principles of spontaneous writing the explicit attitude 'no revisions'. We can see in it Kerouac's way of reinstalling the line-as-trace in the medium of the typewriter, especially when we think ahead to the word processor, in which revision almost automatically becomes the same thing as an erasure of traces. Process versus the processor or procedure; the perfectly polished end-product is no longer the goal of writing. Writing becomes a method for relating to truth, for voicing and communicating stages on a way, not definitive statement. Writing without revising becomes one particular avenue into the experience of truth in the moment of realisation, the now or not-yet at which we, darkly, live – vouchsafed by the handwritten line in one form of writing, in the spontaneous typewritten prose of beat in another.

The history of culture, seen through this light, is the history of the successive and increasing realisation of the function of writing in the development of freedom of thought. This is not a story of simple progress, it is a path itself that is as much interrupted as the written text itself. In a way it is constituted by interruptions, by the appearance of gaps in meaning, understanding and practice that cannot be filled by the simple reference to what was. In those spaces of not-knowing, created by the pen, freedom of thought lives.

Today furthering the culture of freedom of thought requires, among much else that has to do with creating and safeguarding the political institutions that guarantee free speech, the conscious democratisation of acts of writing, in schools, universities, work places, communities and the public sphere. An understanding of the deep psychological and existential function of writing can guide the developments of new practices of writing, new forms of literature, poetry and new styles and genres. Imagine what might become possible, in the way of free thinking, if we break with the uniformity of word processed writing, in the academy and elsewhere, and find new ways to give expression to the individual moment when the written word is put down on paper. People can find a new understanding of the way that moment relates to knowledge, to action, to meaning; to what goes on when we find and cultivate our own writing voice. Then we might stop speaking of the 'death of the author', stop being tied to a once liberating but now stifling critique of western logocentrism which has gone hand in hand with the depersonalisation of style. We might then emphasise the disappearance of the writer as authorial voice and the emergence of the democratised writer, the universal writer who freely lives into the new. People might come to understand themselves as superjects living into the not-yet, creating themselves by expressing the openness and unfinishedness which they are and in that process transforming the world in which they live into something commensurate to our human openness to being itself. This process lies at the foundation of all movements of freethinking in history; it is the process of humanisation, a divine gift if ever there was one.

ISBN: 9781849043014
£16.99 / Paperback / 288pp

Medina in Birmingham, Najaf in Brent

Inside British Islam

INNES BOWEN

Muslim intellectuals may try to define something called British Islam, but the truth is that as the Muslim community of Britain has grown in size and religiosity, so too has the opportunity to found and run mosques which divide along ethnic and sectarian lines.

Just as most churches in Britain are affiliated to one of the main Christian denominations, the vast majority of Britain's 1600 mosques are linked to wider sectarian networks: the Deobandi and Tablighi Jamaat movements with their origins in colonial India; the Salafi groups inspired by an austere form of Islam widely practiced in Saudi Arabia; the Islamist movements with links to religious political parties in the Middle East and South Asia; the Sufi movements that tend to emphasise spirituality rather than religious and political militancy; and the diverse Shi'ite sects which range from the orthodox disciples of Grand Ayatollah Sistani in Iraq to the Ismaili followers of the pragmatic and modernising Aga Khan. These affiliations are usually not apparent to outsiders, but inside Britain's Muslim communities sectarian divides are often fiercely guarded by religious leaders.

This book, of which no equivalent volume yet exists, is a definitive guide to the ideological differences, organisational structures and international links of the main Islamic groups active in Britain today.

'After a decade of fear-mongering, when Islam was portrayed as a unitary threat to the West, here comes a book that cuts through the hysteria. In this short and very readable volume, Bowen shows the complexity and nuances of Islam in Britain. This is a must-read for all people who want to understand the changing nature of Britain and its Muslim communities.' — Marc Sageman, author of *Leaderless Jihad: Terror Networks in the Twenty-First Century*

WWW.HURSTPUBLISHERS.COM/BOOK/MEDINA-IN-BIRMINGHAM-NAJAF-IN-BRENT

41 GREAT RUSSELL ST, LONDON WC1B ⅔
WWW.HURSTPUBLISHERS.COM
WWW.FBOOK.COM/HURSTPUBLISHERS
020 7255 2201

MILOSZ: THE MINDFUL DISSIDENT

Eva Hoffman

Freethinkers often end up as dissident. The poet, writer, translator and diplomat, Czeslaw Milosz (1911–2004) was a specific type of freethinker. He came from a country, Poland, which has had a long history of resistance: to the three powers which partitioned it at the end of the eighteenth century; to the Nazi invasion and war of conquest; and to Soviet domination in the long Cold War decades. Milosz himself was one of the last century's great poets, as well as a thinker of great independence and originality – although his work remained almost totally unknown in the West until he received the Nobel Prize in 1981. He was not by temperament an activist, or a reflexive oppositionist; but his inability to accept any form of oppression, political falsity, group-think or received ideas, made him an intrinsically provocative writer and a dissenting – indeed, a dissident – voice. I recently attended a conference which took place in a manor house previously owned by the Milosz family. The geographical location of the conference – right on Poland's eastern border, in a village set amidst bucolic landscapes and dark echoes of a turbulent past – reminded me once again how much that past had shaped Milosz, and his almost cussed stance of internal and external resistance.

Milosz was born in what was once part of the Polish-Lithuanian Commonwealth, but was then a multicultural, multi-religious region of Lithuania. He came from a Polish-speaking family, but was equally fluent in Polish and Lithuanian; later, he added Russian, French, English and Hebrew to his repertory – the latter acquired in middle age, so he could read the Bible in the original language. He grew up in a period when potent ideologies began to collide with religious faith, and when national allegiances and identities were becoming increasingly strident and divisive. Perhaps his first and formative act of dissidence was to refuse to 'identify' himself as either Lithuanian or Polish. He later wrote a beautiful book,

Native Realm, in which he depicted Vilno, the capital of Lithuania, as a city where several groups and religions – Polish, Lithuanian, Jewish and others – co-existed in a fertile, if sometimes uneasy proximity. Milosz was also stubborn in his refusal to embrace either Catholicism, or Marxism – the two philosophical options presented to him in his education – unquestioningly or uncritically. Catholicism, at that point, seemed to him too morally idealist, and insufficiently aware of the stubbornly mixed 'nature' in human nature. For a while, he was involved in a Marxist group with fellow students in Vilno; but by sensibility and perhaps the quality of an inclusive, poetic intelligence, he seemed to be, from early on, inured to the reductive certainties of ideological systems. As the group became more set in their convictions, and more convinced that they represented History and Progress, he distanced himself from them and devoted himself to studying law, and the pursuit of poetry.

It was a crucial part of Milosz's moral and intellectual development – as it was for all Polish intellectuals of that period – that during World War II, he experienced two totalitarianisms in ruthless close up, and in their full, murderous horror. In 1939, Poland was simultaneously invaded by Nazi Germany from the West, and by the Soviet Union from the East. (The pact between the two powers broke down in 1941, when the Nazi armies attacked the Soviet Union). Under the Nazi regime, there were really two wars in Poland: the war of conquest and eventual enslavement against the Poles, and the war of extermination against the Jews. Milosz spent most of the war in Warsaw, working with underground resistance journals, in what was – against impossible odds – the largest resistance movement against the Nazis mounted in wartime Europe. Earlier than most, he understood the enormity of the Holocaust, which was perpetrated largely on Polish territory; and in an act of prescient conscience, he wrote two poems on the extermination in the Warsaw Ghetto – 'Campo dei Fiori,' and 'A Poor Christian Looks at the Ghetto' – while the destruction was still going on, and in what were perhaps the earliest literary responses to the terrible events by a non-Jewish writer.

After the war, like many artists and intellectuals, Milosz tried to get along with the new, Soviet-sponsored regime. After all, he had little choice. He was wedded to the Polish language – and he also had some initial hope that a new form of 'socialism with a human face' might be created in Poland. But this was not to be; and after working for several years as a diplomat, and a cultural attaché in Paris, he found that he could not accept – could not, to use his word, stomach – the mendacities and corruptions of public and private life, the persecutions of the former resistance members and the suppression of all intellectual freedom, within the new political order. He particularly could not bring himself to perpetrate the lies that were expected of him in his poetry, in the service of 'socialist realism.' In 1951, he defected to France – where, in a bitter twist, he was sabotaged by the pro-Communist leftist intelligentsia, who did not approve of the bad news Milosz delivered to them about the 'socialist Utopia'. A few years later, to avoid penury and cultural censorship, he accepted a job at Berkeley, in far-flung and initially very alien California.

It was from those experiences that his most political book and what might be called his dissident manifesto – *The Captive Mind* – emerged. In that complex, subtle, and in a sense frightening text, Milosz anatomises the strategies and compromises adopted by Eastern European intellectuals in Communist times in order to persuade themselves to accept a destructive ideology and to cooperate with a terrible regime. There were those who hypnotised themselves into self-delusion and denial, which allowed them to accept the New Faith without questions and with serene acceptance. Those intellectuals, in Milosz' formulation, figuratively swallowed a 'Murti-Bing pill' which banished all conflict or doubt – a fictional invention of another prophetic Polish writer, Ignacy Witkiewicz (1885–1939). There were those who played the game of Ketman, which Milosz believed derived from a Persian tradition, in which people with heretical beliefs rigorously hid their true beliefs from the powers that be, and from inferior minds – until, in the Communist context, they could no longer distinguish between their own thoughts and those of their oppressors. There were those who convinced themselves that a higher morality inhered in serving 'the people,' even if this led to the people's persecutions and widespread misery; and those whose need for power or popular success meant that their sense of morality slid imperceptibly and by degrees into collusion with the prevailing dogma. In a sense, Milosz describes in 'Captive Mind' techniques of self-censorship, or what Hannah Arendt later called the inability to think – a state of mind responsible, in her diagnosis, for many heinous crimes (for example, those of Eichmann), and for the willing embrace of mindless fanaticism.

Milosz himself was never able to persuade himself to believe in what he did not believe – or to go along with power for the sake of supposed 'logic of History,' or his own safety. In *The Captive Mind*, he was writing about the Communist archipelago; but in a Foreword to the 1981 English translation of the book, he wrote that 'its subject is the vulnerability of the twentieth-century mind to seduction by sociopolitical doctrines and its readiness to accept totalitarian terror for the sake of a hypothetical future.'

The geopolitical situation has changed radically since Milosz wrote that fascinating book; but the seductions of 'sociopolitical doctrines: and all-explanatory faiths are ever present; and the analysis Milosz offers of minds trapped and imprisoned by ideological blinders continues to be relevant and much needed. The fear of freedom is an underestimated force, especially in today's democratic world, where freedom is too easily taken for granted; and the impulse to give over one's mind and self to a cause, a group, or a supposedly salvational ideology, is ever powerful. Milosz' form of resistance did not involve violence or physical protest; rather, it was moral and philosophical. In times when all incentives were to accept reigning dogmas, he kept his independence of mind, and his fidelity to the truth as he understood it. In his poetry, consciousness is inseparable from conscience, and his devotion is to the fullness of reality, and to human particulars, rather than to any supposedly all-explanatory 'system'. He came from a country which had suffered a succession of tragedies and enormous losses; and his form of fidelity was to remember what was lost, and to cherish it through poetic beauty. He was, ultimately, a humanist, and what might be called a mindful (rather than a mindless) dissident. His difficult and inspiring body of work should be studied as an antidote to the temptations of all totalising beliefs – no matter how idealistic they pretend to be; and to the seemingly opposite, but actually convergent seductions of extremist protest, no matter what their attractions of certainty, supposed heroism or transcendence. Milosz reminds us that we live in a human world, and that a respect for the humanity of others (and of ourselves) is all that matters – and that it is enough.

OUT OF THE OLD BOX

Hanan Al-Shaykh

I began to think about the past as I opened an old box where I kept my journalistic articles. I found a series of interviews I had conducted with more than twenty women, entitled 'Portrayal of prominent Lebanese women'. Looking at their faces on faded sheets of newsprint and in the supplements I could not help but remember the women in my family and neighbourhood who had left their mark on me and who had taken me by the hand to help me embrace womanhood at an early age.

Our house was full of women. We all shared the house with this uncle; and sharing was common among families from Southern Lebanon who had come to Beirut in search of work. Our house was full of women visitors, too, each one a completely different personality. The favourite was a cousin who lived in both Africa and Lebanon and who was twice married. Her social status, in her case based on wealth, was tied in with her strength. She even felt superior to men. She was confident enough to smoke in front of them; to take us to movies whenever she felt like it; to learn to drive a car and to be independent in many other ways. Even her husband asked her opinion about things. When she entered a room, we became like Chagall's women – flying to her from roofs, windows, doors. Housework stopped. Freedom flowed, perhaps from her beautiful shoes, handbags, sunglasses. With her the women were relaxed, gossiping and pushing the shadow of their men from their consciousness. They were no longer frantic to make themselves available as soon as they heard their man's footsteps.

In contrast to this visitor, there was another who came regularly from the South for medical reasons. I remember how she used to choose a corner of our sitting room, never leaving it except to visit the doctor. She spent her days criticising indecent women who were not wrapped from head to toe in black like herself. She spat whenever a friend of my mother's appeared wearing make-up or if she saw someone chewing gum. Gum, according to her, drew attention to a woman's mouth, which she considered to be an obscenity.

But Adila, who lived facing our house, was the one I was most drawn to. I had been pleading with the flock of pigeons which were going round in circles above the rooftop to take me away with them when I heard a voice trying to imitate the coo of pigeons: 'Hurry up and hold my wing and take me away!' I giggled. The voice was Adila's, and she emerged from behind the sheets she was hanging up: 'If you'd begged a cat and not the bloody pigeons, I could have mimicked the sound so well it would have made you shit in your pants!'

I was drawn to her, even obsessed by her, though sometimes she would ask me to leave her alone and go home and play with the other kids or, even better, talk to pigeons. Children assumed that my enjoying the company of someone who was so ancient, forty years old when I was only twelve, was because she was the only one in our neighbourhood who baked cakes and offered us some. But adults assumed that Adila was a mother figure to me since my mother had left home and married her lover.

I would spy on her in the evening from my window, my bird's eye view of what was about to unfold was merely a blurred outline sometimes swaying to reach her hubli bubli. When the water gurgled with a force, I would wonder if she was upset and for what reason? How come she lived alone and no one gossiped about her but found her nonetheless intriguing with her intimidating or witty comments? Why did she choose to sit in front of an open gate in the darkness facing an empty alley, without the daytime commotion when she could observe every movement, every voice with curiosity? She watched over me with the eye of an eagle to shield me from my father's anger. She would gesture to me to warn me if my father had come home from work or from the mosque so that I could pull my scarf from my school bag or untie it from around my waist or race to borrow her scarf to hide my hair and neck before I entered the house. Every time I returned her scarf, she would say 'Good girl, I know why you do this, you feel sorry for your father, but let me assure you that he can look after himself!' And I understood what she meant, whether a few months or a year later I don't recall, when I gathered my courage and confronted him by saying: 'No I will not hide my hair under any scarf. I am sorry but I've been deceiving you all along.' When my father wept instead of scolding me or hitting me, I found myself embracing him, feeling sorry for him.

How did Adila predict everything? How did she know what was going in my mind and my father's when she said, 'I am sure you will be able to protect yourself without your scarf.' When I asked her why she did not wear one, she said, 'I bargained with God, I told him that I couldn't breathe under the veil! Adding that the veil made me feel like a donkey!'

Next day when I told her what happened with my father, she called out: 'Congratulations Huda Shaarawi', referring to a leading Egyptian feminist who took off her veil in public in 1929. I felt so proud. When I started writing, and my essays were published, she nicknamed me May Ziade, a key figure of the Nahda in the early twentieth century and a prolific poet and essayist.

'Who are you Adila?' But I never asked her this question. I thought she was going to live forever and reveal to me the story of her life. I suppose she did live forever as the woman who sparkled and ignited embers in my childhood and youth.

She was fourteen years old when her family took her from her school and married her off. She lived with her in-laws, not unusual in those times, unaware that she had entered a prison: her husband was her jail and his mother his faithful jailer. They both interfered with everything she said, even when she ate pickles as in their opinion pickles were an aphrodisiac! They forbade Adila to wear the gold necklace her grandmother had given her because it outshined what her husband had given her as a wedding present but Adila kept the necklace close to her heart and hid it secretly under her garments.

One day she left it with her clothes to take a bath and couldn't find it. She looked everywhere, asked everyone about it, she wept, asked again. Her mother in law shushed her, but Adila yelled: 'God gave me a tongue to speak, eyes to look and see and brain to think!' She fled to her family. Her mother wept as she hugged her, and her father listened sympathetically to her, and yet they both took her back to her husband, ignoring her tears. Back with her in-laws, days passed as long as years, but then Adila saw that the jasmine had been burned, the only thing she loved and cared for at her in-laws' because its smell reminded her of home. She asked her mother-in-law what had happened to the jasmine and the wicked woman answered,

'It was withered and died because of the many times you buried your face in it.' Next day Adila sneaked out as soon as her husband went to work and her mother-in-law went into the loo. She didn't run away to her family this time but to a nearby town called Saidon. There she asked for the well-known school for orphans. Yes, she was an orphan, but since she didn't carry her identity, she wasn't admitted in the school but worked there as a cleaning girl, until a rich and noble patron of the orphanage who was in need of a maid took her home with her. Adila wept when she was taken to her own beautiful room. She wept even more when she understood that her employer thought that she was worthy of respect and sympathy when her parents had seen her tears but took her back to her in-laws, warning her that she'd better not come back to them if she tried to run away a second time. Her thought was 'What did I do to deserve this cruel fate?'

She found in the big house a library with many books, one section for her employer and the rest for her employer's husband. Reading some of the books, she came to discover the darkness of patriarchal oppression and the tyranny of in-laws claiming that they have the power over daughters-in-law, over her. She understood why she hated her mother-in-law thinking back to when this woman waited by the door on her wedding night until she heard her screaming in pain, grabbed the sheet stained with her virginity blood and yelled in joy as she rushed to show it to the immediate families, relatives and neighbours, 'The angels have cleansed her, the angels have cleansed her!'

Adila stayed with her mistress. When her parents found her after many years and wanted her to come back home, she made peace with them but refused to live with them, 'They need me now to look after them, but my home is here! They should have had pity on me, a girl fourteen years old, from their flesh and blood who pleaded with them. Did you bring me into this life in order to see me crying or laughing?' When her mistress died and left her goodly sum of money, Adila bought a house with a garden in our neighbourhood. Yes, Adila will go on living within me. Once in Fez, Morocco, when I saw the Qairawin Mosque, with its university amongst the first in the entire world, built by Fatima al Fahriah, I thought how Adila used to call one of the girls Fatima Al-Fahriah. I found myself exclaiming, 'Oh, Adila now I know what you've always known.'

I wrote a series of articles between 1974 and 1975 on well-known Lebanese women, famous and respected for their achievements, for what they have done in their society. They encompass politicians, pioneers in medicine and in law, socialites, festival organisers, writers, tribal women, actresses, business women, women who have lifted the veil and who have said 'no' to old stifling taboos and traditions. I started with Fatima Al-Asad (1898–1978), known as Um Kamel (Mother of Kamel). She was raised in strictest seclusion. Her father, Kamel Al-Asad, was the most powerful landowner in South Lebanon. He owned nearly the whole of the South, as it was handed to him by Ottomans. As a father, Kamel As-Asad was possessive. He forbade Fatima and her younger sister to be seen by anyone outside their household or to be heard inside their household. 'I don't wish even for the walls to hear your voices or even your whispers', he ordered. They felt like prisoners. 'He', Fatima told me, 'would only let us leave the house to accompany him for a stroll in the fields, when there was no one else, human being or Jin in the distance'. A woman taught her how to read and recite the Qur'an. This teacher and other women visitors would come from everywhere in the South, visit them and keep them company, but Fatima would listen carefully for any political gossips or news and become totally mesmerised. This interest in politics made her assume the role of her father when he died.

She wouldn't allow her uncle to sell one centimetre from her lands. Soon, she married his son, six years her junior, as both her father and her uncle wanted to secure the lands they owned for the Al-Asad clan. Realising that her husband lacked her judgement, she rolled up her sleeves and became his political brains when he was appointed the speaker of parliament: 'I am armoured with six senses and strength too. I would pick up with one glance who had integrity and who had not. Who was lying and who was honest, I learned by instinct the psychology of men, I would go over tiny details when I was in doubt in order to study matters very carefully and draw my conclusions. My husband was more trusting. Whenever I warned him about someone and asked him to be very careful, he would shrug his shoulder and say, 'Let me judge for myself, and why are you assuming that person was a liar? Why do people have to lie?'

Fatima Al-Asad became known as the mother of the South, and became the Speaker of Parliament, from 1951–1953, but from behind the curtains, the power behind her husband. 'My husband would never take any decision without my input, he would tell the president of the Lebanese Republic: "Let me sleep over this matter, let me think it over". The president and everyone else would know that the speaker of the parliament meant the following: "I need to go home, discuss the matter with my wife, and I will come back to you with my opinion, tomorrow".' They would sit together and study and weigh the consequences before she gave him her verdict. I smiled to Um Kamel upon hearing this coming from her. I remembered her nicknames since she became known among the southerners: 'the ministry of interiors', 'the Israeli jets', since the jets roamed the sky registering every inch of the South and Um Kamel knew everything.

After her husband's death, their son Kamel Al-Asad became the speaker of parliament, from 1964 to 1968. I remembered also how I was hesitant before I asked her if the rumours were true, that she advised her son Kamel on political strategy, even though he was a lawyer and a politician in his own right. With great calmness she answered that she could not deny certain things: 'Though my son didn't need me, and of course he did not listen to me, but I settled as the go between him and the people who needed his help and could not reach him'.

Another woman I portrayed was Anbara Salam Al-Khalidi (1897–1986). When she opened the door, with her dark brown hair mixed with grey in a bun, I asked jokingly: 'Where is your veil?' Anbara Salam was known for being the first young woman to unveil in Greater Syria. In 1927, she stood in front of a crowd with an uncovered face to speak at the Women's Renaissance Society. 'I had consulted first with my father,' she said. 'I told him that the veil blocked my thoughts, suffocated my feelings, it hampered me! I wanted people to see the determination in my eyes and in my expression. My father replied that unveiling is my own decision, and that he would stand by me.' When she made this gesture in public, a furore occurred. Old women lamented in grief, the end of the world had come; religious sheikhs threatened that her and her family's fate would be in hell. Posters condemning her act were hung on every street corner in Beirut; there were articles against unveiling in the newspaper. Some blamed her action on contact with other sects and with the West, on colonial influence, as Anbara had accompanied her father for two years, 1924–1926, to Great Britain, where he had worked while she took the opportunity to study

English. In England, Anbara discovered that life was not ruled by fanaticism and over-strictness. 'I found out how cultural people were, how civilised and yet sympathetic and helpful. The freedom was overwhelming!' She continued: 'I should mention here that before I visited Great Britain, I had been to Egypt, to Cairo, and experienced modernity and segregation. That was 1912. I saw elevators in buildings, watched plays at theatre, walked in beautiful gardens, attended together with almost the entire population of Cairo, the unveiling of Mustapha Kamal's statue, and when I say "people" I mean women as well!'

The retaliation began immediately. Warnings were issued to every woman not to follow Anbara Salam's example: the consequences would be dire. Women would be violently attacked, with acid thrown on their faces, razor-sharp knives would cut them open and slice off their breasts. But in the face of fury, her father, Abu-Ali Salam, remained silent. He and the entire Salam family knew that the revolution against the hijab had begun. Or did it begin much earlier?

Anbara was born into a well-known Muslim family, pious and conservative. One of her brothers became Prime Minister (1952–1973). She felt secure and happy. She never heard arguments in the household. She realised at an early age that her father was more liberal than her grandmother and her mother. He helped her as a young girl at school, and afterwards she was given private lessons at home. When she was ten years old, she was not allowed to play any more in the neighbourhood, but was permitted to continue at school, with one of her eight brothers. This was when the neighbours and passers-by in the street would shout at her: 'Go back to your family and ask them to veil you!' But young Anbara refused to be veiled, though she had to resign herself to wearing a face veil and a black coat instead of a *Milaya* (a cloak which enveloped the entire body).

When I asked her what prompted her to seek liberation from oppressive tradition, she answered: 'The book of Qasim Amin, the great advocate of the emancipation of women. I had managed to get hold of a copy, although it had been banned, and I used to read it secretly under my blanket.' After Reading Amin's *The Liberation of Women* (1899), Anbara felt that she must take a part in the Arab movement – the *Nahda* (Awakening) – he was talking about. She instinctively agreed with him. After all, she followed in the steps of her moderate, liberal father instead of both her grandmother and mother.

Her father read the newspaper daily and was aware not only of what was happening in Lebanon and the Middle East but in the entire world.

Anbara completed her studies of the Qur'an, and won a golden medal for her recitation. She also felt that she wanted to perfect her Arabic, especially when she became involved in political battles and started writing articles. When she asked a noted religious scholar to give her private lessons, he refused, as she was a woman. But she convinced him later to give her one hour's tuition a day. Soon, her voice was the only woman's voice in the nationalist movement current in 1913, before World War I. People assumed that her articles couldn't have been written by a woman. 'I became involved in this political battle, persuading women to have a choice and a voice and to take part in seeking Arab rights in the Ottoman Empire', she said. She even made a speech when World War I was announced in the presence of the Ottoman Jamal Pasha (1872–1922), 'the Butcher', as the Arab Nationalists called him.

'When I knew that the Butcher was attending the gathering, I refused to give the talk. He has brought starvation, fatal contagious diseases and death to Lebanon. But I was advised to go ahead in order to put Ottoman Jamal under pressure. It was crucial that he heard about the strife and the suffering and how much people had to endure. Whoever gave me this advice was extremely wise, because after my speech the Ottomans built shelters, orphanages and halls for the hungry and the homeless. I still remembered how I trembled as I stood in front of him. He looked like a beast with his bushy beard. After he congratulated me on my speech, he asked why I did not know how to speak Turkish. I answered that I had left school in order to assist the needy and the sick in this wretched war.'

By the time she was twenty-eight, Anbara was still unmarried. She proved how wrong people were when they said that her act of lifting the veil was to attract a husband. But she married eventually. She laughs about this. 'Didn't I see, hear and know? I didn't want to depend on the descriptions of matchmakers, and I was blessed by meeting the Palestinian Ahmad Al-Khalidi, a friend of my family. We discussed current affairs in the presence of my family, of course. He was a principal of the Arab college in Jerusalem and a director of education under the British mandate'. Anbara left Beirut for Palestine but continued working and campaigning for women's rights. But the declaration of state of Israel in 1948 caused her to return to Lebanon with her husband and children.

I still remember how I wanted to ask her if she had ever been to a night club. She did, however, tell me about the time she attended a public lecture in a men's club with the help of one of her school teachers. She woke up the following day to another furore. A newspaper's front page screamed: 'Muslim girls in night clubs!' I ended up not asking her, but felt the urge to tell every woman I saw on my way home that I had been visiting Anbara Salam, the first Lebanese woman to defy stifling traditions and taboos.

I returned the mangy articles to the old box. All the women were alive, on the pages and beyond: they had their hands in mine as we walked. I felt that they were pushing me forward, as they had pushed millions of women towards the light.

ARTS AND LETTERS

THE AISHA PROJECT

Alev Adil

The Project is Commissioned

'You've been highly recommended', the caller said before going on to identify herself as the personal assistant of a certain Professor Y, who pending the results of the investigation, preferred to remain anonymous. 'We were impressed with your work on Zuleika, Potiphar's wife', she went on to tell me. I admit, I was flattered that someone was following my research, although that journey into Biblical, Qur'anic and Sufi poetry had seemed more like a detour, rather than a new direction for my enquiries in invocation and possession. The Y project had proceeded through a process of lucid dreaming and haunted dérives searching for Zuleika in Alexandria, Baku, Kuala Lumpur, New York and Nicosia. I developed a mysterious virus and had to take to my bed for a fortnight after I'd finished the Zuleika dream project, or rather the Zuleika dream had finished writing itself through me. I don't like to dwell on the matter of ghosts for fear the process will sound like some kind of otherworldly séance nonsense, which it is not at all. My research is about finding a way into the buried metaphors in the field of the narrative and to putting those metaphors to work again and thus unleashing their transformative force through performance and publication. Don't take me for a mystic. Much of this is solid scholarship, close reading, interpretation and reinterpretation. However it cannot be denied there is a part of the process that is about dreaming, and dream writing, twilight-writing, sneaking up on the subject, the self as subject as well as the subject-object of scrutiny.

A slight cough at the other end of the line made me realise I was thinking out loud. I shut up and listened carefully. I didn't want to come across as a rambling eccentric. I was intrigued. No conventional research body has shown interest in my research to date, so I couldn't help being flattered by this Professor Y's interest, even if it was thus far a rather mysterious request, and by proxy at that, to use my lucid-dream-invocation method to produce some sort of writing, to produce insight into the life of Aisha, the Prophet's beloved third wife. 'A short story or essay', the professor's assistant said. I made it very clear my work was phenomenological research of the most inhabited kind. 'I am not in the business of producing fiction so much as inhabiting metaphor', I told her, rather haughtily, 'and this is new territory for me.'

'Professor Y is certain you are up to the task Dr Adil,' his assistant assured me smoothly, 'in fact he insists you're the only person for the assignment', before hanging up so swiftly that my lack of a response became a de facto assent.

Later, during the long afternoon rains of spring and early summer, I was to wonder why I had taken on the job. My specialism is goddesses, those of my birthplace and surrounding regions particularly: Astarte, Aphrodite and Inanna, but also Cybele, Artemis and the muses – especially the mother of all muses, Mnemosyne. I've been studying them academically, as well as evoking them through poetry for years now. Lately though, I've been invoking them too, inviting them to inhabit the moment through me. The process has been quite exhausting, and whilst I am aware of my friends' concerns for my health, I believe it has been worthwhile. I am still at a slight loss as to how to express, qualify or quantify the knowledge produced by these invocations. Like those closest to me I too sometimes wonder for my sanity. So much of life is spent in exhausting storm-tossed preparatory dreams, lone prowls, maps, solipsistic soliloquies: words, words, and crazed one-off performances. Nevertheless I'm onto something. I'm sure of it.

I dream for a living, that is my current profession. I am dreamed into being through the visions that ensue. I admit this way of being I'm trying to describe is somewhat unorthodox as a research methodology. Let's be very clear I am not a theologist. What follows is not theology. Not history. Not fiction. What follows is somewhere in the cracks between all of those. A seed germinates and blossoms where the breeze takes it. A small wild flower insinuates itself between great slabs of stone, grows out of the mouth of a dead cannon. What follows is interpretation and invocation.

The Research Process Begins

My work thus far has been in the field of deposed gods and goddesses. To venture into the interpretation and invocation of the unstable, metamorphosing metaphors at the heart of Astarte/Aphrodite worship and her continuing presence in contemporary life is not, of itself, dangerous work. Whilst she still has powerful political and economic weapons at her disposal, the people who no longer worship Aphrodite still assert their prerogative to oil fields in her name; not as much is as stake as in the domain of a deposed goddess. Here I am pitching my dreaming tent in the field of a living God, the God, Allah. Aisha is heavily contested territory. Fatwas have been issued for coming to the 'wrong' conclusions about her. She is a controversial figure. For devout Sunnis, criticising Aisha is akin to criticising the Prophet himself. They believe she was his favourite wife. Intelligent and spirited, she was a disciple as well as a companion. Aisha played a leading role as a teacher, interpreter and exponent of Islam. More than two thousand hadiths are attributed to her, some two-thirds of Islamic Shari'a is based on reports and interpretations that have come from her.

For Shia Muslims she is a much more problematic figure, a meddlesome widow who should have stayed quietly at home instead of making mischief as chief instigator of the Battle of Jamal at Basra against Ali Ibn Abi-Taleb's Caliphate. Those outside the faith are most troubled by her age at marriage. In truth, many within Islam are troubled too. There are fierce scholarly debates. The *Sahih al-Bukhari*, one of the six major hadith collections of Sunni Islam, compiled over twenty-four years and completed in 846, considered the most authentic text of Islam after the Qur'an, is clear that she was six at the time of her *nikah* and nine at the time of her wedding.

This estimation of her age remained unchallenged until the Islamic scholar Maulana Muhammad Ali's Urdu translation and commentaries on *Sahih al-Bukhari* in the 1920s and '30s put forward the hypothesis that Aisha must have been much older, more like nine or ten when she was betrothed and a less alarming fourteen or fifteen when the union was consummated. Subsequent scholars make her even older. Abu Tahir Irfani estimates she was fourteen or fifteen at betrothal, nineteen at marriage.

I try to begin at her beginning, but it's unclear when that was, even whether was she born before the Call or after. Nevertheless, after their betrothal when the Prophet came to visit her he let her play with her dolls in his presence. Her friends scattered at his approach but he called them back to come and join her in her games. Yet only a year after that marriage we see her helping during the Battle of Uhud, her ankle bracelets visible, her robes tucked up out of the filth of war, as she hurries through the throng with a water skin on her back, offering sustenance to the wounded. My reading proceeds in several different directions simultaneously – biographies, fictionalisations, hagiographies, hadiths. I quickly get bogged down in history, in detail, in genealogies and chronologies. I become addicted to a website, www.searchtruth.com, a digital archive which you can search for any word in the Hadith from *Sahih al-Bukhari*, *Sahih Muslim*, *Sunan Abudawud*, or *Malik's Muwatta*. Before beginning the dreaming process I feel I need more facts to hand, but the facts undulate, shape-shift, accumulate and then disappear, like sand dunes, clouds, faces in the moon. The problem is not solely one of verifiability. There are too many facts.

Aisha is given to over-sharing. In her hadith fragments she tells us about washing semen spots from the Prophet's clothes, that he goes to prayers with the water not yet dried upon the stains; she passes on his postcoital clean-up routine, his advice for menstruating women… She's bursting with hygiene tips. No other Prophet has had his private life described so intimately and in such domestic detail, how he did his share of the household chores, milked the ewes, mended his own clothes, dealt with squabbles amongst his wives. Aisha is also very cheeky. The Prophet notes that when she's pleased she says, 'Yes, by the Lord of Muhammad,' but when she is angry, she responds 'No, by the Lord of Abraham.' Always playing tricks, for instance she persuades him another wife's honey makes his breath foul, Aisha is forever getting the Prophet to confirm she is his Special One. They drink from the same cup; they play together and race each other. Her bitterest jealousy is reserved for his first wife Khadija, because the Prophet mentions her so fondly and frequently.

Much that Aisha has to say relates to the domestic sphere but she has a keen sense of politics too, and how the two are intimately related. She says, 'The things which annul the prayers were mentioned before me. They said, 'Prayer is annulled by a dog, a donkey and a woman if they pass in front of the praying people.' I said, 'It is not good that you people have made us women equal to dogs and donkeys. Allah's Apostle prayed while I used to lie between him and the Qibla and when he wanted to prostrate, he pushed my legs out of the way and I withdrew them." And when she wanted to get up she would, and slip away, stepping between the Qibla and her praying husband.

I on the other hand am neither praying nor sleeping. Thus far I've been staying up until the early hours collecting too many stories. This is frustrating because I don't aspire to the truth, these hadiths however impeccable their lineage can't be any more than hearsay, they're archived hundreds of years after the events they describe. I don't want to produce more cheap fictional clutter. Orientalist soft, poor corn about jewels and medinas repels me. I must return to my methodology, and move beyond these narratives through dream, sleep-gleaning the stories for particularly sharp or intriguing metaphors. Metaphor drives and gives form to every idea from hard science to poetry; it is the engine of actualisation. It is through metaphor that metamorphosis occurs. Yet I am nervous. For days on end I chain smoke and forget to eat. I forego sleep to stay up late, collecting fragments from the hadiths and taking notes. What metaphors will Aisha reveal to me through these shards?

In the Small Hours

A man, he has dark eyes, but they're flecked with amber when he gazes down at you, because he really looks at you, in you. There is flurry in the household. The child is told to bring a cup of cold water. An important visitor has come. She balances the cup carefully on a tray, taking care not to spill it. He is smiling and indicates she should sit on his lap. Such a beautiful child, they all agree. The man strokes her head; her hair is very short and fluffy, just growing back. You can tell from her pallor that she has been very ill. He tells her parents not to discipline her.

I wake up, and find I'd fallen asleep slumped over my desk. Hunting in the mess of cups and papers for a pen I write 'Why? Do they hit the child too much? How did he know — were there marks on her? Or rather is she a mischievous or willful little girl? Which hadith is this? What was she sick with? Cross check sources'. My face is sore, a pen and the corner of my laptop have left red lines on my face. My back aches. I feel like I've been on a long haul flight. I'll go to bed in a minute, I tell myself. I just need to find the source for this. No, there's nothing in my research notes about this event, just a reference to websites with furious online debates about whether and how hard Muhammad hit/slapped/pushed her, later, when they were married and she followed him out unbidden to the graveyard in the middle of the night.

I'm ready to go to my bed too when my laptop begins emitting that little tune, something between the rhythm of a nursery rhyme and an ambulance siren, that tells me Nilüfer is Skyping me.

'Hello Alev abla' she booms, her voice is clear although there is loud music in the background, live I think. 'What are you up to? You should be here. We've just come from a read-in, a sit-down protest at Taksim Square. I've posted some pictures online, take a look.'

A link, a tiny URL, pops up in the speech box. I click on it and it takes me to a website called *kaldırım taşlarının altındaki plaj* which translates from Turkish as 'the beach beneath the paving stones'. The photographs are of Nilüfer and her friends sitting in Taksim Square holding up books.

'See the one of me?' Nilüfer says, 'I'm holding up Bachelard's Poetics of Reverie, just for you cuz.'

Most of the images on her site are from various Gezi Park protests. The images I find most intriguing are of street dogs hanging out with the protestors, even defending them in the riots.

'Sweet. Thank you janim. How's your work going?' Nilüfer is an artist, mainly sculpture and installations, her most famous piece *Family* is an installation of domestic furniture, a facsimile of her childhood living room, the pastiche Baroque furniture covered in giant upholstered tumours. Her installation was exhibited in the Istanbul Modern in 2010 and met with international interest. She was really going places, but since last year both her head and her heart are only in one place – Gezi Park.

'We're preparing for the anniversary demonstration. I won't say too much online…'

The camaraderie of protest has consumed her and given her the glow that you see on the faces of pregnant women, those who have just fallen in love, gone mad, or found God. I can't begrudge her that happiness and newfound sense of purpose. But I'm less enamoured of the righteous indignation that comes with it, too close a dialectical reflection of Erdoğan's belligerence. It's not that Nilüfer and I disagree entirely but even when we agree she makes me feel I don't agree enough. I worry about her.

'And what are you doing? Why have you had your Skype switched off for the last week? Why are you up so late? Have you been eating?' She worries about me too.

'I'm doing a new project. Another one of my invocation things...'

'But abla, I thought you were going to stop this, last time you became so ill. You're not taking any weird pills or anything?'

'No, no, just vitamin B6 and lots of chicken. I haven't started yet though... I'm still preparing, researching. It's about Aisha.'

'Ayşe hala?'

' No, not our auntie – Aisha the Prophet's wife.'

'You're kidding? *Abla*, have you gone nuts? Have the Gülenists got to you?' She makes an impassioned speech about Muslim piety that is partly drowned out by the music and the time delay on our call. Her image keeps pixelating, freezing, reforming. It's not just the corruption and repression, the relentless neoliberal profit driven brutality of the current government. It's not just Erdoğan's arrogant responses to the death of Alevi children in the riots and the horrors of the Soma mining disaster that enrage her. She goes on at some length about the small-minded Muslim puritanism that makes everyday less joyful, making it harder and more to expensive to appreciate the view over a raki or three, about people being arrested for kissing in the street. Then her discourse gets darker and roams farther, the woman stoned to death by her family outside the courthouse in Pakistan, the pregnant woman, about to give birth, imprisoned in Sudan, the kidnap of hundreds of school girls in Nigeria... Whatever Islam is/was supposed to be, face it, it's never good news socially or politically these days. Where is Shari'a Law anything but barbaric?

'This project is not about contemporary Islamic politics, or about fundamentalism, terrorism, it's not about any of that. It's about Aisha, the metaphors that sing out from her words across the centuries. It's about the poetics of dreaming.'

'Well, you can take to your bed and ignore the world all you like, but all this is not about to disappear. The place of women in Islam is unavoidably a part of that story. And didn't he have sex with her when she was six?'

'Nine.'

'Nice.'

'I know. Though some scholars....'

'These could be very heavy dreams. And what will you do with them when they're dreamt?'

'I know. I don't know.' It's time to hang up. Nilüfer and her friends are off for breakfast by the Bosphorous.

The Dreams

I prepare for the dreaming time with vitamin B6 supplements and chicken at every meal, bananas at bedtime. I have also developed a morning and evening yoga and meditation sequence. But it is very difficult to direct the dreams, to conjure them up. After the fugitive dream of the glass of cold water Aisha refuses to appear at all in my thin dreams. My sleep is poor. I fidget and tangle the sheets up night after night and try not to worry, after all Aphrodite refused to properly and vividly appear until three months into the project. After two months an email arrives from the efficient assistant. Professor Y wants to see a preliminary report. I request an extension and ignoring all the unanswered messages in my inbox, I turn off the laptop and give myself to the business of dreaming. However it is more than a week later when the shriek of a car alarm wakes me from the first dream.

I am tightly swaddled in a rough blanket. I have a fever. I am not sure who I am. I am a child. There is a sandstorm outside. My blanket is cochineal coral. The light around the woman's dark braided hair is golden. I hear the palms thrashing outside. 'Hush now my precious one' she presses her cool long rough fingers against my forehead. 'Where am I?' I ask her. 'Who am I?'

'Yathrib, my beloved. You are the beloved child of Yathrib. Watch the movement of the clouds, of the branches in the breeze. Listen carefully to your dreams.'

I wake up realising I really do have a fever. I am bound up in my duvet. As I drink the dream soiled stale water by my bed I wonder, was that Aisha? Or was it the Prophet himself? I had no sense of being a boy or a girl. Perhaps that was Aminah who held me in her arms? She took the Prophet to Yathrib as a child. She was to die as they returned to Mecca. The child was six. Somehow I know that from the dream, the child is six.

I make coffee but my throat is sore and it tastes burnt and bitter. I can't drink it. I take two Paracetemol and gulp down some water. I press my forehead on the windowpane. London is lush and green outside my window; a blossom-laden branch wags a gnarled finger at me. A steady sleet of light summer rain is falling. Turning back into the room I begin a list of metaphors thus far gleaned:

> A cup of cold water (stone cup?)
> The movement of the clouds
> The movement of the branches in the breeze
> The sound of wind in the palms:
> The fever child of Yathrib
> is six years old.
> I am burning up and go back to bed.

I have the same deep coral blanket wrapped around me, rough against my cheek. There is a copper bowl of water before me with fragrant rose petals in it. I lean over it and catch my reflection; it is I, not Aisha. The woman with the healing hands comes in, the fragrance of crushed thyme about her she takes me in her arms as though I was a child.

'She was his most beloved they say, but such childish competition is meaningless. And if we were to compete, I would say I won — I loved him the most.' She pours me a sweet cold drink of diluted honey and vinegar. 'I had already built up my business when I saw him, I made a good living. I was happy to pay the bills and to raise the babies, those that survived. I wanted to marry and support him not just because I loved him when I saw him, but also because I believed his dreams were divine. I knew from his eyes.'

'What about Aisha? What do you know of Aisha?' I ask her.

'Why Aisha? Why don't you even ask my name? I am a tree of a woman; she was a twig of a child. He was nurtured by me alone for twenty-five years, slept in my arms alone. The Apostle of Allah slept by her side for nine short years, and not even every night, but taking turns, in a shared throng. Is it because I didn't cause trouble? Are you only interested in women who start wars?' Her voice is gentle but I feel ashamed I have not shown her the respect that is her due.

I wake up without any sense of what day or time it is. It is twilight outside, but whether it's early morning or evening I have no idea. I pad barefoot to the kitchen and search for vinegar and honey to make myself a hot drink. I have run out of honey but find some Basra date syrup and use that instead.

'We are the Ansari women, we come to speak of her'. The most remarkable thing about this dream is its rich auditory qualities. Their voices sound like a single voiced

multiplied with a slight time delay, an acapella echoey disorientation like Bulgarian
choral folk music.

'Ā'ishah bint Abī Bakr, A'ishah, Aisyah, Ayesha, A'isha, Ayşe, Aishat.' The Ansari
women are a wedding party, they sing and sway these ululating vowels and the
sound becomes the rhythm of a rope swing between two palms.

'He will bend her but no one will break her.
The young branch bends and bounces back
in a greenstick fracture.
Her hair has grown back; it has passed her ears.
We have passed more than three times
through the cycle of the years.
Dress her with silk, dress her with stone.
Child-woman came from Mecca in the Call
to Yathrib, you are to be His alone.
Hurry now, you can bring your doll.'

Aisha is about fourteen when I next see her, her hair is a wild tangled storm. She
is feverish in her bed and wakes still searching for the lost necklace she now holds in
her hand. She won't plead her innocence. Since Allah is all-seeing He knows she is
innocent. She throws herself at His mercy, not the Prophet's. He consults the Ansari
women. Buraira steps out of the wedding chorus to bear testimony and the others
sing too in their echoing uncanny misharmony.

'Her only faults are those of her young age,
she is so easily moved to laughter, jokes
that turn to sulks and tears, even rage.
The thing we'd complain of most though,
is how she neglects her household chores
and lets the goats wander and eat the dough.'

I am in a cave. There is pile of bones in one corner. Flies congeal over a freshly
killed goat. A television is on. A report on fresh atrocities from the war in Syria is
being broadcast on a large television. A figure rises out of the corner with a lion at
her side, a palm frond in her hand. Of course, I should have known... Still, I was
not expecting to see her here.

'Weren't you now?' she laughs. She can read my thoughts. 'Perhaps I can say the
same. Once you sought me out in my birthplaces as Astarte/ Aphrodite and now I
find you sniffing around my grave.' She is a huge, naked warrior and she turns, leans
over me emits a terrible torrent of awful wailing, the deposed goddess of love and

war, caught always in the midpoint between the two, the goddess of lament. Her lion roars with her.

'*You're worried about the Desert Princess, the Mother of the Believers? You're snooping around for her in dreams?*' *She grabs me by my hair. Her lion looks at me quizzically.* '*You want to know whether she was innocent or guilty? Is that it? You've come to me for her war record?*' *She turns my head to television.* '*Many would say that's her war record too.*' *The lion sniffs me. I can smell his meaty breath.* '*When the Christians deposed me in your birthplace they smuggled me into the heart of their religion as Mary. My lament for Adonis became the Pieta. They veiled my power in royal blue, stuffed my mouth with suffering. But her Muhammad had my temples razed. I am Al-Lat of Taif. Ask your Aisha about me, about what they did to my followers in Taif.*'

Who knows, I'm really not sure. I have consulted my calendar but I am still not sure how many days I lost in those fever dreams. When I'm well enough to log on to my email again I find a slew of new messages, most are group mailshots from galleries, theatres and publishers, some are phishing exercises requesting my bank details, three are from Professor Y's assistant and one from Nilüfer with the subject line 'happy birthday?'.

'Alev *abla*, how are you? I've been offline for a while. I'm fine but some of my friends were arrested last night during the anniversary demonstrations. I would have been too, but just as I was about to follow them one of the wild dogs I've been photographing in the park started howling madly, and distracted me; I thought he'd been wounded. In the confusion I lost my companions in the crowd. Then the dog gave me a look as if to follow him, and trotted down a side street away from the riot unguarded by the cops. So I did. I slipped away. I escaped.'

Nilüfer had attached an article on the history of street dogs in Istanbul. I read it as I search the kitchen for something to eat. It has been days since I have shopped or eaten properly. Over toast and more Basra date syrup I read a chilling account of the Ottoman practice of banishing the dogs to barren islands in the Marmara Sea. In 1911 the governor of Istanbul released tens of thousands of dogs onto Sivriada, a tiny island to which Byzantine rulers once exiled criminals. A yellowed postcard shows hundreds of dogs on the beach. The citizens of Istanbul complained that they could not sleep because their haunted howls could be heard even at great distances. An earthquake occurred a few weeks later and was taken as a sign of God's displeasure. The dogs that had survived were brought back to the city.

In the Rain

I am shaky on my feet, my nerves jangled. I call Qais and ask if he can meet me. He's in the British Library. I haven't been outside for days and can't face a crowded café. I suggest we meet in Tavistock Square. I misremember it as having a cute little tea kiosk, which it doesn't. That's Gordon Square. Tavistock Square has the statue of Gandhi and the tree planted as memorial to the victims of Hiroshima. It's raining hard and yet the canopy of leaves protects us from the worst of it. We shelter under a large Beech tree near a small lugubrious bust of Virginia Woolf. Qais is a scholar of Ottoman and Persian literature and the person I know who is the most knowledgeable about Aisha.

'So let me get this straight, this is another of your crazy poetic projects? Will it end with a performance like the Aphrodite project? Have you recovered? Has London?' Qais roars with laughter whilst puffing on something that looks like a fat pen, he keeps pressing a small button and then exhaling clouds of vapour.

'Ah yes, do you like my little portable *nargile*? An e-shisha they call it. Amusing no? Try it.'

'So what do you think Qais? Nilüfer thinks I'm just asking for trouble. I can't get my head around all the history, or get past the whole child marriage thing…'

'Well, she might have been lying about her age? Women are always lying about their age.'

'Oh Qais, come on. Granted she might have been hazy about her birthdate, even underestimated her own age a little, but still, there are so many references to her youth and playing with toys, all that. And who would lie about being nine when they were nineteen. She must have been a child.'

'But she wanted it. The Prophet didn't take her against her will.'

'Are a nine year old girl child's desires anything but crushed if they're acted upon?'

'Mary was twelve, Joseph an old man.'

'Why is that relevant?'

'Well they are both virginal portals to the divine my dear. An angel has one, the Prophet the other. Are you sure you should you visit your twentieth century political correctness on all this?' he exhales a calligraphy of vapour, poems that vanish in the rain.

'Of course not, you're right. I'm not interested in judging him, or turning her into a passive victim. I just want to find out...'

'Lesley Hazelton's books, which are very good about Aisha, are *The First Muslim* and *After the Prophet*. The second will serve your purpose particularly well.'

'I've been proceeding more through dreaming than reading but I did read Karen Armstrong's biography of the Prophet.' Qais raises an eyebrow and stares back sadly at the bronze visage of Virginia, 'There's rather a good hagiography, *Hadhrat Ayesha Siddiqa: Her Life and Works* by Allamah Syed Sulaiman Nadvi. You could consult that too for your story.'

'It's not a story. I'm not interested in fictionalising or providing neat narratives out of the hadith fragments but in having a sense of the presence of this woman, who I already feel, through my hadith readings, was vigourously and assertively worldly – driven by a muscular sense of entitlement through her aristocracy, her rightful place through birth, marriage and love at the heart of Islam.'

'Which translation of Bukhari are you consulting? I can give you some guidance on the pros and cons of the various translations.'

'Actually I've been using www.searchtruth.com. You can do word searches of the entire Hadith. It's really brilliant.'

'Hmm. I really rather doubt that. So the point of this is neither fiction nor scholarship? Or both?'

'I want to discern what was divine about her. She was the only woman in whose bed the Prophet received divine revelations. He loved her the most of all his wives. He died in her lap. She was his child-bride, in fact or at heart. She was the girl, not the woman (that was Khadija) of his life, that too I find very moving.

The girl I glimpsed was very un-Lolita-ish, this Aisha girl-child who unlocks a very special divine tenderness in the Prophet. His love for her was remarkable and remarked upon then and is transgressive now.'

'A love story then?'

'No, I can't. I find the Prophet's married life so alien. He's monogamously married to a woman he loves deeply, then after she dies, after the age of fifty he takes on, is it ten, more wives, one still a child?'

'It was political.'

'Yes, very. Anthropological, historical and hysterical. They seem to have been a handful for him to manage too.'

'It seems to me that most important thing about her, if you think of the consequences for Islam, is her part in the Battle of Jamal. Whether she is really guilty of bringing about the schism in Islam.'

'I guess you're right. I've been so caught up in thinking about how she helps the Prophet reach the divine; that she is a threshold to the divine, like you were saying.'

'And yet you find that in her day to day life she is the desert Arab version of (almost) any other spirited Byzantine or Borgia princess?'

'You put it so well Qais.'

And then I hail a taxi and we go for tea at the Wolsey because we are damp from the rain. It is to be my treat for we have encircled the statue of Gandhi and been glared at by Woolf, both of whom Qais detests, many times that afternoon.

The Last Dream

I hear her voice, just her voice and the wind. All I can see is a heavy woven curtain flapping in the wind. 'He had returned from a war, was it the expedition to Tabuk or Khaybar? I cannot be sure. He brought the wind with him. The draught raised an end of the curtain that was hung in front of my cupboard, revealing some of my toys. He asked me, 'What is this?' Perhaps he thought I would have disposed of them by then, I was sixteen or seventeen. He picked the horse with wings made of rags, and asked, 'What is this I see among them? A horse with wings?'

'Have you not heard that Solomon had horses with wings?' I teased him and the Apostle of Allah (peace be upon him) laughed so heartily that I could see his molars.

Then I rise from my bed, the wind seems to be coming from an open window, and the rain has soaked the curtains. I lean out of the window, the moon is full and low and golden on the horizon. I see a slim figure walking down the street in a long dark shift. I rush out of the house and follow her down Southampton Row. She grows thinner and taller as she glides towards the Kingsway. A pack of dogs slink out of the side streets and accompany me padding silently towards the river. She is taller than Bush House as she reaches Aldwych. Aisha turns as she reaches Waterloo Bridge.

'*The hounds of Hawab, Allah's Apostle warned us, I thought the interdiction was for another, but he said it for me. "Turn back when you hear the hounds of Hawab howl". I understood that when I heard their unearthly cries.*'

I am surrounded by hundreds of dogs but they don't make a sound at all.

The Report

Dear Professor Y,

Apologies for the delay in completing my report. My research methodology proved particularly physically taxing, hence the delay. Qualitative and quantitative data will follow shortly but below is the key data that has emerged from my dream investigations:

The fever child of Yathrib,
the girl on a swing strung between two palms
is a greenstick fracture,
spirit undaunted, will unbroken,
fighting her corner,
but alone.
Some horses have wings.
Most beloved.
He died in her lap.
A bride, a widow, never a mother,
she was always a fighter when cornered.
The hounds of Hawab howl to warn her
the warrior in her has wandered too far,
as is her destiny, as the widow-queen of Islam
who learnt his dreams by heart.
Greensticked spirit, will unbroken,
fighting her corner,
but alone.
How they howl.

WRITERS IN ISTANBUL

Mohamed Bakari

In the spring of 2010, the Istanbul high-brow literary afficionados were treated to a feast. V.S. Naipaul, Hanif Kureishi and Gore Vidal were coming to the town. The events took place in different venues, with V.S. Naipaul reading from his essay on his evolution as a writer at the Sabanci Museum's *The Seed* amphitheatre. Hanif Kureishi was part of a panel consisting of Naipaul and Elif Shafak, a leading contemporary Turkish writer, held at the the ultra-modern art gallery, the Istanbul Modern. The presence of these writers was courtesy of the Liberium organisation, an NGO dedicated to the promotion of cross-cultural dialogue and societies, founded by a young man with the improbable name, at least to me, of Pablo Ganguli.

V.S. Naipaul, frail and looking exausted, walked, or was rather helped on to the stage, by his protective wife, Lady Nadira. He was in an oversized black suit, large black shoes and what appeared to be white ankle-cap, since he walked with some effort. He almost seemed to mimic the stereotypical Oxford don in his attire. His session was chaired by the Rome editor of *Vogue*, Franca Sozzani. As she took charge of the proceedings, it became obvious that this was a glamour event. Naipaul invested the proceedings with some dignity by his lugubriousness: after all this was the famous no-nonsense Naipaul. Sozzani made the introduction in heavily-accented English. Almost immediately, businesslike, Naipaul started reading from his *Reading and Writing*, published in the *New York Review of Books Classics* series. I have always been a fan of Naipaul, to the total perplexity of my friends, who have sometimes been so indulgent as to grudgingly send me books on what they consider his unfair portrayal of our third world. But my friends and children have forgiven me because they know that Naipaul and I stand on opposite ideological spectrums. The author thinks that he is ideologically neutral, although the very positions he takes are ideologically loaded. His position is analogical to someone considering themselves asexual, an impossible position to maintain for a functioning person. I have been reading Naipaul since my undergraduate days. As a graduate student at the University of York, I took the opportunity, in my moments of laziness, to escape from the precision and rigour of linguistics, to the comedy and cynicism of Naipaul's spare and elegant prose.

Vidia, to take the liberty of calling him by the name used by those closest to him, read a few paragraphs, pausing every now and then to elucidate on his views. This elucidation turned out to be what he had articulated in his fiction and essays: that writing is a travel-mate of vanity. In his younger days he had dreams of celebrity, not knowing the hazards of a writer's vocation. That writing is lonely, painful and unpredictable; writers are easily prone to discouragement when things do not seem to go the way they expect them to. In other words, they are just like the rest of us – the less glamourous. Writing has its own fulfillments and rewards, but the anti-climax is reached when the manuscript is completed and dispatched; then begins another round of the search for new subjects and the whole process starts all over again, with all the attendant anxieties and uncertainties intact.

It turned out Naipaul has now completely shaded off his West Indian lilt, and speaks with cut glass British, or more accurately, upper class Oxbridge accent. This is not surprising given that Naipaul left Trinidad at the age of eighteen swearing not to return to that nondescript place. The reading itself did not take more than twenty minutes before Lady Nadira, who was not chairing, intervened to cut the proceedings short and demanded written questions for Naipaul to answer. The censor was of course her ladyship. Lady Nadira is best known for her cavalier and abrasive manner through Patrick French's no-holds-barred biography of V.S. Naipaul, *The World Is What It Is*. Questions were vetted and read by Nadira on the lectern, while Sir Vidia remained seated. She insisted that only three questions should be asked, and sure enough, she got what she wanted. This was partly because there were only about fifty people in the large lecture theatre, perhaps because of the bad press he received in Turkey when he won the Nobel; and partly because Turks had never read him. He was perceived by a large swathe of the non-secular Muslim reading public as pathologically anti-Muslim, although this is hard to fathom given that his wife is herself a Muslim.

I was one of the fortunate few. My question was read by her ladyship; and allowed. It was an innocuous question on Naipaul's fascination with classical and late antiquity, as reflected in scattered and ubiquitous references to ancient Rome in both his essays and fiction. Naipaul's face lit up, he loved the question. No one, it seems, had put this question to him before this moment. The question did not touch on any of his controversial positions: the bugbear of Islamic fanaticism, modernist gay writers and intellectuals that he despised, like E.M. Forster, or Africans and Afro-Caribbeans. Or Derek Walcott. The Ancient Rome question animated him and took him back to his late adolescence when he was reading for his A Levels. He described how he came under the spell of this charismatic history teacher who came to class without a book but who was in complete command of his subject. He was sufficiently interesting to inspire the young Naipaul to take an abiding interest in ancient Rome. He had, he said, through a slow accumulation of knowledge, through follow-up readings, come to appreciate Roman history through its incremental accumulation of imperial power and its challenges.

It became obvious that Naipaul had been heavily influenced by Edward Gibbon's *The Decline and Fall of the Roman Empire.* Early on Naipaul borrowed lock, stock and barrel, Gibbon's pithy style, his raw scepticism, and of course, his cynicism about religion. Gibbon is one of the great stylists of the English language. Naipaul must have read him over and over again to get a handle on that style. And he did. He has turned out to be the master of that turn of phrase, just as the master himself, Gibbon, was. This is a little understood influence on Naipaul, hidden from public view and Naipaul has a genius for hiding early influences.

As someone born inside one of the last empires, Naipaul could gradually, with maturity, understand the desire of the other to go to distant places to colonise for God and Glory. In fact, the model for British Empire was not classical Roman imperialism, but Ottoman, the difference being that the latter Empire was inclusive whereas the former was decidedly exclusive. In both the Roman and Ottoman empires there was the figleaf of citizenship, whereas the British wanted subjects and not citizens. One of the earliest references to ancient Roman history and culture appeared in the first of his Indian travel books, *An Area of Darkness*, his back-to-roots book. On noticing the Indian habit, or rather the habit of some Indians, to defecate in stark public view while fully engaged in a conversation, he remarked: 'In India, like in Imperial Rome, defecation is a social activity'. As expected, this did not endear Vidia to the citizens of his ancestral home, however comic or Naipaulesque the turn of phrase might be. A lot of Indian intellectuals were stung by Naipaul's perceived anti-Indian posturing. The late Indian poet and essayist, Nissim Ezekiel was stung enough to write a reposte to Naipaul's keen eye, in a memorable essay entitled 'Naipaul's India and Mine'. Naipaul got what he wanted, he provoked Indian writers into action.

Naipaul went on to add that he needed to know more about this theatre of ancient history than he had cared to look into; he noted that Turkey was a fascinating place; he was sorry that it had eluded his gaze and it would have added to his passion for antiquity if he knew more about it; after all, that father of historical studies, Herodotus was born and wrote in Halicarnassus, circa 484 BC in what is now Bodrum in the Western Turkish Aegean shore. He could have been amazed, even more, if he had known that his own prototype, Diogenes the Cynic, was born in the Turkish Black Sea city of Sinope in 412 BC. Having spent a few days in Istanbul, Naipaul was unlikely to have gone back as an unreconstructed islamophobe.

At the botton of the paper where I had posed the Roman question, I politely indicated that I was the late James de Vere Allen's friend. Jim Allen was a naturalised Kenyan citizen, a historian born in Britain who studied history at Oxford. In the colonial and ex-colonial places, an Oxford degree counted for a lot. Armed with that kind of credential you could move mountains. Jim ended up at Makerere where he taught history at a time when Naipaul was offered a Fellowship in creative writing. They immediately struck a rapport, and many years later when Naipaul was looking for a subject for his next book, he must have happened on Jim Allen again, this time in Kenya. The novel he wrote won him his Booker; on reading *A Bend in the River* one is struck by Jim Allen's influence in the view Naipaul takes on the Swahili and the Indians of the East African diaspora. Jim Allen had an encyclopaedic knowledge of East African history, especially Swahili and coastal society.

Jim Allen later relocated to the University of Nairobi where we were colleagues and later very close friends. It was from him that I learned that he played host to both Vidia and Shiva Naipaul (his younger brother). Shiva was to write an acerbic travel book on East Africa, *North of South*, in the wake of Idi Amin's expulsion of Asians from Uganda. Naipaul was touched by my mentioning Jim Allen and could not resist talking about him, and mentioning how when he was about to set out for Kenya again, he heard that Jim had passed away. I had gone to visit Jim in hospital all the time he was there, before he died of abdominal cancer. Like Naipaul, Jim had his views and thought against the current of historical thought in the Department of History at Nairobi. He was really there on sufferance, in the midst of historians of all kinds of ethnic and racial and ideological persuasions, outside his way of thinking. These were revolutionary historians hell bent on toppling the infamous view about African history of the British historical school, influenced by Sir Hugh Trevor-Roper. Trevor-Roper, the Regius Professor of History at Oxford, was certain that the African continent had no history. That what was there was simply 'a phantasmagoria of nothingness', little more than 'a record of the activities of Europeans', and that the rest was 'darkness, and that darkness was not a subject of history.' When I went to the podium to get my *A House for Mr. Biswas* autographed, I identified myself as the person who asked that Roman question. He again became animated and asked me how long I had been in Istanbul. 'Twelve years', I retorted. But Nadira was hovering around and wanted to protect Vidia from us. In any case, she had announced unilaterally that only three people would get the autographs. As it turned out only three of us, myself, and my two students, Fatih Esenboğa and Roman Nikolaev, formed our little British queue.

Naipaul went an extra mile, and despite Nadira's sharp eye, not only autographed, but remembered our mutual friend by inscribing in my copy 'For Jim Allen & friend.' It was quite touching for both of us. Then, the real faux pas: as we were trooping out to get back to our seats, Nikolaev asked to be photographed with Naipaul. He had given his mobile phone to Fatih Esenboğa to take the photograph and asked me to join him. Unknown to us, Franca Sozzani was also standing behind Naipaul and her own official photographer was about to take the snap unaware that we were not supposed to be part of the scene. 'Oh, my God!' Nadira shrieked. 'Stop!',

obviously unhappy that we should be in the snapshot that was especially
meant for the glamourous *Vogue*. We, the unglamourous, sheepishly vacated
the platform for the glitterati.

   A question that inevitably arises, and which people raise when Naipaul
gives readings (he almost never gives presentations because he says in one
of his essays he has no stomach for academic work) is the whole question
of the future of the novel. While Roland Barthes had proclaimed the death
of the author, Naipaul is dead certain that a requiem for the novel is
overdue. Although one of its best practitioners, even earning him a cover
of *Newsweek* in 1980 entitled 'Master of the Novel,' Naipaul is pessimistic
about its future. He still believes that it has no future, given the rise of new
media, the internet and its various metamorphoses. In the world of Twitter
and YouTube that endorses short concentration span, surely novels, and
especially tedious long novels, hardly have a place in the modern world.
Now every wannabe novelist can have their five minutes of celebrity on the
net by posting their writing there. The high noon of the novel was the
nineteenth century. The surest indicator of the death of the novel, Naipaul
lamented, is the proliferation of creative writing programmes in
universities. And of course all manner of weird courses started in the US.
Even British universities are not immune from the American contagion of
creative writing. *The Guardian* now runs creative writing courses for God's
sake! Naipaul's expression of nostalgia for life before creative writing
courses were willed into being, reminded me of the postscript Chinua
Achebe had written immediately after the death of James Baldwin. 'I had
all my schooling in the educational system of colonial Nigeria', Achebe
said, 'in that system Americans, when they featured at all, were dismissed
summarily by our British administators as loud and vulgar. Their
universities, which taught such subjects as dishwashing, naturally produced
the half-baked noisy political agitators some of whom were now rushing
up and down the country because they had acquired no proper skills.' It
would be pretty unfair to lump together Naipaul with other anti-
Americans, like Dr Samuel Johnson. In fact one of the best travel books
Naipaul has written is *A Turn in the South*. At the session, a colleague of
mine, an American academic in Istanbul, handed in a complementary note
to congratulate him for his graphic and lyrical description of the
quintessential American hillbillies, the rednecks. She said that was the best

description of rednecks she had ever read. Naipaul just smiled in acknowledgement.

Creative writing programmes, Naipaul declared, were responsible for the uniformity of the novel as it exists today because everyone thinks that they have a novel lurking inside them and no wonder now that these novels are mass produced, once you have read one, you have read them all. He felt nostalgia for real novelists, those who were self-taught and developed the skill through sheer endurance. He said writing was a lonely vocation and that drawing on one's life experiences and autobiographical details ran the danger of exhausting one's store of themes. For this reason he sought other genres, other ways of seeing. Travel writing provided alternative ways of exploring the world.

The vocation of a writer is a fraught one. It is a life of isolation and loneliness. He felt himself, he said, following a routine of seeking a subject, ruminating on it for days and grappling with it. Its completion signalling the end of just one cycle in a series of endless cycles of creative outbursts and denouement. Writing creates a sense of purpose for living and fills the void of idleness, despite its anxieties. When asked whether he will continue writing he admitted that there must be an end to everything. He feels that he has now come almost to the end of his vocation – after all, he is in his eighties now. But he could learn a lesson or two from the iconoclastic Indian writer Nirad Chaudhuri. Niradbabu had his last piece of writing appear in *Granta* magazine, which was then celebrating India's fiftieth birthday anniversary. Chaudhuri was 102 in 1999. He was dubbed 'the last Englishman' by the Indian novelist and essayist, and Naipaul protegé, Pankaj Mishra. Chaudhuri was an early influence on Naipaul but like all his early influences, he tried to distance himself from this trace by running him down in that anthology of acerbic, gonna-get-you essays entitled *A Writer's People*. Unsurprisingly, Nirad Chaudhuri is in the company of Naipaul's other nemeses like Derek Walcott and Mahatma Gandhi. This book is a celebration of his own exceptionalism, one aspect that he grudgingly shares with the Americans' self-perception.

On the second day after Naipaul's gig at The Seed, we congregated at Istanbul Modern to hear Hanif Kureishi, Elif Shafak and Lady Nadira. These speakers were supposed to describe their writing experiences as Muslims:

Muslim majority countries in the case of Elif Shafak and Lady Nadira and a Muslim minority country in the case of Hanif Kureishi.

Right from the outset Hanif Kureishi wanted to assert himself as a pro-homosexual writer. Elif Shafak made it clear that she was enthralled by the Islamic Sufi tradition, with its benign tolerance of popular practices that sometimes went contrary to the dictates of textual Islam practised by her more fundamentalist co-religionists. Lady Nadira must have been included for the sole purpose of stoking the embers of anti-fundamentalism. Elif opened the discussion by noting that writing fiction in a conservative society where readers find it hard to separate writers from their writings is not easy. As an illustration, she said that she always has to be cautious about what she writes because locally, her fictional characters may automatically be taken to be the alter-ego of the novelists or assumed to undergo the actual experiences of the novelist. She said in one of her novels there is an episode of rape and she feared that her readers may assume that it was the novelist herself who undwerwent the trauma. This is invariably taken to be so because in the larger society, those who undergo disgraceful experiences always tell stories that are true to life, from their own experiences and narrate them through the voice of a third person. She feared that on reading the book her own mother might be horrified. She might think that her daughter had repressed the unpleasant experience only for it to emerge in her fictional characters.

This view is alarmingly close to the Freudian return of the repressed. Elif Shafak celebrates folk religiosity embodied in her maternal grandmother's religious syncretism, where shamanistic, sufi and strict orthodoxy find happy coexistence. In contrast her paternal grandmother preached to her the Islamic version of fire and brimstone, more frightening than Dante's fifth circle. She said she is influenced by the philosophy of Mevlana Jelaliddin Rumi who preached a tolerant Islam; she deeply immerses herself in Islamic philosophy and spiritual tradition from which she draws her inspiration. Asked about the sensitivity of writing about sex in a conservative Muslim society, she answered that it was hard to touch on that subject if one wanted to attract mainstream readership. To write on unconventional subjects, she noted, one had to be living on the margins of society, like lesbians, for example, because society does not take them seriously and expects them to write outrageous things about sex.

Kureishi was scandalised by Shafak's position. She insisted that this was the Turkish reality and writers would be foolhardy to ignore the intensely macho and male dominated context. On his part Kureishi was over the top about homosexuality and went on to describe what he must have thought were shocking situations. It is with respect to this element of surprise, and shock, that Kureishi believes his fiction shows the way forward.

The following Sunday Kureishi's *My Beautiful Laundrette* was shown to the Istanbul public. Istanbul has now been hijacked by country dwellers who are extremely homophobic, contrary to the press representation of the city as open and broad-minded. You see them all over the city in their pointed shoes, Groucho Marx moustaches and worry beads. Each one looking like the traditional *mahalle kaba dayi* or *efe*, the neighbourhood enforcer of local morality. And the love that dares not mention its name, does not work here. Transvestites meet constant harassment and violence from the general public. James Baldwin got a taste of this when he was roughed up as a softie. Turkey considers itself a macho haven. This is still a Manichean world, and gender ambiguity is not easily tolerated. Kureishi's vehement defence of gay culture did not go down well with the audience here, although they already knew the script before watching the movie. Those of us who had different views about homosexuality did not see great art in the movie. Indeed, Kureishi's aggression looked like an attempt to impose his worldview on others. Just like the fundamentalists he railed against.

Kureishi's antagonism contrasts sharply with the gentleness of James Baldwin who spent a good decade in Istanbul and came to know the old city well. There are endearing photos of him sitting on ablution slabs at the Sultanahmet mosque, in the Sultanahmet neighbourhood; along the Haliç bridge, taking sanctuary from rain or holding babies; in the popular Istiklal Caddesi, Istanbul's own Oxford Street; in a fish restaurant in Eminönu; and in other snaps as far as Kilyo, Bodrum, in the Aegean Sea. He was completely integrated within the small circle of his Muslim friends. Everyone saw him as 'arap', a generic term for all those who are a shade darker. He was of course able to get easy acceptance because he did not wear his sexual orientation on his sleeve. He was also in the good company of other homosexuals, like the late transvestite crooner, Zeki Muren, a household name in Turkey even today. His other close friend, who is still alive, and appears often on talk shows and films, was the actor Ali Poyraz.

It was here that some of his most productive work was produced. His novel *Another Country* is datelined Istanbul. It was here that he polished his signature moral indignation, *The Fire Next Time*. It was here that Baldwin developed, in the memorable phraseology of the Irish novelist and essayist Colm Toibin, the 'high faggot style.' The decade that Baldwin spent in Istanbul was probably one of the happiest in his life. He could work and play, both before celebrity and after, anonymously.

It was in Istanbul that Baldwin came to know Muslims at close quarters because his close circle was entirely Muslim. In fact it was the young Engin Cezzar whom Baldwin took home after a night's rave in a Harlem nightclub who invited Baldwin to Istanbul. Engin had just graduated from Yale Drama School. Engin and his wife, another well known Istanbul socialite, Gülriz Sururi, adopted him as their own and introduced him to the literary and artistic uppercrust of Istanbul and Turkey. It was from this easy familiarity with Muslims that Baldwin was able to confront Elijah Muhammad's distortion of the spirit of Islam and its non-racial worldview. Baldwin's perceptive questions to Elijah Muhammad in *The Fire Next Time* can only be understood within this Istanbul context. It also forced him to change, somewhat, his earlier view of white people. Just as Mecca had changed Malcolm X's hardened views about the 'White Devil', Istanbul was Baldwin's moment of epiphany, too.

To win friends in Istanbul you should not overstate your case.

BLASPHEME

Peerzada Salman

Before I died – beaten black and blue by a lynch mob with a watchman's stick, an iron rod, fists, kicks and head-butts – and before I committed blasphemy, I was a moderate believer. Now that I'm dead, I'm a nonbeliever. Not an atheist, but a nonbeliever.

There's a difference between an atheist and a nonbeliever. The atheist doesn't subscribe to the idea of God. He defies divinity. He doesn't think life is controlled by an outside force, an extra-terrestrial entity. He doesn't buy the notion of the divine, amorphous omnipotence. He says 'no' to Yazdan, mocks Zeus and looks at Shiva with a wry smile.

The nonbeliever just doesn't believe. His grouse is about the truth. Truth – the virgin whore.

Before I died, I was a young man who was into philosophy, literature and music. Or had become one. It is a bit of an anomaly in a country like Pakistan where these subjects aren't deemed fit to lead either a comfortable life or to do well in the Hereafter.

My mother wanted me to become a banker or a teacher at a government-run school. Being a banker would've meant that I had the facility to take loans to build a 120 square feet house and buy an 800CC car. And teaching at a government school would have ensured a pension, a decent amount, so that when I grew older I had something to fall back upon, apart from a son-bearing fecund wife who never missed her period and bled like a jilted lover's heart.

My father, on the other hand, is a science buff. He wanted me to obtain a master's degree in physics or chemistry or any such discipline which allowed me to get into a lab and do all sorts of experiments that made things go bump in the night. But damn that beautiful girl, that virgin whore, Shiba!

Shiba, my classmate in college where I was studying the application of the quadratic equation and the directly proportional relation of volume and temperature, introduced me to that idiot Descartes and that nincompoop Nietzsche. She also made me read the unending ramblings of Leopold Bloom and the pusillanimous poetics of the Prince of Denmark. And that smart cookie, that cunning raconteur Scheherazade. Damn. I liked them all.

So all of it made me run after that virgin whore.

Shiba, like me, comes from a Muslim family. But she belongs to a different sect – a sect that in Pakistan is looked down upon. Their mosques are not even called mosques. They are referred to as 'places of worship'.

I fell in love with Shiba primarily because she is beautiful. The fact that she is into literature, music and philosophy is secondary. Shiba has the face of a firefly and the body of Diane Lane. Is there a sexier woman in the world than Diane Lane?

I didn't know that Shiba once went out with Ayub, the rich, upcountry bugger. Something happened between the two of them, thank God for that, and they broke up. She says they weren't compatible, whatever that means, and Ayub's friends argue she was too opinionated for him. He doesn't like girls with opinions. Girls, he thinks, only have an aesthetic value; they aren't meant to think deep. Deep-thinking makes them lose their marbles. Shiba, being a bluestocking of sorts, took strong issue with Ayub's chauvinism and split.

As long as Shiba was single, it didn't prick Ayub. But the moment she started seeing me, and not even going out with me, just seeing me, because 'seeing' implies the beginning of the 'going-out' phase, it got his goat. I could see that he didn't like it one bit. I could see that his nostrils were getting bigger and bigger. I could see that his upcountry red face was getting redder and redder. I could see that his thick bushy moustache was making funny shapes when he twitched his long, well-placed nose, the nose that could mistake him for a Jewish hobo if he lived in Europe. By the way, Ayub's Christian equivalent is Job. I have no idea what its Jewish equivalent is.

So Ayub was irritated, annoyed and all those words that can be lumped in this category. Shiba told me on our first date at Burger King (my God, what juicy burgers, loved their stuff, and the pickles and veggies, just heavenly) that he got in touch with her and asked her to revisit their relationship. To put it simply, he wanted them back together. To which Shiba replied that she couldn't, she's over him and that that bridge couldn't be built anymore. I heaved a huge sigh of relief and planted a wet kiss on her luscious lips then and there in front of the two dozen burger-chewing men, women and children.

After we were done with our second date, at McDonald's this time, I reached home to start reading 'Immortality'. Of course, Shiba had recommended it. As I slipped into my pyjamas my mobile phone rang. It wasn't a number fed into the phone book or sim card.

'Hello.'

'Hi, this is Ayub.' [He spoke decent English, had done his A Levels from the most expensive school in Lahore.]

'Oh, hi.'

'Listen you twit, if I see you with Shiba again, I'm going to beat the pulp out of you.'

'You hold your tongue mister...'

'Don't tell me to hold anything, you have no idea what I can do to you. I'll have you disappear, vanish into thin air and your parents will keep looking for you for the rest of their lives.'

'Listen Ayub, I'm telling you, don't threaten me, you cannot make me do anything against my will, go and scare off goats and sheep.'

'Ok *bachu*, you'll see...'

He banged the phone down so hard that it hurt my ear. To be honest, his call did affect me but I was so in love I couldn't care much about it. When you are in love, the only thing that you are afraid of is to lose the object of your love. Love toughens the meekest of persons in ways that can shock the cruellest of persons out of their wits.

When I told Shiba she said, 'He barks, he never bites. Trust me, I've been his girlfriend.'

I don't know why, but that gave me a strange pleasure and at the same time put me under pressure. He never bit her. She's unbitten. Did I need to bite in order to be a worthy boyfriend? What's with me and desultory thoughts!

The next day the unthinkable happened. Ayub, along with four or five sturdy boys that one usually sees in the movies as the villain's wingmen, came to Shiba's flat. It was 9 in the morning, which meant that her father would be at work. In case you're wondering where her mother was, well, she died of hepatitis C when Shiba, her only child, was fourteen. Ayub knocked on the door gently. In the next few minutes she was forced to get into his car, pulled by her arm and pushed from behind by two of Ayub's wingmen. Luckily her neighbour, Shahmir, who is my second cousin, saw the whole episode and as soon as they sped away, he phoned me.

I tried to track Ayub down but nobody knew where he was. He and his cronies had gone to, using the phrase used in Pakistan's newspapers, an undisclosed location. For two full days, fuller than the full moon, there was no trace of Shiba. The police were hesitating in filing an FIR because Ayub's father, whom I had the misfortune of shaking hands with at a college event, was a well-connected politician. The police reasoned that, according to their information, the girl had run away with the boy with her own consent, and that she did so because her father opposed their relationship.

Feeling helpless like a bird in a cage, I decided to stage a protest against Ayub in front of his house. I took a big portrait of Shiba, made by an artist at a shopping mall for a paltry sum of Rs100 that I had asked him to make, and reached Ayub's bungalow located in the city's posh locality. Finding myself in a bit of a quandary as to what to do next, I started shouting typical slogans that you hear during political rallies.

'Ayub, you dirty dog, you filthy dog, dirty dirty dog, free Shiba or I'll stage a hunger strike right like Kafka's hunger artist here and die in front of this big mahogany gate...'

I kept repeating these words, in different orders of course, sometimes 'Ayub you dog' came later and 'free Shiba' earlier, sometimes 'I'll stage a hunger strike' became louder and 'die in front of this mahogany gate' got mellower. I managed to get a decent audience. People, mostly young men, started gathering around me looking at me as if I had gone dotty. It was the eleventh time when I said 'Ayub you dog' that Ayub's father came out on the balcony and shouted: 'He is cursing Prophet Ayub, he is cursing him. Can't you hear? Don't you hear? He is abusing our Prophet Ayub, he is constantly calling him a... Are you deaf? Aren't you all Muslims? Don't you know he is seen with that girl whom we all know what group of *kaffirs* she belongs to... and they talk about philosophers who don't believe in God... and all that stuff... He is cursing Prophet Ayub... don't you get it?'

'What?' This was the last word that I ever uttered when I was alive. The crowd which had assembled to see what I was chanting about, got worked up and rushed towards me. One man punched me in the face, another head-butted me and blood plopped out of my nose like red paint dripping off Francis Bacon's brush; then came a heavy slap on my neck... At that point, I saw a boy, about 18-years-old, picking an iron rod used as construction material that a labourer may have left behind, and the old, bearded watchman holding on to his stick tight like never before... I was stunned from the first blow of the iron rod in my back and a second in the forehead made me feel as if I was high on a drug that causes pain and pleasure in equal measure. Gosh, thank God I'm dead.

I'm dead. Dead as a dodo. The good thing is, I can still read. I don't know how. But I'm a non-believing reader. And writer.

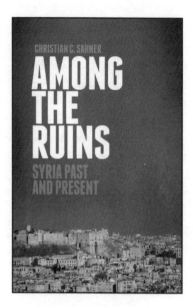

AMONG THE RUINS

SYRIA PAST AND PRESENT

CHRISTIAN C. SAHNER

As a civil war shatters a country and consumes its people, historian Christian Sahner offers a poignant account of Syria, where the past profoundly shapes its dreadful present.

Among the Ruins blends history, memoir and reportage, drawing on the author's extensive knowledge of Syria in ancient, medieval, and modern times, as well as his experiences living in the Levant on the eve of the war and in the midst of the 'Arab Spring'. These plotlines converge in a rich narrative of a country in constant flux — a place renewed by the very shifts that, in the near term, are proving so destructive.

ISBN: 9781849044004
£20.00 / Hardback / 240pp

Sahner focuses on five themes of interest to anyone intrigued and dismayed by Syria's fragmentation since 2011: the role of Christianity in society; the arrival of Islam; the rise of sectarianism and competing minorities; the emergence of the Ba'ath Party; and the current pitiless civil war.

Among the Ruins is a brisk and illuminating read, an accessible introduction to a country with an enormously rich past and a tragic present. For anyone seeking to understand Syria, this book should be their starting point.

'*Among the Ruins* is a uniquely vivid evocation of the past of Syria and a prescient record of its present state. Deeply humane and drawing on subjects from all walks of life, Sahner has a gift for presenting them against a past that is as varied and as ancient as the country itself. We are brought to the edge of the precipice over which, alas, a magnificently diverse society appears to have stumbled. We will be both better informed and wiser for reading it.' — Peter Brown, Rollins Professor Emeritus of History at Princeton University

WWW.HURSTPUBLISHERS.COM/BOOK/AMONG-THE-RUINS

41 GREAT RUSSELL ST, LONDON WC1B 3
WWW.HURSTPUBLISHERS.COM
WWW.FBOOK.COM/HURSTPUBLISHERS
020 7255 2201

TWO GHAZALS

Marilyn Hacker

For Farkhonda and Bina

Ghazal One

Laughter, music, voices singing verses can be heard outside the door.
The little girl is memorising every word outside the door.

Light in the stairwell, seen through the judas-hole:
is that the visitor you longed for or you feared outside the door?

Long hours in lamplight practising his scales,
in counterpoint to solfège of a bird outside the door.

The diplomat entering the leader's office
forgets the Copt, the communist, the Kurd outside the door.

Praise for the leader, loyalty till death!
Another imprecation is whispered outside the door.

The first love left, the second packs her bags.
Are those the nervous footsteps of the third outside the door ?

Self is a mirror, poster-colour bright,
but notice how the colours become blurred outside the door.

The revolutionaries' nameless laundress
wonders 'What happens to a dream deferred ?' outside the door.

Ghazal Two

The moment's motion blurs the pose you hold for it
as if you knew what future were foretold for it.

Is there a course in loss and cutting losses,
and what ought I to do to be enrolled for it?

I could walk to the canal and watch the barges
from the footbridge, but this morning it's too cold for it.

However the diplomat flattered the dictator
or threatened him, ten prisoners were paroled for it.

Who wants to push poems on reluctant readers?
Keep them in notebooks, wait to be cajoled for it.

A lover's hand reaches for the beloved's
hand, as yours would too. Are you too old for it?

Yâ 'ainy, if revolution shakes your stupor
awake, open your eyes, your arms, be bold for it!

REVIEWS

ANWAR'S OUTLOOK

Merryl Wyn Davies

According to the old adage, history repeats itself first as tragedy then as farce. Personally, I think history is not that particular about order and precedence. History, after all, is in the eye of the beholder or, more precisely, the historian. And one should never overlook the possibility of simultaneity, that things are both tragedy and farce at one and the same time. It is much like slapstick comedy which is not to everyone's taste. While there will always be those who guffaw at the carnage of missteps and pratfalls and see only the farcical there will necessarily be others of my disposition who see nothing but cruel and inhuman treatment meted out to undeserving put-upon victims which makes one prone to weep rather than laugh.

As I survey recent events around the Muslim world there is little to make one laugh and no suspicion of slapstick – just a lot of torture. Yet a famous line from that genre often comes to mind: 'Another fine mess you've gotten us into'. This was the constant refrain of Oliver Hardy forever turning the blame for their latest predicament onto the guileless Stan Laurel as Stan scratched his head and wondered how what had seemed so logical and obvious had somehow turned to disaster. It makes one want to weep. In this perspective the Arab Spring is akin to that most iconic of silent slapstick movies *The Plank*. Clearly, in this analogy the plank is symbolic: new building, hope for the future. The narrative, however, turns out the same: man carries plank and gathers a crowd of interested and intrigued followers. Inevitably something makes the man turn and the enthusiastic host who follow get smashed in the face. The man, oblivious to the innumerable dangers in his path, continues on his way turning and turning and with each turn the plank keeps on smashing into innocent followers. Think of the plank of wood as the serial elections that have followed the outpouring of euphoria in Egypt's Tahrir Square and you see what I mean.

What the Arab Spring has proved beyond reasonable doubt is that it is not sufficient to hope and demonstrate, even with the consummate courage these acts of defiance require in nations that, whatever they lack, are amply supplied with well-equipped repressive dragoons of police and army. It is also evident that something more than elections is necessary to create a genuine new dispensation of sustainable democratic good governance. Authoritarian rule is not just about figureheads, familiar dictators. The power they manipulate to maintain themselves is institutionalised, embedded in deep structures of privilege that corruptly deliver a nation's bounty into the hands of a chosen few. Institutionalised authoritarian power constructs the terrain of nationhood as an obstacle course designed with determined purpose to forestall and frustrate all efforts to effect change by mere popular will. Simply putting the X in another box is only part, the lesser part of the task.

Nowhere better demonstrates the complex nature of the challenge that so far has confounded the Arab Spring than Malaysia, where the definition of the problem and quest to achieve sustainable democratic good governance began some years before the outbreak of the Arab Spring and remains ongoing.

The conventional narrative of Malaysian politics in turbulent times is presented as a succession struggle centred on the fate of Anwar Ibrahim. Anwar was considered the heir apparent to the long serving Prime Minister, Mahathir Muhammad. It was Mahathir who had brought the radical activist Anwar into the fold of the ruling UMNO (United Malays National Organisation) party and then rapidly advanced his ministerial career. The most charismatic and popular figure in Mahathir's lacklustre administration, Anwar rose through the ranks to become Finance Minister and Deputy Prime Minister. The question clearly was when would Mahathir, whose actual age is never precise but was well into his eighth decade, step down? Much had been achieved, much was changing rapidly in Malaysia and much needed remedying. Speculation was rife that the time for a generational change was at hand. Out with the old making room for a new better cleaner dispensation in government with Anwar in the lead. Camps were aligning themselves as Anwar or Mahathir loyalists. There were naïve and overzealous efforts to bring the issue of succession to the top of the political agenda. In a culture where gossip is an art form as well as a national pastime the capital, Kuala Lumpur, is sufficiently small and coherent: the concentrated living space for all interested in politics, business and administration for the rumour mill to be in overdrive 24/7.

What actually happened was not among the scenarios debated at the tea stalls. On 2 September 1998 Anwar was summarily sacked from his cabinet posts and later expelled from the ruling party UMNO. The ostensible reason concerned a swirl of allegations of sexual misconduct and misuse of office. Anwar was arrested and badly beaten while in custody by none other than the Inspector General of Police. The legal proceedings that followed came to be known as Sodomy I, which led to a sentence of six years imprisonment for Anwar, with Sodomy II the legal morass that continues to embroil Anwar today. In Sodomy II his acquittal on the charges can become guilty on appeal and more appeals await.

Charles Allers, *Anwar Ibrahim: Evolution of a Muslim Democrat*, Monsoonbooks, Singapore, 2013; first published as *Evolution of a Muslim Democrat: Life of Malaysia's Anwar Ibrahim*, Peter Lang, New York, 2013.

The court cases have been truly Dickensian in their serpentine course and duration as well as lending as much support as possible to Dickens' dictum that 'the law is an ass'. Anwar and his lawyers have consistently sought to argue, and been denied the right to present this defence, that the charges are politically motivated fabrications designed to destroy his reputation. Several libel and defamation cases, which Anwar has won, have accompanied the main drama. International observers such as Amnesty International and Human Rights Watch have deemed the trials political and criticised the nature and conduct of the proceedings. And yet, as opinion polls have shown, the greater part of the Malaysian public still does not believe any of the charges to be true. Nevertheless the trials achieved their clear objective by ensuring Anwar has been unable to stand in most of the elections of the last seventeen years.

Politics, however, is more than elections. When Anwar was sacked from government he became the focus of an unprecedented outpouring of popular protest in a country and culture groomed for quiet acceptance and respect for authority. Yet Anwar is more than a figurehead or emblematic cause celebre victim. He is the principal articulator of the analysis of genuine reform, thoroughgoing change to sweep aside the structures of authoritarian control and the inequity they beget and that sustains them. His analysis reveals the context in which events occur and pinpoints the problematic eventualities that become the normal practice that orders an environment of corruption, cronyism and nepotism where democracy is made into a gerrymandered veneer to serve and keep the powerful in power. It is the diligence and energy Anwar applies to broadcasting an alternate vision of good governance that have made him an important voice not only in Malaysia but around the Muslim world.

Charles Allers' book seeks to track what he calls the evolution of a Muslim democrat. Therein lies part of the problem. Evolution – descent with change – infers and presumes one does not begin as a Muslim democrat. In this heavy hinting, Allers is in line with all the array of writers and commentators on Malaysian politics that he quotes and references. The possibilities for democracy within the context of Islam is a subject to be interrogated, it is a questionable category. The generalised lack of democratic instincts in Muslim populations, a standard trope of Western analysis since the sixteenth century, explains why authoritarian rulers proliferate and tyranny has such easy reign in nation after nation. When Muslim democracy is the rare beast being tracked through the jungle it is little wonder that a lot of the important landscape and topography slips out of focus.

Like many commentators, Allers starts with Anwar's early career as an activist and founder of ABIM, a Malaysian Islamic youth movement. He gives the familiar context of the post-independence condition of Malaysia a multi-ethnic, multi-religious country where the indigenous Malay population were marginalised, impoverished and sensitive to being swamped by the Chinese, who dominated the economy, and Indian populations that had been imported to serve the colonial regime. In this context to be Malay is to be Muslim. Therefore it is little surprise that Islam serves as the natural rhetoric for justice and equity which has special reference to the specific conditions and needs of the Malays but does not necessarily, certainly not inevitably, imply a lack of tolerance or openness. And yet it could easily be otherwise.

Anwar was active in protesting the conditions of rural Malay poverty at a time of particular tension. It was at this time that Mahathir Mohamma was writing *The Malay Dilemma* a book which excoriated the West condemned the colonial era and was heavily apologetic and chauvinistic about the Malay condition. Circumstance can make for uneasy political cohabitation. Both Anwar and Mahathir considered the Malaysian government was not making sufficient effort to uplift the condition of the Malay majority and therefore failing to deliver on the promise of independence. Agreement and collaboration on policy is pragmatism, the particular political disease which inoculates politicians allowing activity without common identity of outlook. It could and should be said that Anwar began as a natural democrat using the rhetoric of Islam and Malay issues while Mahathir began as a natural authoritarian with an insular ethnic bias. What brought them together was politics, or as British Prime Minister Harold Macmillan so succinctly described it 'events dear boy, events.' To be political is to deal with the events of the day along with all other array of politicians engaged in events. Islam and Malayness are not invariable givens that impact on individuals in exactly the same way.

That Muslim democracy is the natural and best way is the leitmotif of Anwar's career. That Islam is the source from which he draws his inspiration as a democrat, his ideals of justice and equity, tolerance and openness is evident in the quotations Allers selects from a busy life of speech making and writing. What Allers, like so many political commentators, is less willing to acknowledge is the business of politics. Principle is forever, policy is all adaptation, changes in the articulation of how principle is to be translated into policy. Politics is events, change and circumstance that have to be harnessed and ushered as best they can to the objectives of principle. Politicians are constrained by their environment and access to power. Radical politics, the politics of change, however much it may irritate theorisers, is impossible without access to the levers of power. One must gain control before one can shift those levers in more democratic equitable and just directions.

It is the specific nature and orientation of the levers of power in Malaysia that are the concern of Anwar's career in politics. Malaysia has been ruled since independence by a coalition of communal based political parties: UMNO for the Malays, MCA (Malaysian Chinese Association) for the Chinese, MIC (Malaysian Indian Congress) for the Indians, that issues and interests could transcend ethnic boundaries was not on the list of political possibles. After the race riots of 1969 a New Economic Policy (NEP) was crafted as a national objective for growth and development with redistribution designed to redress and advance the participation of Malays in education and the economy. The communal based political parties were conduits of patronage through which the benefits of the NEP would be distributed. By definition government would be the central actor in fashioning economic growth and effecting redistribution, which thereby tied the populace to the communal party political structure. Malaysia became a totally politicised country, a nation where calculating the political runes and operating accordingly if one hoped to succeed, but especially if one worked in any arm of government, public service or business, is first nature.

Mahathir became Prime Minister in 1981, a post he held for 22 years. Throughout his career Mahathir has enjoyed a following across the Third World, the formerly colonised nations of the South as a radical critic of the West and all its nefarious ways. His cachet goes hand in hand with his various updating of the NEP through the Look East phase, modelling economic planning on the economies of South Korea and Taiwan to make Malaysia part of what was called the East Asian Economic miracle. Then there was Vision 2020, the plan to make Malaysia a fully industrialised country by that year. It survives his deregulation and privatisation policies which created the nexus of cronies who have become the mega rich, the Malaysiarchs. It also endured through the vanity mega projects he conceived, from building a new capital city to a Formula 1 race track. Deregulation and privatisation has made no difference to government as central to the structure of inequitable wealth and power distribution. Government must work with the powerhouses constructed under its tutelage and business gets business from government. This is the legacy of Mahathir's stamp on power. He purposefully designed the concept of strong business corporations controlling crucial sectors of the economy as the essence of being a fully developed economy. In doing so he was working to the Western economic playbook. Far from creating an alternative to the dominant system he formed a locally controlled offshoot.

Cronyism and nepotism became endemic during the Mahathir years. Corruption was the staple of tea stall gossip because it was normal practice. The problems came to roost with the contagion of the currency crisis which began in Thailand and rapidly spread around the region. In Malaysia many overstretched cronies were in dire trouble. Much like the banks in the West in more recent times they clamoured for cover from government. Mahathir again donned the mantle of scourge of the West by insisting on currency controls and rudely rebuffing the IMF. Behind his closed currency walls, however, it was the revitalisation of the inequities of crony capitalism that was to be effected by the diversion of public funds. And therein lay the rub. Anwar opposed the currency controls and refused to go along with using public funds to rescue reckless capitalists, notable among them Mahathir's own son. It was at that point that Anwar was summarily sacked.

The charges of sodomy were a façade drawn over the substantive political difference that existed. From the moment he was sacked crowds flocked around Anwar. In no time at all he formulated the agenda of Reformasi which has matured, grown in rhetorical sophistication of argument rather than substance in the subsequent years. At the heart of the reformation of Malaysia is the deconstruction of the communal based view of politics. During his years in government, Anwar kept developing the theme of Malaysia as a truly multicultural nation. The logical culmination of this outlook is a new development policy which replaces the dependency growth of Malay economic interests with affirmative action according to need, irrespective of race or ethnicity. The political party of which Anwar is now de facto leader, Keadilan, is indeed a multicultural, multi-ethnic, multi-religious party of Malaysians. It is doubtful any other politician could have effected such a momentous sea change. Perhaps one ought to stop wondering whether Anwar needed to evolve as a democrat and start realising it was the circumstances of Malaysian society and politics that had to alter.

Allers offers a painstaking track through the life and times of Anwar Ibrahim. His book is the most copiously footnoted I have ever read. Sadly it reads like a student dissertation and one that would have been well served by better editing. Anyone seeking a compendium for resources about Malaysia will be well served by his footnotes and bibliography.

However, the cautious framing of his questioning and relentless focus on the person of Anwar rather than the context of circumstance and events leads Allers to miss some of the most salient points. It is the deep structure of inequity that are the substance of the issues articulated by Anwar that matter most. The inequity, for example, of the gerrymandering of constituencies that meant the opposition triumphed in the popular vote in the 2013 elections yet won fewer seats than the UMNO dominated Barisan. Election fraud is beside the point if governments can cling to power by rigging the entire system. To change an inequitable system requires more than one man. It needs all those officials who turn their eyes to and take their cue from political masters to accept their own responsibility for running judiciary, police, electoral commissions, anti-corruption agencies and the like without fear or favour. Politicians exhort, it is people who deliver change.

Anwar Ibrahim has been consistent in making a coherent and increasingly cogent case for open, tolerant democracy. Allers fails to note that Mahathir not only left the imprint of inequitable development on Malaysia but continues to be the *eminence grise* who manipulates from behind the scenes. In fact Mahathir is the icon and spokesperson of the embedded structures' inequity. Allers would have done well to note that Mahathir has seen off one successor Prime Minister, Abdullah Badawi, and publically speculated about his willingness to replace the second, the current incumbent Najib Tun Razak. As Najib founders in the wake of his electoral weakness and the debacle of the handling of the loss of the MH 370 airliner, he is trimming his supposed reforms to the familiar contours of Mahathir's preferred plan. Electoral weakness means only one thing to Mahathir: Malay insecurity. There can be no mistaking the support and encouragement he has given to the openly racist Perkasa movement, a sort of local Malay defence league.

Malaysia is a beautiful country, rich in resources and possibilities. It is a test case of the real agenda for change and democracy in the Muslim World. It is clear that in Malaysia, as elsewhere in so many other countries, change will come at personal cost. Change will require more than just elections: it requires dismantling the institutional structures of inequity, most of all it will depend upon building the strength and capacity of civil society, the plethora of organisations and associations by which ordinary people hold their governments to account. The quest for democracy and good governance is not unique to the Muslim world. The democracy deficit is rife in Britain or the United States too. The motion that the democratic instinct is unique to the West and somehow deficient in the Muslim world is absurd. Power prevents and power has to be confronted for democracy to reign supreme. Not all the power that prevents and prevaricates the democratic quest comes from within Muslim nations. Anwar has spent his career speaking for and articulating an agenda of politics as the art of what we wish were possible. Making it so is everyone's assignment.

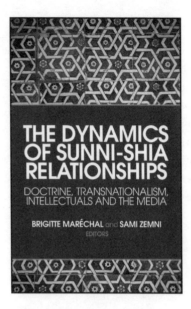

The Dynamics of Sunni-Shia Relationships

Doctrine, Transnationalism, Intellectuals and the Media

Edited by Brigitte Maréchal and Sami Zemni

ISBN: 9781849042178
£39.99 / Hardback / 320pp

Before the immense changes of the 2011 'Arab Spring', it was Sunni-Shia sectarian rivalry that preoccupied most political analyses of the Middle East. This book presents wide-ranging and up-to-date research that sheds light on the political, sociological and ideological processes that are affecting the dynamics within, as well as the relationships between, the Shia and Sunni worlds.

The growing tensions and occasional clashes between believers in the two main strands of Islam have been major concerns. Upheavals within the Shia sphere of influence had altered the relationship: the Iranian revolution of 1979 changed the politics of Iranian Shiism, and impacted on Shia communities regionally, while the 2003 Anglo-American invasion of Iraq initiated a new phase of tension in Sunni-Shia relations. The spectre of a sectarian war in Iraq, a diplomatic and military offensive against the Lebanese Hezbollah and a potentially nuclear armed Iran (along with Tehran's support for Hamas) prompted King Abdullah II of Jordan to warn of an emerging 'Shia crescent'. However, away from such grand geopolitical gestures, Sunni-Shia relations are being rearticulated through an array of local, regional and global connections.

This book presents wide-ranging and up-to-date research that sheds light on the political, sociological and ideological processes that are affecting the dynamics within, as well as the relationships between, the Shia and Sunni worlds. Among the themes discussed are the ideological and doctrinal evolutions that are taking place, the contextualisation of the main protagonists' political practices, transnational networks, and the role of intellectuals, religious scholars and the media in shaping and informing this dynamic relationship.

'A must-read for anyone seeking to understanding Sunni-Shia dynamics in the wake of the Arab Uprisings.' — Peter Mandaville, George Mason University, author of *Global Political Islam*

WWW.HURSTPUBLISHERS.COM/BOOK/THE-DYNAMICS-OF-SUNNI-SHIA-RELATIONSHIPS

 HURST PUBLISHERS

41 GREAT RUSSELL ST, LONDON WC1B
WWW.HURSTPUBLISHERS.COM
WWW.FBOOK.COM/HURSTPUBLISHERS
020 7255 2201

PANAHI'S RUMINATIONS

Suhail Ahmad

It was one of Orson Wells' most iconic creations, Harry Lime, who made the point that culture thrives on conflict and antagonism. And if you view art to be a refined expression of culture, then you'd be hard pushed to find a better example of Lime's words than the achievement of Iranian filmmaker Jafar Panahi. Charged on 1 March 2010 for disseminating 'propaganda against the Islamic Republic' (by supporting those who were protesting the re-election of the Iranian president Mahmoud Ahmadinejad), the authorities marked Panahi out as a dangerous freethinker. He was subsequently placed under house arrest and banned from writing scripts or making films for the next twenty years. And so this highly decorated filmmaker was cast into purgatory, the remainder of his career consigned to drown in the amniotic fluid of his unbirthable movies. But Panahi refused to accept the punishment. He turned the camera on himself, made himself the subject of a 'non-cinematic' event, and in doing so has managed to capture – with incredible dignity and aplomb – the agony of an artist who cannot tell his stories.

It shouldn't be that much of a surprise, really. Somehow art manages to find a way to burrow out of even the heaviest slab of censorship, and, better still, assume an edge that is sharper and more piercing as a result of these constraints. Indeed, the Iranian film industry bears testament to this phenomenon. The numbers alone tell a story: in 2012, more than 150 films were made in Iran, many of which have garnered worldwide recognition. It appears that Iran's draconian laws are doing little to dampen the creative spirit – in fact censorship is clearly seen as a challenge by its film industry and is having the opposite effect. As hardliners nibble away at human rights while censors continue to turn the screw on what's permissible, the arthouse faction has become more introspective, subtle and nuanced in the way it is exploring the effects of suppression on the human psyche. This has seen a rise in character-centred narratives shot in cramped settings which contrasts with the more expansive Iranian films of the 1990s.

In the case of *This Is Not a Film*, however, there wasn't any kind of plea-bargaining with the authorities. The film was made and then reportedly smuggled out of Iran in a USB stick, which was hidden inside a cake as it crossed the border and arrived at the Cannes Film Festival to take its place amongst grand cinematic pieces such as Terrence Malick's *The Tree of Life* and Lars Von Trier's *Melancholia*. This makes the film something of a celebration, a victory for freedom against the odds, not to mention a testament to Panahi's creative genius thriving despite the woefully limited means of production at his disposal. After finding out that their film had reached Cannes, one can only imagine the tears of joy Panahi and co-director, Mojtaba Mirtahmasb, must have shed.

Shot partly on a digital camcorder and partly on an iPhone, we are taken through a day in the life of Panahi, and are made voyeurs in what appears to be an artless video diary and, at best, a documentary running at a little over 75 minutes. Idle and uptight, Panahi is living out his days in the prosaic comforts of his high-rise apartment, which somehow makes his situation feel more desperate. A director whose debut feature, *The White Balloon* (1995), picked up a prize at Cannes and whose subsequent films have impressed audiences the world over, he finds himself puttering alone in the house, seemingly marooned, the middle years of his life now bleeding away in a state of incarceration. It is the eve of the Persian New Year, and his wife and daughter have gone to visit family, leaving him in the company of their pet iguana Igi, who is given licence to roam the apartment and whose interactions with Panahi offer moments of light relief.

From the outset the film has a deliberately downplayed demeanour. It is as if Panahi is mindful not to make his statement any more than what is it and risk presenting himself as some kind of martyr and turn his project into a polemic or protest film. No, that would run counter to an oeuvre that has forgone delivering big blows to empire in favour of creating characters whose tacit rebellions tell a more nuanced story. Yet, even with such a straightforward and seemingly uninspiring set up (a man holed up in his house), what follows is a subtle interplay between Panahi's ruminations on the processes of his own filmmaking, the artless businesses of his daily life, the sense of danger attached to the risk he is taking by breaking – if not severely bending – the terms of his ban, the sum of which is bound together in a subtle yet wonderfully cinematic meta-narrative that manages to blur the line between fiction and reality. In the wake of the final act, one wonders whether we spent the last hour and quarter in the company of a despairing man or in fact caught in the spell of a consummate storyteller. Despite the seemingly unstructured nature of the film it is interesting to note that the film was shot in four sessions over a ten-day period; some parts were written, some sketched out, and others came about through happenstance. Indeed the amusing interludes with the pet animals are just one of many clues that suggest reference to certain narrative conventions. As such the film is completely conscious of what it is and what it claims to be, and it is anything but an artless home movie or video essay.

This Is Not a Film directed by Jafar Panahi and Mojtaba Mirtahmasb, written by Jafar Panahi, produced by Jafar Panahi and distributed by Kanibal Film Distribution (France).

In Persian, 2011.

The film opens with a still shot of Panahi alone, sitting at his breakfast table. He is putting jam and spread on his bread, and then tinkers with his mobile phone whilst eating. He has an idea to lift his spirits: unable to make his last film project, he will talk about it instead. He calls his friend Mirtahmasb, a documentary maker, and asks him to come round to record his telling of the story. What is made clear from the start is that in order to make this 'documentary' and be seen to be obeying the terms of his ban at least, Panahi must relinquish his role as director and stay in front of the camera, giving Mirtahmasb complete creative control. It is a situation that is footnoted later on in a poignant moment when Panahi says 'cut' which Mirtahmasb must ignore, unable as he is to take directions from the banned Panahi. This precaution is purely semantic, of course, and merely thrusts a spotlight on the severity of his plight.

After taking a shower we see Panahi talking to his lawyer on speakerphone for the latest update on his court appeal against his sentencing. The news isn't promising (while there is a chance the length of the ban might be reduced, he will definitely have to serve the prison sentence): 'So from what you're saying I should pack my bag and put it by the front door,' he says ruefully. Although underpinned by a stoic acceptance, Panahi's dejection is palpable.

Tense and alone, Panahi cuts a tormented figure lounging around his apartment, not so much like the auteur figure he is, but a creature that has had its wings clipped and is kept in a gilded cage. All the while, we hear what sounds like gunfire going off outside in sporadic bursts, but what turns out to be traditional New Year fireworks, albeit defying government prohibition (as suggested by a news report Panahi watches on TV). Nevertheless, these sounds exacerbate Panahi's sense of isolation. One suspects they aren't coincidental but a planned addition to the mise-en-scene that show the extent to which the authority is out of touch with the people. Indeed, standing on his balcony, Panahi films the celebrations with his iPhone, and in doing so shows that the authorities cannot stop acts of expression, be they his own or the country's at large.

While he is clearly not wanting for food, Panahi is starving creatively and his daily frustrations have mounted so high that he appears on the brink of an onscreen meltdown. We see Panahi hunched over, clutching his arms in mental agony; eventually he dispenses with the film's fourth wall convention and stares directly into the camera: 'I think I should remove this cast and throw it away.' It is a wonderful moment that borrows the modus operandi of Brechtian theatre. By addressing the camera so calmly, Panahi shakes the viewer from passively accepting what is unfolding on screen. He wants his audience to judge the film with a critical mind. In a way, unable to make the films he wants, he uses the opportunity to direct the viewer instead, opening their eyes to the power of art.

It is at this juncture that we arrive at the film's intellectual soul. Panahi discusses the art of filmmaking while showing the viewer clips from his previous movies. His eyes and soul come alive – a god waking from a giant slumber. It is an exhilarating evocation of how his films are painstakingly made, how thought is given to the smallest detail, and how the strength of artistic expression lies in nuance. He begins the seminar by alluding to one of his films, *The Circle*, and discusses the organic nature of an amateur actor's performance – the surprising improvisations that he could never have thought of and how they enhanced the scene's dramatic effect.

Secondly, in another one of his films, *The Mirror*, he shows us a child actor breaking character and throwing a tantrum and explains how her emotional outburst becomes more interesting than the scene itself. And, thirdly, he explains the power of *mise-en-scene,* while playing a series of shots from a film showing a woman running through a corridor. This master class offers a clue that what we're watching is far more than a day-in-the-life documentary. The passage serves as a kind of hall of mirrors in which each example would later be reflected in the seemingly real world of the video diary. It is almost the equivalent of a mastermind killer leaving clues for the chasing detective, so they could marvel at the man's ingenuity. What's more, the signposting of these elements attests to the filmmaker's artistry in defying the laws of his ban while pouring more irony over the film's title. In laymen's terms, it is nothing short of sticking two fingers up at the authorities.

Once Mirtahmasb arrives, he handles the camera and sound while Panahi sits astride a chair holding the screenplay of the film that never got made. He explains that by telling the story, as opposed to filming it, he will not be violating the court's order. Soon he gets up and begins staging the setting of his film (which also happens to be a house where his protagonist is imprisoned, although these parallels are left unspoken). In the living room, he uses tape to mark out the space representing the house, indicating the position of props and actors, the length of the shots, and he even reads out parts of the dialogue. Like a sudden burst of Technicolor, Panahi's passion fills the screen; he is on creative overdrive trying to channel the ideas that have been turning circles in his imagination for a long time; in this brisk sequence one sees how every atom of his being is perfectly honed to the task of telling a story. However, amidst this rush of childish abandon, in a heartbreaking moment, he suddenly pauses and, drained of all enthusiasm, addresses the camera: 'If we could tell a film, then why make a film?' It is here that we realise how much the man is suffering. One suspects that here is a man who is willing to die for his art.

That sacrificial act arguably comes in the final act of the film. Just as Mirtahmasb is about to leave for the night, having set up the camera so it can continue filming Panahi, a young man arrives at the door. He is a friendly college student who is collecting the apartment's rubbish and is filling in for regular bin man. Charmed by the young man and sensing that the camera will warm to him, Panahi grabs the camera and begins following him down the lift. For all his charm, the man is evasive about who he is and what he is studying. It is at this moment that one wonders whether the young man is the bait that will lure Panahi outside with camera in hand, and dispatch him red-handed into waiting cuffs of the authorities. It is a truly Kafkaesque finale that forces us to reflect on everything we have seen so far, more so because it echoes the storyline of the film that was never made in which the imprisoned girl falls for a young man who turns out to be a snitch for the secret police.

This Is Not a Film is a wonderful achievement. While it may have a quiet voice, which will barely register with the mainstream sensibility so accustomed to explosions and excess, it delivers an epic message about the power and intelligence of art. Panahi's life is not simply documented in the film – it is pulled apart, examined, reconstituted and dramatised. In Panahi's hand (speaking metaphorically of course), the camera is a storytelling device masquerading as a transparent lens. What we are presented with isn't a video essay, but a piece of cinema that is very much comparable to his other films such as *Crimson Gold* (2003) and *Offside* (2006) in which his protagonists suffer from daily humiliations that they have to find ways to deal with. So while technically this is a film with all meat stripped off the bone, it is this shortcoming that gives the film its unique strength. Indeed, in many respects *This is Not a Film* is a masterpiece with a sleight of hand that the great Orson Wells would have been proud of.

ARENDT'S EICHMANN

Iftikhar H. Malik

Hannah Arendt focuses on her life in New York during the prime of her academic career. In 1961, she was asked by William Shawn, the editor of *The NewYorker*, to write an eyewitness account of the trial, in Israel, of Otto Adolf Eichmann, the German Nazi colonel and a major organiser of the Holocaust. Mostly in English, though it sometimes turns to German and occasionally Hebrew, it begins with the capture of Eichmann. A torch holding, stooped man of medium build is shown walking down the road like those miners of yesteryear heading towards now closed Welsh pits. He is effortlessly bundled into the back of a truck. The Israeli agents had been stalking his movements and uncovered his rather obscure life in Argentina. This scoop and the future trial of a leading Nazi engaged Jewish communities in a heated debate, since it promised an iota of accountability and a semblance of redress to the memory of Holocaust victims and their near ones, while heralding Mossad's transregional capability in netting such high-profile but underground criminals. By that time, Arendt was already an established academic writer and commentator on political philosophy with special interest in totalitarianism of which she was both a witness and victim.

There is much about Arendt's life that we ought to know before the events depicted in the film. Arendt was born to a liberal Jewish family in Hanover, Germany. She began studying philosophy at eighteen at the University of Marburg with the German philosopher Martin Heidegger (1889-1976). Both soon developed a passionate relationship though subsequently they took separate ideological pathways, as Heidegger became a Nazi supporter, which not only compromised his own stature, but critics also used this against Arendt when she subsequently covered the Eichmann trial. She later moved to Heidelberg where, still in her twenties, she was able to finish and publish her doctoral research on the concept of love in St Augustine's thoughts under the supervision of existentialist philosopher, Karl Jasper (1883-1969). However, she could not formally 'habilitate' because of her Jewishness. Her research on Anti-Semitism in Germany incurred investigations by the Gestapo, which made her flee to France in 1933. In 1937, Arendt was deprived of her German nationality, and three years later she married Heinrich Blucher (1899-1979), the German Marxist philosopher. Following the German conquest of France, Arendt was arrested in 1940, labelled as 'enemy alien' and taken to Camp Gur. She was able to escape within a few weeks through the timely help of Hiram Bingham, an American, who had reputedly helped 2,000 Jews to flee from Nazi sleuths. She found her way to the United States accompanied by her mother and husband.

Hannah Arendt directed by Margarethe von Trotta, written by Margarethe von Trotta and Pam Katz, produced by Heimatfilm.

In English, German, French and Hebrew. Germany/France, 2013.

As a vocal part of a German Jewish émigré group, she helped younger Jews migrate to Palestine-Israel and held a visiting fellowship at Berkeley and Chicago until she became the first ever faculty woman at Princeton in 1959. Her circle in New York included the Jaspers and Mary McCarthy, the noted contemporary American author. It was during this early phase of her life in the United States that she published *The Origins of Totalitarianism* (1951). It caused quite an intellectual uproar. Her Leftist critics felt that by juxtaposing Nazism with Stalinism as two sides of the same coin, she had been irreverent to progressive ideas of Marxism. Having experienced Nazism first hand and cognisant of Stalin's purges, she had no qualms in coupling them together as two parallel and stupendously violent manifestations of totalitarianism that denied public space, frowned upon dissent and made individuals commit violence against fellow citizens in the name of a unilateral ideology. Nazism and its large-scale violence against Jews and Romas had been exposed. But Stalin's stance on Western imperialism and construction of a Soviet utopia on the ruins of Tsarist travesties still enjoyed a significant following during the Cold War. Arendt had touched some raw nerves. Her fellow co-religionists and intellectuals accused her of attacking Marxism in the guise of dissection of totalitarianism. She ended up antagonising both traditional and secular Jews in the United States and Israel.

She also had another demi-god in her sights. In her early works, Arendt had detected human vulnerability to collective violence attributable to a wide variety of disparate sources including an uncritiqued modernity, which, to her, was binary and even Hydra faced. Arendt was herself a product and keen witness of this Western modernity especially in its postulations hinging on democracy and scientific progress, yet saw in it the shrinking of public space leaving individual to a solitary and certainly vulnerable existence. According to Arendt's *The Human Condition* (1958) modernity had caused the eclipse of tradition, family and religion. While it allowed space for some private introspection, it was essentially overwhelmed by systemic interests. At a sinister level, it augured the age of bureaucratic administration featuring only anonymous labour, resulting in the triumph of *animal laborans* over *homo faber*. These negative portents of modernist hierarchical hegemonies, to her, led to the totalitarian movements such as Nazism and Stalinism since they tended to homogenise community in an inherent conformist mould. In *The Human Condition*, she appears more focused on negative aspects of modernity. This may be due to her own bitter experiences with nationalism in Europe assuming a more exclusivist and coercive shape. Perhaps, she also felt like Muhammad Iqbal (1887–1938), who a generation earlier, had alerted his readers to the viciousness of a virile and highly masculinised form of nationalism that not only eliminated moral ethos but also regimented a recourse to militarism. Not an historian herself, Arendt still felt confident enough to suggest that modernity had created a rupture in Occidental history rendering many of our hitherto political and moral categories meaningless. To her, the Holocaust and Gulag both were the causes and results of a rupture in the experience of modernity. Her celebration of human *narrative*, of art and literature, stemmed from a greater respect for history and poetry, which kept human virtues and valour alive for successive generations by ensuring inclusive and more supporting public space. Arendt, essentially banking on Western historical discourse, saw the emergence of modernity in two distinct stages: the first from the sixteenth to the nineteenth century, while the second falling within the complex and volatile matrix of the twentieth. One may differ with her on two counts: her almost total negative understanding of modernity, and secondly, her insistence on separating the public and private, and the social and political. In the later case, she somehow failed to see their fluid boundaries, which, in several instances, obviated their dialectical interface. For instance, in her personal and intellectual preoccupation with totalitarianism, she could not fully grasp the significant expansion of justice and rights blurring the boundaries between private and public, or between social and political spheres.

Her most famous phrase, 'the banality of evil' emerged from the coverage of the Eichmann trail. In the film, we see Arendt observing the trial in Jerusalem and jotting down an unending medley of notes. She meets an old friend, Kurt Blumenfeld, who tells her that Eichmann appears in the trial as an unimpressive, ordinary man. She too is taken aback by Eichmann's ordinariness and mediocrity. She had assumed he would be uniquely dripping with evil and cruelty writ large on his persona; instead, he appeared more like a routine individual of rather slim build without any aura of being uniquely sinister. She could not bring herself around to accept the dictum that the man held in the dock had so much of Jewish blood on his hands. The film, in fact, shows the original archival material from the Israeli court proceedings where a wooden Eichmann speaks in a monotonous, emotionless way to the Israeli judges and lawyers without displaying any repentance. Over the cafe conversation, where a reference is made to the Faust story, Arendt refuses to accept that Eichmann was in any way Mephisto, the evil, or a noxious embodiment of psychopathic hatred.

The film is neither a documentary nor a full reportage on Arendt's life; instead it focuses on the trial and the discursive controversy about her own understanding of the role of violent totalitarianism in turning ordinary people like Eichmann into unquestioning murders. It is fascinating to see Jewish émigrés getting into heated discussion in German on Arendt's reports with their American colleagues sitting mute trying to make sense of their passionate gesticulations. Arendt comes out as a complex character embodying intellectual courage, creativity and even complicity. Her views cause controversy and pain yet he she refuses to budge. The film is exceptionally well directed and has some strong performances at its core. It raises a string of questions but they are all left in the air.

Arendt was aptly sensitive to the exigencies of citizenship, pluralism and freedom seeing in them the core of a participatory political system that would disallow totalitarianism. She also gave primacy to work ethics, sounding more like a neo-liberal. But Arendt enveloped it with imagination so as to ward off a mechanical conformity to work ethics. Perhaps this was the very trait that she did not detect in people like Eichmann, who despite the enormity of their share in committing heinous crime, still did not seem to ever possess second thought about it.

In a sense, the film is a reconstruction of Arendt's role as a thoughtful chronicler of Eichmann's trial using it to study the whys and hows of collective violence, where ideologies become the straightjackets of uniformist hierarchies with human agents simply morphed into robots. This total heedlessness, to her, was the callous banality lacking critique and imagination while parading itself as the sole authority. She had finally found the answer to her instinctive question: how come ordinary, normal and even otherwise well-meaning people can commit such horrendous atrocities? Her analysis went beyond a typified blanket caricature of stern-looking Nazi criminal and instead saw him as a cog in a machine awash in a form of mechanical indifference, devoid of any of his own conscientious views on what he was doing. To her, larger forces drained the critical and moral faculties of such individuals so they end up performing malfeasance of a stupendous magnitude as a job like any other. Eichmann was an organisation man. Such a premise was not going to sit well with people who held a unitary view of all Nazis per se and saw them at par with one another, consciously and intently primed to enforce the Holocaust. Here critics saw her position as ironic form of diminution. Arendt attempted to defend herself in her private meetings, through her writings and by using public forums including a lecture to the younger audience in the university, with which the film ends.

Arendt's essays on the trial were published in 1963 as *Eichmann in Jerusalem: The Banality of Evil*. The book incurred a severe backlash from Jewish groups who felt as if by looking at a broad picture she was partially absolving Eichmann of the enormity of his crimes. Letters, death threats and serious annoyance even from closer relatives and associates did not deter her from further research on violence and human nature and she came to be known as a preeminent philosopher on the subject though she preferred to be known only as a political theorist. A chain smoker, she stayed loyal to Heidegger's ideas on primacy of thinking—which further inflamed her critics—as she viewed politics to be a major human preoccupation where revolution, violence, reformism and even 'banality of evil' would happen depending upon structural realities in a given society where normal bureaucrats like Eichmann may commit brutalities as mere instruments and not as architects. She died in 1975 of cardiac arrest and was buried in Bard College which also contains her archives.

It is interesting to note what contemporary Jewish intellectuals would make of Arendt's position. While it is convenient for commentators like Bernard Lewis, Daniel Pipe, Paul Berman, Pamela Geller and others to depict entire Muslim heritage as Islamofascism, in league with European totalitarianism, one wonders about their defence of statist and societal travesties against the Palestinians. Many of my Jewish friends and groups certainly feel uncomfortable how their history has taken a strange and rather ironic turn. On the one hand, they now have their own state, which is increasingly powerful and negates all those stereotypes about Jews being a permanent minority and too docile to fight. On the other hand, their state has unleashed a serious moral dilemma: it is responsible for the exile of generations of Palestinians who, in fact, had no issues with Jews as such. The dispossession of 750,000 Palestinians in 1948, who number three million now and remain displaced through no fault of their own, is constantly underpinned by a denial of their right to return by those very people who apply the same justification to bring in Jews from all over the world. Violence through settlements, detentions and sheer invasions with horrible portents like the massacre of Sabira and Shatila may never recede and, on the contrary, have led to people like Avi Shlaim, Noam Chomsky, Primo Levy, Judith Miller, Illan Pape, Uri Avnery and many others abdicating the whole project. They have turned into avowed and conscientious critics seeing in it expansionist, exclusionary and dangerous dimensions. While there is no scarcity of Ariel Sharons, Ben Gurions, Netanyahus, Baruch Marzels and their new compatriots from across the Caucusus and Atlantic, questions about the recent direction of Jewish humanism under the strong Zionist panoply are no less valid. Thus, Israel is a home from home but its walled existence does not remove the alien and persistent denial of realities all around. I am reminded of my academic friend who took me to a sumptuous lunch at the Faculty Club in Jerusalem, then led me up the hill behind one of the research centres built by her co-religionists from New York, and pointing down below towards the Wall, she observed: 'we are a very privileged nation but in a rather surreal way. We have built the Wall not to keep away the bombers but simply to foreclose encountering the reality around us'. I wondered what Arendt, a supporter of Aliya – the project to settle younger European Jews in Israel – would have made of this banality of dispossession!

Arendt's searchlight on people mechanically becoming perpetrators of heinous offenses does not absolve them of their crime nor does their impertinence lessen the extent of their travesty. But it is the higher and more far reaching forces that turn people into mass murders totally impervious to self-questioning. In recent times, we have seen millions of deaths in Congo (formerly Zaire) with the largest number of women having been gang raped, followed by Rwanda and Bosnia – in all these cases perpetrators are 'normal' individuals from 'next door' who might be former neighbours and class fellows. In Sarajevo, Radovan Karadzic led Europe's longest siege with the full knowledge that his own friends and colleagues were the targets. In Banja Luka, Mostar and certainly in Srebrenica, Serbs and Croats ensured ethnic cleansing on a horrendous scale including elimination of their own Muslim friends. In India, Narendra Modi, now the Prime Minister, is implicated in supervising the massacres in Gujarat in 2002 while more recently, in Muzaffargarh, the cheerleaders of anti-Muslim pogroms were local thugs, fully identified by the victims and their relatives. In Pakistan, various militant outfits within and outside the Tehreek-i-Taliban Pakistan (TTP) pursue selective, indiscriminate and ruthless killings of fellow Pakistanis with a complete nonchalance. Suicide bombers and target killers assume attitudinal indifference by extricating themselves from all kinds of human considerations as if they happen to sleep walk into some nightmarish abyss. Certainly, violence often ushers nihilist monsters such as Eichmann, Karadzic and Tudjman, and if given a chance could, in a banal way, turn victims into perpetrators.

REZA PANKHURST

THE INEVITABLE
CALIPHATE?

A History of the Struggle for Global
Islamic Union, 1924 to the Present

ISBN: 9781849042512
£18.99 / Paperback / 256pp

THE INEVITABLE CALIPHATE?

A History of the Struggle for Global Islamic Union, 1924 to the Present

REZA PANKHURST

While in the West 'the Caliphate' evokes overwhelmingly negative images, throughout Islamic history it has been regarded as the ideal Islamic polity. In the wake of the 'Arab Spring' and the removal of long-standing dictators in the Middle East, in which the dominant discourse appears to be one of the compatibility of Islam and democracy, reviving the Caliphate has continued to exercise the minds of its opponents and advocates. Reza Pankhurst's book contributes to our understanding of Islam in politics, the path of Islamic revival across the last century and how the popularity of the Caliphate in Muslim discourse waned and later re-emerged. Beginning with the abolition of the Caliphate, the ideas and discourse of the Muslim Brotherhood, Hizb ut-Tahrir, al-Qaeda and other smaller groups are then examined. A comparative analysis highlights the core commonalities as well as differences between the various movements and individuals, and suggests that as movements struggle to re-establish a polity which expresses the unity of the ummah (or global Islamic community), the Caliphate has alternatively been ignored, had its significance minimised or denied, reclaimed and promoted as a theory and symbol in different ways, yet still serves as a political ideal for many.

'Reza Pankhurst provides a unique and probing examination of modern thinking on the caliphate. ... This detailed analysis of the ways in which the Muslim Brotherhood, Hizb ut-Tahrir, and al-Qaeda as well as smaller groups reformulate and use the concept today is both judicious and informed. It provides the most reliable guide available to an idea and political symbol that holds attraction for many Sunni Muslims while inciting anxiety, even fear, among others, including many non-Muslims and Shi'a.' — Professor James Piscatori, Durham University

WWW.HURSTPUBLISHERS.COM/BOOK/THE-INEVITABLE-CALIPHATE

41 GREAT RUSSELL ST, LONDON WC1B 3
WWW.HURSTPUBLISHERS.COM
WWW.FBOOK.COM/HURSTPUBLISHERS
020 7255 2201

ET CETERA

ON MAD, BAD AND DANGEROUS

Merryl Wyn Davies

Lady Caroline Lamb's famous epigram elegantly sums up the problem of free thinkers: they are 'mad, bad and dangerous to know' as the Lady declared in one instance. Few who dare to think freely, who boldly go beyond accepted conventions escape being considered either mad or bad or dangerous in any or all senses and applications of that perilous word. And who can argue? Love them or loathe them, if they cannot be classified as mad, bad or dangerous there would be little in the ideas thinkers put forth worth more than a moment's passing reference. Disturbing the waters and ruffling the feathers is not the way the world turns. It is the great tsunamis, the eruptive larval outpourings, the earthquakes of insight that put us in thrall and debt to free thinking individuals. Nothing would be as it is, for good or evil, without the contribution of the free thinker.

Actually, her famous epigram could be applied to Lady Caroline (1785-1828) herself. She ended mad and was notorious for being bad in a way most dangerously destabilising to the social expectations of the rich and famous in the era the novelist T.H. White dubbed the 'Age of Scandal.' One can hardly blame the lady for becoming mad. She is remembered most for just one quip though she wrote a number of novels, was a capable poet, an erudite, puckish and accomplished observer of the life and letters of her time. She was married to a rising politician, later to be the Prime Minister Lord Melbourne (1779-1848), till her death despite her famous indiscretion. In an age when physical and mental disability were hidden and hurriedly confined to asylums the Lambs tended their own disabled son at home. Yet, as a female, Caro, as she was known, was subsumed by the ruling (and seemingly eternal) double standards concerning female contributions which eradicate her achievements, deny her any claim to being a free thinker, and condemn her as bad bad bad for free living and madly emotionally unstable for refusing to fade quietly when her 'amour inappropre' tired of her attentions. It is depressingly dangerous to be contrary, to be not what convention will tolerate.

So what of the object of Lady Caroline's barb? Lord George Noel Gordon Byron (1788–1824) was the original 'celeb', the socialite heartthrob, the quintessential romantic hero, the literary 'rock' superstar image conscious poet sensation of the age, perhaps more infamous for his lifestyle than his poetry while both life and letters should properly be understood as expressions of his thought, his ideas about what and how the world should be. It is by no means only the peccadillos of his private life, though they were varied and many, that made Byron mad, bad and dangerous to know. He provided new impetus to old orientalism and dedicated himself to a new-fangled modern style exclusive nationalism by denigrating Ottoman tyranny as he championed the cause of Greek independence. Thereby, he regenerated the idea of the impenetrable rift between Europe, whose birth was in classical Greece and Rome, and Asia the distinctly Other, inimical to all that was Europe no matter how interesting its exoticism might appear. This cavernous abyss beyond mutual understanding had been opened in the febrile imagination of the humanist thinkers of the Renaissance when they determined to eradicate their civilisation's debt to the predominantly Muslim world of Asia in favour of sole affiliation and loyalty to newly recovered classical learning. Byron's literary construct, the romantic hero, is another pestiferous blot on the imagination who has stalked the pages of literature and arts and on into film and television ever since. This hero is a figure of passion and opposition, or 'anti-establishment radicalism and anarchy', as the novelist John Updike put it. He achieves his rebellious objectives by the marriage of licentious personal freedom of the free living individual who cares not for convention with the quest for freedom from restraint by oppressive power of state and church and all other such institutions for which, ultimately this tormented world weary hero is ready to embrace self-destruction/sacrifice. The romantic hero's ultimate cause is, as Byron wrote in Canto IX of his most acclaimed poem, Don Juan, freedom of thought:

And I will war at least in words (and should
May chance so happen deeds) with all who war
With thought…

So why is free thinking always deemed dangerous? Quite simply, it means pondering the way of things as they are, asking questions without restraint, traversing the known knowns with a quizzical intent, interrogating the known unknowns and venturing forth into the realms of the unknown unknowns, daring to contemplate that there are things we do not know. Whoever thought I would end up quoting Donald Rumsfeld, US Secretary of Defense and architect of the Iraq War? This strange circumstance, surely, is the essence of free thinking: finding the hooks that lead to productive thought in unexpected places and with meaning and purpose quite other than its source may have intended or suspected. It only goes to show that not every useful utterance needs to come from a free thinker or indeed a revolutionary, some can be gleaned from reactionary warmongers as well.

The revolutionary is always presented as a free thinker, like the romantic hero, which perhaps explains why they are so often conflated in the world of art and culture. The revolutionary seeks rebellious overthrow of the established order. Free thinking, however, can come in more mundane less easily recognised yet just as profound categories. It can mean seeing so clearly how things are that new arrangements, new connections, new possibilities, alternative understandings of what is established and accepted become apparent. The path of patient dedicated reform can be the outcome of radical free thinking. Yet radical reform can also leave in place much that is cherished that is called tradition, heritage handed down from the point of origin. One can assert, as I most emphatically do, that tradition is change or it is no longer tradition that is relevant and fertile but rather ossified dead letters and the outpourings of dead good men that can lead whole civilisations into the error of defending what has become indefensible. Reform that keeps tradition mobile, adaptable and pertinent to contemporary need by constant amendment, permanent small (or large) adjustment, does not necessarily render itself any less dangerous to vested interests than revolution that would sweep society clean of the old ways for the sake of what is claimed to be a new utopia.

Thought, the ability to reason is what makes us human. Yet thought operates always in a context, the context of the world, the culture, the time and circumstances in which we live. Pure thought is a true utopia, a nowhere no place that is as delusional as it is illusory. We think with the materials we have acquired from history. It is how freely, how widely, coherently and cogently people are prepared to think with the materials available in their world that determines just how mad, bad or dangerous the results are likely to be.

The tyrants and dictators, the despots and potentates familiar from history are easily categorised as both bad and often mad. They are the evil geniuses who manipulate power and seek relentlessly for absolute power to impose their will on others. In modern times they have been joined by the familiar cultural construct of the mad scientist, either the benevolent naïve kind that remain oblivious, deaf, dumb, and blind to the uses their thought can be put to by unscrupulous power hungry establishments or megalomaniacs. Or there is the truly bad mad scientist ready to destroy humanity for its failures. Tyrant or scientist mad or simply bad their evil influence is a result of thought, their perverse, perverted thinking which is freed from moral and ethical moorings and restraint. Such monsters we know to be wary of, to oppose (if only we could as we know we should) and generally to avoid as best we can. These familiar bogeymen of history and cultural stereotype are personifications of free thinking in its worst sense. The dangers such living or imagined monsters pose is evident. The trouble is there are whole troves of other monsters lurking in the world of thought that escape scrutiny, odium or even earnest interrogation of their faults and methinks this is much more dangerous.

In the world in which we live thought not only happens in a context it happens in neat compartments that we call disciplines of knowledge. Each discipline has a history, a process of genesis framed by asking questions. It is a function of the questions one asks that they inevitably contain assumptions and lead to the accumulation of facts, mounds of information that answer to the predicates of the questions posed, the information sought. Therefore the necessary accompaniment of knowledge is ignorance, ignorance of the questions not asked, not considered relevant, excluded by our assumptions and predicates. We all accept the existence of ignorance, such is the accumulation of facts and information available in our world that it is no longer possible to know everything. We are a world awash with experts. It is easy enough to accept that an astrophysicist may know an inordinate amount about his or her discipline and yet be as uninformed as the average lay person about medicine, history, philosophy or literature. The age of the polymath is past and not even the best search engine means we genuinely can know everything. The danger of thinking then is accepting and respecting the boundaries that have been constructed and ignoring the ignorance these boundaries entail. The complexity of the realities of the world in which we live is shaped and fashioned from the knowledge and expertise that comes to us through the history of the disciplines of knowledge. All these disciplines, the structure and operation of modern academia, originate in the western world and employ its characteristic cultural ways of thinking and attendant assumptions as a further set of exclusionary boundaries. There are other traditions of reasoning, ways of framing questions and different starting assumptions. It is not a denigration of free thinking of the western way to argue that cross fertilisation, thinking beyond one's own conventions – as the rest of the world has been required to do – might be a dangerously useful means to attain new insights.

The greatest danger we face is how circumscribed our freedom of thought, exercised as free inquiry, has become along with the reliance we place on knowledgeably ignorant experts who are the products of our highly structured systems of thinking – more commonly known as academic disciplines. In a complex and ever more interconnected world it is entirely possible to think ourselves into a new era of serfdom, shackled to the bidding of interlocking networks of the rich and powerful, the mega corporations that command and control the choices of our lives, to become powerless servants of a system running out of control beyond our ability to think and therefore act, create and operate otherwise. If that seems alarmist, dear readers, the evidence is in – we already are!

We live in a dangerously unequal world, a world riven with haves and have nots within and between regions, countries and continents. The map of inequality is daily growing more complex and exaggerated. We live in a globalised world of international capital where money washes around the globe as blips on computer screens by the nanosecond and the bulk of it always comes to rest in the pockets of the few who were, are and ever yet shall be wealthy. The institutions and operatives who manage this system are the architects of such fiendishly devious schemes to generate wealth that it is almost beyond the wit of a sane mind to comprehend. Assuredly they are beyond moral hazard since the enterprises they operate are deemed so essential that they cannot be permitted to fail and hence are beyond effective regulation or oversight. We call this system liberal capitalism and we know it has failed us. Yet we are asked to accept this liberal capitalism as the apotheosis of history, the dispensation towards which humanity has been making an inexorable march. The hope of the human future has therefore to be placed in the warped vessel of global capitalism in the unlikely eventuality that it will do what it says on the tin and somehow, no one knows how, turn into a self-regulating mechanism where hidden hands will make it all turn out for the best in the best of all possible worlds by essentially returning to the assumptions, predicates and procedures that delivered us into the maw of a global economic crisis in the first place.

If ever there were a time for critical free thinking it is now. Fortunately, cometh the hour cometh the book, the thought and ideas we all need to take seriously. I speak of the sensation of Amazon and the *New York Times* bestseller list *Capital in the Twenty-first Century* by the French economist Thomas Piketty. Piketty has built a cogent, reasoned argument that the present situation where wealth is concentrated in few hands is no aberration. The concentration of wealth to levels incompatible with democracy and social justice and the creation of levels of inequity that are unsustainable are automatic outcomes of capitalism, he argues. The book gathers the evidence that we are on an inexorable march which while it may include a rise in living standards – the supposed promised land – nevertheless does so in a context of increasing inequality. Wealth gathers to itself disproportionate accumulations of more wealth.

Conventional theory holds that while the early stages of industrialisation were fraught with inequality this lessened with the advance of industrial society. The proof offered is to point to the post World War II era characterised by the expansion of the middle class, state funded social provision and high taxation of the wealthiest. Indeed there was a fashionable export of this supposed commonplace. It was the underpinning of the economic miracle said to be taking place in East and Southeast Asia.

The various ferocious beasts that became the epithets for the various economies all managed to work best and produce the most marked results through their more marked equality of wealth. A few decades on and the shallowness of this view is clear to see. High performing economies in rapidly developing countries materialised not through the prudential application of economic theory but because each of the countries concerned was of special interest to the Western powers in their battle with communism and therefore received high levels of aid and investment. While there might have been growing equality once upon a time, the long term effect of the excursion with capitalism has produced enormous wealth concentrated in few hands which will ramify burgeoning inequality down the generations. Croney capitalism of the Asian kind is the self-selecting elitist handmaid of global capitalism with all its attendant features. What once looked like a possible alternative has become a case of the same old same old that afflicts western nations.

Piketty is able to demonstrate that many of the shibboleths of what economics calls theory are either barely defined or demonstrably false. The Kuznets Curve, generally accepted within the realms of academe, supposedly shows the inequalities at the outset of industrialisation flattening as economies mature. Piketty has gathered the evidence to show the curve goes in the opposite direction taking the global economy back to the gross inequalities with which we began the failed adventure of industrialism. There is a central myth to capitalism which is wielded as its shield or moral armour by politicians, theorists and thinkers of many stripes. The myth is that wealth is the outcome of effort, ingenuity, hard work, wise investment and risk taking. Sadly, this is the conjuror's illusion dangled before the gullible audience of the populace. In contemporary times one stands a better chance of getting some purchase on wealth by becoming a footballer's WAG (Wives And Girlfriends), as so many young girls apparently aspire to be, or rock superstar. Provided they have the suitable hedge fund manager not of the Bernie Madoff variety then their wealth can grow down the generations in an environment where the rate of return on capital outstrips the rate of growth. Under such conditions, inevitably, inherited wealth always outstrips earned wealth. Today's nest egg becomes the growing trust fund of future generations for only the few who are or are gradually inducted into the ranks of the super rich.

It is no secret to the general public how this depressing state of affairs keeps on proliferating inequality. It happens by the co-option of the managerial class that can succeed in paying itself ever increasing salaries boosted by perks irrespective of its productivity, the stagnation or even the obvious failure of the enterprises they manage. It's the bankers' bonuses and eye watering stock options on top of huge basic salaries of the fat cat section of the economy.

The basic proposition of economics is that human beings are selfishly self interested and when they act on these instincts they create perfect markets where the rational choices of individuals as buyers and sellers will equalise fair outcomes. The right goods will be made available at the right price and supply and demand will even make sure the workers get a fair wage. In other words economics is based on a set of idealised assumptions which made sense to those who devised them, way back in other times, as means of answering the questions that interested them. Today, critical free thinking finds them wanting and hardly satisfactory as a basis for devising policy to right all the imperfections which distort society and burden it with increasing inequity that makes a nonsense of social justice and eunuchs of the power of the people as the supposed basis of democracy.

Piketty is clear that the problem of wealth and income, concepts to which he has given free thought and careful definition, can be addressed. His remedy is 15 per cent tax on capital, 80 per cent tax on high incomes, enforced transparency for all bank transactions and the use of inflation to distribute wealth downwards. In other words he is suggesting the turkeys vote for Christmas. Even Piketty describes some of his solutions as 'utopian'.

And there dear reader we meet the problem with free thinking. It is the essential critical tool to gain insight into what we do not know yet urgently need to know. Free thinking is dangerous because it unmasks the imperfections in our world, the assumptions that have installed themselves in power and pervert and divert the course of justice, equity and full equal representation for all. The most dangerous thing about free thinking is when it proves reason is powerless and impotent to effect moral change, and adherence to ethical norms that would distribute justice with equity and enable the people to determine their fate is irrelevant in the status quo.

The final and most dangerous stage of free thinking is finding effective, peaceful means to change the equation of powerless impotence that envelops the world today for a reasoned programme of competent reform. Thinking of that order would be sane and good. The dangers inherent in not thinking freely and leaving things as they are should be enough to stir anyone's critical juices.

TEN FREETHINKERS TO THINK ABOUT

Freethinkers have three basic characteristics. First, they actually think – often outside or against the dominant modes of knowing, doing and being. They revel in ideas. They write; and often they write a lot. The thinking is free in the sense that it does not prescribe to the single, monolithic meaning that prevails: it does not accept one interpretation or submits to one truth or authority. There are more than one way to think; and, therefore, more than one way to be human. Second, they think towards a purpose. Free does not mean 'free for all', or 'anything goes', as postmodernists tends to suggest. If 'anything goes' then 'everything stays': the status quo is maintained. Freethinkers aim to transform the existing state of affairs to promote social justice, equity and pluralism. Third, a corollary of the first and second, they maintain a respectful distance from most forms of power. The thought, structures, authorities and individuals freethinkers tend to criticise naturally upsets those who wield cultural, intellectual, religious and political power. So freethinkers have a tendency to upset the powerful. Those that freethinkers criticize are sometimes keen to include them inside the tent, knowing that this is an effective way to blunt their influence and criticism. The mark of truly dangerous freethinkers is to refuse such offers. They know that the closer they come to power, the harder it becomes to speak the truth.

So if you subscribe to the *Foreign Policy* list, and think that Malala Yousafzai and Aung San Suu Kyi (who is happy to turn a blind eye towards the massacre of Rohingya Muslims in Myanmar) are 'global thinkers', then you are clearly not living on the freethinking planet. Lists too are designed to preserve the status quo, provide the route map to familiarity with the essential landmarks of political, cultural and intellectual orientation – and cast doubt on other people's power of reasoning. On this list are thinkers who question the familiar, wish to travel in a different direction, and attempt to provide an alternative route to what is possible.

1. Noam Chomsky

The Godfather of freethinkers has been exposing unpleasant truths about the US, its free-booting liberal intelligentsia, military-industrial complex, corporations, intelligence services and the 'unholy alliance' between the state and the corporate media for decades. But he made his intellectual reputation in linguistic with *Syntactic Structures* (1957), which is regarded as a landmark work. He established the idea that every child has an innate capacity to master the structure and grammar of language; and all languages have the same basic structure of 'depth grammar'. His outrage with the status quo and deep commitment to social justice is evident from every word of his countless books, articles, essays, interviews and films. In the hands of US imperialists, democracy has become an ideological tool, Chomsky has argued. For the US, a society is democratic only if its commerce and business are subordinate to American corporations and US interests. The 'free press' is an instrument of capitalism and works to support the hegemony of American finance. Get hold of *Manufacturing Consent* (1983), *Necessary Illusions* (1989), and his more recent work, *How The World Works* (2012) and discover what free thought is all about.

2. Ashis Nandy

The author of the concise classic, *The Intimate Enemy* (1983), and the ground breaking *Traditions, Tyranny and Utopias* (1987), is quite simply one of the great thinkers of our time. But he is not easy to understand. He operates on a non-dualistic logic where relationships of similarity and convergence are more important than cold rationality. He functions beyond (rather than outside) the established conventions of western thought. Both the man and his ideas span a different universe, a universe that includes 'the West' but only as a victim of its own thought and instrumental rationality. Nandy takes the side of the victims of history and the casualties of the present – fatalities and suffers of an array of grand western ideas such as Modernity, Science, Rationality, Development,

Nation State. He seeks both to unite the victims and to increase the awareness of their victimhood. Even though he was trained as a psychologist, Nandy has no respect for disciplinary boundaries. Indeed, to accept the disciplinary structure of modern knowledge is to accept the worldview of the West. But Nandy's scholarship is not interdisciplinary or transdisciplinary in the conventional sense; he is no 'Renaissance Man'. He is a polymath is the traditional understanding of the word: he operates beyond the disciplinary structure of knowledge and regards all sources of knowledge as equally valid and all methods and modes of inquiry as equally useful.

3. Edward W. Said

Well known for *Orientalism* (1978), Edward Said (1935–2003) was a dangerous freethinker in part because the book's core message rattled an audience that was used to having it all its own way. Said's thesis, that orientalist scholarship is tied to the discourse and project of imperialism, was aimed at those who provide it with academic and intellectual justification, and it had a major impact on its intended target. The thesis itself was not new; it had been outlined by the Syrian scholar of Islam, A L Tibawi (1910–1981), and Egyptian political scientist and Marxist, Anouar Abdel-Malik (1924–2012), and others before. But Said framed it within the discourse of literary criticism and the academy has never been the same. The great Orientalist-era scholars of his age, men such as Bernard Lewis, Albert Hourani and William Montgomery Watt, were far less troubled by the writers who had preceded Said, so much so that they rarely bothered to respond. Only after *Orientalism* were they woken up to produce an avalanche of books, essays, pamphlets, lectures, and countless media appearances attacking Said. Said effectively forced them into introspection, and the need to explain in public the discourse, methods, the donors, the wider politics and their own personal motivations for their work.

4. Jerry Ravetz

The mild-mannered and self-effacing author of the seminal *Scientific Knowledge and its Social Problems* (1972) is not an obvious candidate for the 'dangerous' label. But Ravetz, who trained in mathematics before heading up history and philosophy of science at the University of Leeds, is a giant among the philosophers of the twentieth and twenty-first centuries. He was among the first to draw attention to the changing nature of science, especially the absence of certainty in the scientific method, and the dilemmas of making decisions based on incomplete information. His pioneering work on risks and post-normal science will stand the test of time. No wonder he is shunned by the science establishment.

5. Fatema Mernissi

Sociologist Fatema Mernissi began writing on patriarchy in Islam in the 1970s onwards, when the default position among many Islamic states, writers, thinkers and faith-based civil society activists was that women have more protections under Islam and theocratic environments than in secular ones. The outspoken Mernissi, a long-time professor at the King Muhammad V University, shattered these illusions. In *Women in Islam* (1991) she explored misogyny in the earliest Islamic societies, highlighting members of the Prophet Muhammad's inner circle among the perpetrators. That's getting too close to the edge; and would have attracted death sentences had she been based anywhere but Morocco. In *The Forgotten Queens of Islam* (1994) she uncovered the names of women who have held state power going back fifteen centuries. Through a string of such books as *Beyond the Veil* (1975) and *The Veil and the Male Elite* (1987), Mernissi pioneered Islamic feminism and established the path for others to follow.

6. Sisters in Islam

The Malaysian based Sisters have not been too far behind Mernissi. The Sisters, a group of scholars, lawyers and journalists, came together in 1987 to advocate, and fight for, gender equality, human rights and social justice. That means taking on the Shari'a; and the Sisters have been anything but shy about telling the truth to Medina. The shaping of the future is not something that can be left to 'religious scholars', they have argued. Rather, it is the task of all to rethink the Shari'a and foster an enlightened and contemporary understanding of the Qur'an. The Sisters have helped countless women seek legal redress through the Shari'a courts. Led by the journalist Zainah Anwar, the Sisters have included the sociologist Norani Othman and American scholar and activist Amina Wadud, amongst its ranks; although, an occasional brother, such as the legal scholar Mohammad Hashim Kamali, is allowed into the inner sanctum. The only group of genuine freethinkers to come out of Malaysia, the Sisters are constantly attacked and maligned by the conservative Muftis and religious scholars.

7. Hernando de Soto Polar

Peruvian economist Hernando de Soto was tackling capitalism long before Thomas Piketty, the current flavour of the month. And unlike Piketty, de Soto does not suggest that simply taxing the rich will solve the problems. De Soto is known for his influential book, *The Mystery of Capital: Why Capitalism Works in the West and Fails Everywhere Else* (2000). What makes rich rich, he argues, is property rights – that is, they own property in all sense of the word. They could own land, housing, businesses, intellectual property. The poor are denied these rights – that's why they remain poor. Or in other words, the free market should really be free – for the rich as well as the poor. Between 1988 and 1995, de Soto put his ideas to work by producing a string of legal reforms and designed the administrative reforms of Peru – allowing poor farmers and peasants to own land, and giving titles to families which allowed them to move from the black market to the formal economy. Peru's economy was transformed. He helped introduce similar initiatives in El Salvador and Haiti. There is only one problem. The World Bank and the IMF like his ideas. As we said, the powers that be are keen to bring freethinkers inside their circumference.

8. Nurcholish Madjid

No Muslim country has produced as many freethinking activists as Indonesia, scholars and intellectuals as diverse as Haji Misbach (1876-

1926), who argued that Islam and socialism were compatible; Dawam Rahardjo, who at the age of seventy-one continues to champion pluralism, religious freedom and defending minorities, such as the Shia, from the wrath of the conservative establishment at considerable risk to himself; and writer and academic Kuntowijoyo (1943–2005), who championed plurality and democratic accountability both in his fiction and non-fiction. Most Indonesian freethinkers are not known outside their own country as their works seldom get translated and never get the attention they deserve. The freethinker who we would like to champion is Nurcholish Madjid (1939-2005), who was the student of another great freethinker, the late Pakistani American scholar Fazlur Rahman (1919–1988). Affectionately known in Indonesia as Cak Nur, Madjid worked for modernizing Islam from within. Islam, he argued, is all about ideas; and to fight the battle for ideas, it must embrace tolerance, pluralism and democracy. 'The Islamic State Does Not Exist', he declared in a famous correspondence with one of the leaders of the Indonesian war of independence; and coined the slogan: 'Islam yes, Islamic parties no'.

9. Eduardo Viveiros de Castro

The Brazilian anthropologist specialises in looking at Christianity and the West from the perspective of American Indians, as illustrated by the title of one of his books, From the Enemy's Point of View: Humanity and Divinity in an Amazonian Society (1992). He has transformed our understanding of the Amazonian society, culture, cosmology and rituals almost single handedly. De Castro shows that the Amazonian peoples, such as the Arawete tribe, have a dynamic, complex and tragic vision of the world, and their societies were astonishingly open and transformative. Moreover, some even had the cultural integrity to face and overcome the vicious forces of European imperialism and modernity. In a discipline renowned more for being the hand-maiden of colonialism than originality, he is a refreshing, freethinking voice.

10. Roger van Zwanenberg

And finally to someone who provided a platform for the voice of freethinkers. You have probably never heard of economic historian-turned publisher Roger van Zwanenberg. He is the founder of not one, but two independent publishing houses: Zed Books and Pluto Press. He is chairman of the latter. Between them, both publishers have provided a home for freethinkers around the world for nearly a century. Pluto is often the publisher of choice for authors from the Middle East and North Africa, where, until quite recently, independent publishing in English and Arabic was barely tolerated by state authorities. Pluto's authors include Noam Chomsky, Nick Robins, author of *The Corporation that Changed the World*, one of the best histories of the East India Company, and our very own Ziauddin Sardar (now there is a dangerous freethinker to boot).

CITATIONS

The Circumference of Freethought by Ziauddin Sardar

Sun-Mi Hwang's deceptively simple, elegant and moving novella *The Hen Who Dreamed She Could Fly* is published by Penguin (2013). Richard Scholar's article 'Two Cheers for Free-Thinking' appeared in *Paragraph* 29 (1) 40-52 (March 2006), and *Montaigne and the Art of Freethinking* is published by Peter Lang (Oxford, 2010). Karl Pearson, *The Ethics of Freethought* was published in 1901 (Adam and Charles Black, London). On the western history of freethought, and its association with atheism see Martin Priestman, *Romantic Atheism: Poetry and Freethought, 1780–1830* (Cambridge University Press, 1999)

Jahiz: Dangerous Freethinker?
by James E. Montgomery

The quotations from Al-Jahiz, in the order they appear, are from: Al-Jahiz, *Kitab al-Hayawan*, ed. Muhammad ʿAbd al-Salam Harun (Beirut: Dar al-Kitab al-ʿArabi, 1969), 7.55.13-58.15; Al-Jahiz *Kitab al-Bayan wa-al-tabyin*, edited by Muhammad ʿAbd al-Salam Harun (Cairo: Maktabat al-Khanji, 1989), 3.374.15-375.2; Al-Jāḥiẓ, *Theological Epistles*, edited and translated by James E. Montgomery (New York: New York University Press, forthcoming); *Kitman al-sirr wa hifz al-lisan*, in *Majmuʿ rasaʾil al-Jahiz*, edited by Paul Kraus and Taha al-Hajiri (Cairo: Maṭbaʿat Lajnat al-Tàlif wa-al-Nashr wa-al-Tarjama, 1943), pp. 37-60 (38.10-39.9); and *Rasàil al-Jahiz*, edited by Muhammad ʿAbd al-Salam Harun (Beirut: Dar al-Jil, 1991), Volume 4, pp. 232.2-14 and 235.6-11. The translations of this epistle are taken from my forthcoming translation and edition, Al-Jāḥiẓ, *Theological Epistles*, for *The Library of Arabic Literature*.

I have based the discussion on the biography of Jahiz given by Charles Pellat, 'Al-Jāḥiẓ' in *ʿAbbāsid Belles-Lettres: The Cambridge History of Arabic*

Literature, edited by Julia Ashtiany, T.M. Johnstone, J.D. Latham, R.B. Serjeant and G. Rex Smith (Cambridge: Cambridge University Press, 1990), pp. 78-81; the quote from Pellet is from p.80. The quote from Isaiah Berlin is from 'Two Concepts of Liberty,' in Isaiah Berlin, *Liberty*, edited by Henry Hardy (Oxford: Oxford University Press, 2007), pp. 166-217; 'The Boasts of the Blacks over the Whites,' has been translated by Tarif Khalidi, in *Islamic Quarterly* 25 (1981), pp. 3-51; and for the wider implications of the debate between Jahiz and his interlocutor, see J.E. Montgomery, *Al-Jāḥiz: In Praise of Books* (Edinburgh: Edinburgh University Press, 2013), pp. 134 and 327-31. My thoughts on Jahiz as a free-thinker have benefitted enormously from Richard Scholar, *Montaigne and the Art of Free-Thinking* (Oxford: Peter Lang, 2010).

Ibn Rushd's Dangerous Idea by Oliver Leaman

This article is based on the Muslim Institute Second Annual Ibn Rushd Lecture, delivered on 4 June 2014 at Art Workers Guild Hall, London.

Two major works by Ibn Rushd that have a significant discussion of the issues raised here are: *Averroes on the harmony of religion and philosophy*, translator George Hourani, (Luzac, London 1961) and *Tahafut al-Tahafut* (Refutation of Refutation), translator S. van den Bergh, (Luzac, London, 1954). Borges' short story about what he calls the tragedy of Averroes is 'Averroes' search', translated by J. Irby, *Labyrinths: Selected stories and other writings*, edited by D. Yates and J. Irby (New Directions, New York, 1964) pp. 148-55. Yusef Chahine's 1997 movie is called *Destiny* (*al-Masir*) France / Egypt. The works which have influenced the reception of Ibn Rushd in the modern Arabic speaking world are Ernest Renan's (1986) *Averroes et l'averroisme* (G. Olms, Hildesheim, 1986), a nineteenth century work; while F Antun, (1988) *Ibn Rushd wa'l-falsafahtu*, (General Egyptian Book Organization, Cairo), A al-ʿIraqi, (editor) *Ibn Rushd mufakkiran ʿarabiyyan wa ra'idan li al-ittihan al-ʿaqli*, (Cairo, 1993, np) and M Abd al-Jabri, *Bunyat al-ʿaql al-ʿarabi*, (Beirut, 1987) represent important modern work.

Some detail on Ibn Rushd's ideas and cultural environment is provided in my books, *Averroes and his philosophy* (Routledge, London, 1997), *Introduction to classical Islamic philosophy* (Cambridge University Press, 2002) and *Islamic Philosophy* (Polity, Cambridge, 2009). A variety of different perspectives may be found in Urvoy, D. *Ibn Rushd (Averroes)* translator O Stewart (Routledge, London, 1991), R Arnaldez, *Averroes: A rationalist in Islam*, translator D. Streight (Notre Dame University Press, 2000), Fakhry, M. *Averroes (Ibn Rushd), his life, works and influence*, (Oneworld, Oxford 2001).

A very balanced account of the whole issue of the impact of Ibn Rushd on both the European and Arab Enlightenments is provided by Stefan Wild in his 'Islamic enlightenment and the paradox of Averroes', *Die Welt des Islams*, 36, (1996), pp. 379-90; Anke von Külgegen, *Averroes Und Die Arabische moderne: Ansätze zu einer Neubegründung des Rationalismus im Islam* (Brill, Leiden, 1994) and in many of the articles in M Wahba and M Abousenna, editors, *Averroes and the enlightenment movement* (Prometheus, Amherst, 1986). A good account of why Wittgenstein thought that language games cannot be evaluated is found in his *On Certainty* translated by D. Paul and E. Anscombe, (Blackwell, Oxford, 1969).

Al-Hallaj's Truth, Massignon's Fiction by Robert Irwin

Massignon's *La Passion de Husayn ibn Mansur Hallaj* was first published in 1922 in two volumes by Geuthner. A new expanded edition in four volumes was published by Gallimard, Paris, 1975. The English translation by Herbert Mason of the second edition appeared as *The Passion of al-Hallaj: Mystic and Martyr of Islam*, 4 volumes (Princeton, New Jersey, Princeton University Press, 1975). Quotation beginning 'The huge gory setting of the gibbet...' is found in *The Passion*, vol. 1, p.361. The quotation beginning 'in the depths of the imperial harem...' is in vol.1, p.36. 'We recall a man after his death...' is found in *The Passion*, vol.1, p.630. 'We glimpse the precious ordered setting of Ibn Dawud's death...' vol. 1, p. 361. Hallaj's verses are quoted from F. Harb, 'Wine Poetry (*Khamriyyat*)' in Julia Ashtiany, T.M. Johnstone, J.D. Latham, R.B. Serjeant and G. Rex Smith, *The Cambridge History of Arabic Literature: 'Abbasid Belles-Lettres*, (Cambridge,

1990), p.233 and Martin Lings 'Mystical Poetry', in idem, p.246. 'This? It is Iblis...' *The Passion*, p.290. The comparison of Hallaj to a torch appears in Mary Louis Gude, *Louis Massignon the Crucible of Compassion*, (University of Notre Dame Press, Notre Dame, 1966), p.115. 'contemplating beautiful faces...' *The Passion*, vol. 1, p.398. 'A slow difficult work...' *The Passion*, vol.1, p.lv. The quotation from 'Ali Shariati appears in Elizabeth Sirriyeh's *Sufis and Anti-Sufis: Rethinking and Rejection of Sufism in the Modern World* (Richmond, Curzon Press,1999). Carl Ernst's *Words of Ecstasy in Islam* (Albany, State University of New York Press, 1985) is, as its title suggests, a close study of the seemingly wild boasts made by Sufis while in a drunken state of ecstasy. Alexander Knysh's, *Islamic Mysticism: A Short History* (Leiden, Brill, 2000) is a good guide to the Sufi background. His *Ibn Arabi in the Later Mystical Tradition: The Making of a Polemical Image* (Albany, State University of New York Press, 1999) has some penetrating observations about Hallaj's afterlife in the Muslim community. Jeffrey J. Kripal's *Roads of Excess, Palaces of Wisdom: Eroticism and Reflexivity in the Study of Mysticism* (Chicago, University of Chicago Press, 2001) has a chapter on the sexual element in Massignon's approach to Hallaj.

Al-Biruni: Against the Grain by Bruce B Lawrence

For the biography of Al-Biruni, see C. E. Bosworth et al, 'Biruni, Abu Rayhani Life' in *Encyclopaedia Iranica* Vol. IV, Fasc. 3, pp. 274-276. And for the ongoing, perhaps endless debates about why he did not have a proper *nisbah* or last name, see F.A. Shamsi, 'Abu Al-Raihan Muhammad ibn Ahmad Al-Bayruni 362/973-ca. 443/105i' in Hakim Mohammed Said, ed., *Al-Biruni Commemorative Volume* (Karachi: Hamdard National Foundation, 1979):260-288. Quotations regarding Al-Biruni's correspondence with Ibn Sina are taken from Ahmad Dallal, *Islam, Science, and the Challenge of History* (New Haven: Yale University Press, 2010): 74-80. A wonderfully concise summary of al-Biruni's scientific achievements is provided in Christina Healey, *Al-Biruni* (ebook), published in Toledo, Ohio: Great Neck Publishing, 2006, summarized here in the section on al-Biruni's major scientific achievements. A similar popular exposition of his pioneering endeavours as a research scientist with multiple, overlapping interest can be found in Bill Scheppler, *Al-Biruni:*

Master Astronomer and Muslim Scholar of the Eleventh Century (New York: The Rosen Publishing Group, 2006). The quote from *The Chronology of Anciei Nations,* translated by C.E.Sachau, London, 1887, reprinted in Frankfur¹ 1969 are from p.315; and the quotes from *Alberuni's India,* also translated by. C. E. Sachau, 2 volumes, London, 1888, then 1910, are from p.24, 50 and 68. An attractive abridgment of Sachau's translation of *India* has been done, with introduction and notes by A.T. Embree, *Alberuni's India,* New York: Norton, 1971. And for the final section on Al-Biruni's labour in and on India, I have used my own earlier article: Biruni, Abu Rayhan viii. Indology' iin *Encyclopaedia Iranica* Vol. IV, Fasc. 3, pp. 28ɔ-287.

Abbasid Culture and the Universal History of Freethinking Humanism by Aziz al-Azmeh

This is an edited version of my Cantemir Lecture deliver at the University of Oxford on 26 February 2013.

The Darwin quotations are from the Darwin Correspondence Project: www.darwinproject.ac.uk/letter/entry-1924; the quotes from Al-Shahrastani are from *Kitab al-Milal wa'l-Nihal,* editor. W. Cureton (London 1846), 1:5-7; quotation from U. J. Seetzen is from *Reisen in Syrien etc.* (Berlin 1854-59) 3:171-2;

For the Qur'anic references to Adam and Satan, see 2:34, 7:11-13, 17:61-62. On Abu Nuwas and his jest with Satan see P. Kennedy, *Abu Nuwas* (Oxford 2005, 43-47); and on Satan as a tragic figure see P. Awn, *Satan's Tragedy and Redemption: Iblis in Sufi Psychology* (Leiden, 1983). On unbelievers in the Abbasid era (including Bashshar b. Burd) see M. Chokr, *Zandaqa et zindiqs en Islam au second siècle de l'hégire* (Damascus, 1993). On the theme of the three impostors and works with this title over a period of nearly a millennium in Europe see G. Minois, *The Atheist's Bible,* translated by George Minois and L. A. Weiss (University of Chicago Press, 2012). Works that treat this phenomenon in general and in some detail, include: A. Badawi, *Min Tarikh al-Ilhad fi'l-Islam* [Of the History of Atheism in Islam]

(Cairo 1945); D. Urvoy, *Les penseurs libres dans l'Islam classique* (Paris, 1996); S. Stroumsa, *Freethinkers of Medieval Islam* (Brill, Leiden 1999).

On al-Ma'arri, see H. Laoust, 'La vie et la philosophie d'Abu-l-'Al-Ma'arri," *Bulletin d'Études Orientales, 10* (1944), pp. 119-156; on Razi and Galen, see S. Pines, "Razi critique de Galien," *Actes du VIIe Congrès International d'Histoire des Sciences*, Paris, 1953, pp. 480-487; on and by al-Warraq: D. Thomas, 'Abu 'Isa al-Warraq and the history of religions,' *Journal of Semitic Studies*, 41 (1996), 275-290; D. Thomas (editor and translator.), *Early Muslim Polemic against Christianity* (University of Cambridge Press, 2002); on Euhemerism and classical skepticism towards gods and myths about gods: B. Graziosi, *The Gods of Olympus* (Profile Books, London 2013), chapters 3 and 6; on Muslims as pagans, see for instance B. Septimus, 'Petrus Alfonsi on the Cult at Mecca', *Speculum*, 56/3 (1981), 517-533 and John V Tolan, *Saracens* (Columbia University Press, New York 2002); and on the views of Varro, see Augustine, *City of God*, vi.4. See also E. Renan, *Averroes et l'Averroisme* (Paris 1852); and on seventeenth- and eighteenth-century philo-Islamism in Europe, which is a growth area in scholarship, see J. Jacob, *Henry Stubbe, Radical Protestantism and the Early Enlightenment*, (Cambridge University Press, 1983); Z. Elmarsafy, *The Enlightenment Qur'an* (OneWorld, Oxford 2009) N. Matar, *Henry Stubbe and the Beginnings of Islam: The Original and Progress of Mahometanism* (Columbia University Press, New York 2014).

Al-Ma'arri's *Epistle* is now available in English translation: *The Epistle of Forgiveness*, translator G. van Gelder and G. Schoeler, 2 volumes (New York University Press, 2013).

Adonis' Heresy by Stefan Weidner

Adonis, *Aghani Mihyar al-dimashqi* (The Songs of Mihyar the Damascene) (Dar Majallat Shi'r, Beirut, 1961) and *al-A'mal al-shi'riyya al-kamila* (Complete Works) (Dar al-Auda, Beirut, 1985). Various translations of his poetic works are available, see: *Mihyar of Damascus: His Songs* (BOA Editions, 2008); *If Only the Sea Could Sleep: Love Poems* (Green Integer, 2003); *The Pages of Day and Night* (Northwestern University Press, 2000);

and *Victims of a Map: A Bilingual Anthology of Arabic Poetry* (Saqi Books, London, 2005). Translations of two of his best known books are also available: *Sufism and Surrealism* (Saqi Books, London, 2005); and *An Introduction to Arab Poetics* (Saqi Books, London, 2003).

See also: Stefan Weidner, 'A Guardian of Change? The Poetry of Adunis between Hermeticsm and Commitment', in Stephan Guth, Priska Furrer, Johann Christoph Bürgel (editors), *Conscious Voices. Concepts of Writing in the Middle East* (Steiner, Stuttgart, 1999, 277-292); and 'The Divinity of the Profane', in Ed de Moor and Gert Borg (editors), *Representations of the Divine in Arabic Poetry* (Rodopi, Amsterdam, 2001, 211-225).

Neo-Modernity of Soroush by Mohammad Moussa

Abdolkarim Soroush's works are largely in Persian. However, his most important articles and essays have been translated in English as *Reason, Freedom and Democracy in Islam: Essential Writings of Abdolkarim Soroush*, translated and edited by Mahmoud Sadri and Ahmad Sadri (Oxford and New York: Oxford University Press, 2000) and *The Expansion of Prophetic Experience*, translated by Nilou Mobasser (Brill: Leiden, 2009). A number of his interviews are available online at *www.drsoroush.com*, including: 'A Congregation of Bees, not a Congregation of Parrots: Interview with Abdulkarim Soroush by Bizhan Mumivand and Hossein Sokhanvar,' April 2009; 'Intellectuals, The Powerless Wielders of Power: Conversation with Abdolkarim Soroush,' 1 January 1999; 'I'm a Neo-Mu'tazilite: An interview with Abdulkarim Soroush by Matin Ghaffarian', July 2008; 'Islam, Revelation and Prophet: An interview with Abdulkarim Soroush about the Expansion of Prophet Experience,' February 2008; and 'Muhammad's Word, Muhammad's Miracle: Interview with Abdulkarim Soroush by Kargozaran newspaper,' February 2008.

For further information on how prophecy was conceived by medieval Muslim philosophers see Fazlur Rahman's *Prophecy in Islam: Philosophy and Orthodoxy* (Chicago and London: The University of Chicago, 2011). The quote from Fazlur Rahman is from *Islam* (Chicago: The University of Chicago, 2002), p. 31. See also: Abbas Milani, *Lost Wisdom: Rethinking Modernity in Iran* (Washington, D.C.: Mage Publishers, 2004); and Farzin

Vahdat, *God and Juggernaut: Iran's Intellectual Encounter with Modernity* (Syracuse, New York: Syracuse University Press, 2002).

Mahmoud Taha: Heresy and Martyrdom by Abdelwahab El-Affendi

The account of Taha's execution is based on the official website of the Republican Party, which houses a large number of documents and books relating to the history and thought of the movement. See his 'official' biography at the Republican website: http://www.alfikra.org/index_e. php. My account of his life and politics are based on: Abdallah al-Faki al-Bashir, *Mahmoud Muhammad Taha wa'l-Muthaqqafun: Qira'a fi'l-Mawaqif wa Tazwir al-Tarikh* (Mahmoud Muhammad Taha and the Intellectuals: Reading in Stances and the Falsification of Histroy) (Ruya, Cairo, 2013); Mohamed Mahmoud, 'Mahmud Muhammad Taha and the Rise and Demise of the Jumhuri Movement', *New Political Science*, 23: 1 (2001), pp. 65-88; and George Packer, 'Letter from Sudan: the Moderate Martyr', *The New Yorker*, September 11, 2006, which can be accessed at: http://www.newyorker. com/archive/2006/09/11/060911fa_fact1?currentPage=all.

Quotations from Taha are from *Al-Risala al-Thaniya fi'il-Islam* translated as *The Second Message of Islam* (Syracuse University Press, 1996); I am using the 1996 edition published by the Sudanese Human Rights Organisation. The quotes are from pages 78, 46 and 121. The last Taha quote is from al-Bashir, *Mahmoud Muhammad Taha wa'l-Muthaqqafun*, p. 604. The Abdullahi Ahmed An-Na'im quote is from, 'Mahmud Muhammad Taha and the Crisis in Islamic Law Reform: Implications for Interreligious Relations', *Journal of Ecumenical Studies,* 25:1 (1988), pp. 1-21.

See also Abdelwahab El-Affendi, 'Political Culture and the Crisis of Democracy in the Arab World', in Ibrahim Elbadawi and Samir Makdisi (editors.) *Democracy in the Arab World: Explaining the Defici* (Routledge, London, 2010), pp. 12-40; and 'Arab Spring, Islamist Ice-Age: Islamism, Democracy and the Dictatorship of the "Liberalism of Fear" in the Age of Revolutions', Introductory Essay in the AJISS Special Issue on 'Islamist Spring', AJISS, 30: 4 (2013), pp. 1-18.

The Devil's Interpreter? by Nazry Bahrawi

Interview with Nasr Hamid Abu Zayd, 'My life fighting intolerance', can be found at: http://www.youtube.com/watch?v=_d7WGgHKfXc. The quotations are from his *Rethinking the Qur'an: Towards a Humanistic Hermeneutics* (Humanistics University Press, Amsterdam, 2004), p.36, 22; and 'The "Others" in the Qur'an: A Hermeneutical Approach', *Philosophy and Social Criticism*. Vol. 36, nos. 3–4 (2010): pp. 281–294. I have used Yusuf Ali's translation of the Qur'an throughout.

The Ziauddin Sardar quote is from *Islamic Futures: The Shape of Ideas to Come* (Mansell, London, 1985), p.108. The quote from Mohamad Hashim Kamali is from his article, '*Maqasid al-Shari'ah*: The Objectives of Islamic Law', *Islamic Studies,* 38 (1999): pp.193–209. See also his *Maqasid al-Shari'ah, Ijtihad and Civilisational Renewal* (IIIT, London, 2012) and Jasser Auda, *Maqasid al-Shari'ah: A Beginner's Guide* (IIIT, London, 2008). Mohamed Mahmoud's quote is from his Review of *The Concept of the Text: A Study of Qur'anic Science,* in *Journal of Arabic Literature,* 25, 2 (July 1994) 181-184. Hassan Hanafi quote is from *Volume 8: Al-Yasar al-Islami wa al-Wihda al-Wataniyya* (The Islamic Left and National Unity), part of the series *Al-Din wa al-Thawra fi Misr: 1952-1981 (Religion and Revolution in Egypt), 8 vols* (Maktabat Madbuli, Cairo, 198 8-89). Harold Bloom's comments on New Historicism can be found in his *The Western Canon* (Harcourt Brace and Company, New York, 1994).

The Use of the Pen by Johan Siebers

All quotations are taken from Jack Kerouac, 'Essentials of Spontaneous Prose', 1959, which can be downloaded from: www.analepsis.files.wordpress.com. Tim Ingold's *Lines: A Brief History* is published by Routledge, London 2007.

Milosz: The Mindful Dissident by Eva Hoffman

Czeslaw Milosz's *The Collected Poems, 1931-1987* (Ecco Press, Hopewell, NJ, 1988) contain the two poems, 'A Poor Christian Looks at the Ghetto,' and 'Campo dei Fiori'. *The Captive Mind* is available in several editions, including a new Penguin Classics edition (2001); his *New and Collected Poems, 1931-2001* is also available in Penguin Classics (2005). See also: *Visions from San Francisco Bay*, translated by Richard Lourie (Farrar Straus Giroux, New York, 1982); *Native Realm: A Search for Self-Definition*, translated by Catherine S. Leach (Farrar Straus Giroux, New York 2002); and *Proud to Be a Mammal: Essays on War, Faith and Memory,* translated by Catherine Leach, Bogdana Carpenter and Madeline G. Levine (Penguin, New York, 2010).

Writers in Istanbul by Mohamed Bakari

V.S. Naipaul's books mentioned in this essay – *Reading and Writing*, *The World Is What It Is* (biography of Naipaul by Patrick French), *An Area of Darkness*, *A Bend in the River, A House for Mr. Biswas, A Turn in the South* and *A Writer's People* – are widely available in paperback.

Shiva Naipaul's *North of South: An African Journey*, originally published in 1978, is available in a new 1996 Penguin Twentieth Century Classics edition. James Baldwin's *Another Country* and *The Fire Next Time* are available in the Penguin Modern Classics series.

Hannah Arendt's Eichmann by Iftikhar H. Malik

On Hannah Arendt, see *The Origins of Totalitarianism*, (Harcourt Publishers, New York, 1951); *The Human Condition* (University of Chicago Press, Chicago, 1958); *Eichmann in Jerusalem: The Banality of Evil* (Penguin, New York, 1963); and the two volumes of *The Life of Mind* (Harcourt Publishers, New York, 1978). See also Bonnie Honig, editor, *Feminist Interpretations of Hannah Arendt* (Pennsylvania University Press, Philadelphia, 1995) and the entry on 'Hannah Arendt' in *Stanford Encyclopaedia of Philosophy* (Stanford, 2006).

Last Word: On Mad, Bad and Dangerous
by Merryl Wyn Davies

On Cara's life and works, see *Lady Caroline Lamb: A Biography* by Paul Douglass (Palgrave McMillan, London, 2004) and the 1973 film of the same name. Thomas Piketty's *Capital in the Twenty-first Century* is published by Harvard University Press, 2014.

CONTRIBUTORS

Alev Adil, Head of the Department of Communication and Creative Arts at University of Greenwich, London, is still trying to figure out Aisha ● **Suhail Ahmad** is a writer and a regular reviewer for *Critical Muslim* ● **Aziz al-Azmeh** is CEU University Professor in the School of Historical and Interdisciplinary Studies, Central European University, Budapest ● **Hanan Al-Shaykh** is a world renowned novelist ● **Nazry Bahrawi** is a research associate at the Middle East Institute, National University of Singapore ● **Mohamed Bakari** is Professor of English at Fatih University, Istanbul ● **Merryl Wyn Davies** has recovered fully and is (allegedly) taking her responsibilities as co-director of the Muslim Institute seriously ● **Abdelwahab El-Affendi** is co-ordinator of the Democracy and Islam Programme at the Centre for the Study of Democracy, University of Westminster ● **Marilyn Hacker**, renowned poet and critic, is Professor of English at the City College of New York ● **Eva Hoffman** is a Polish American writer and critic ● **Robert Irwin** is the author or editor of seventeen works of fiction or non-fiction, of which the most recent is *Memoirs of a Dervish* ● **Bruce B Lawrence** teaches Islamic studies at Duke University and Fatih Sultan Mehmet University, Istanbul ● **Oliver Leaman** is Professor of Philosophy at University of Kentucky ● **Iftikar H Malik** is Professor of History at Bath Spa University ● **James E Montgomery** is Sir Thomas Adams's Professor of Arabic, University of Cambridge ● **Mohammed Moussa** is currently transforming his PhD thesis on the Islamic tradition and modernity into a book ● **Peerzada Salman** is the pen name of Mohammad Salman, playwright, filmmaker and senior reporter with *Dawn*, Pakistan ● **Johan Siebers** is a philosopher and senior lecturer in religious studies at Middlesex University ● **Stefan Weidner** is Editor-in-Chief of *Fikrun wa Fann* (Art&Thought)